the BINGE WATCHER'S guide to

RIVERDALE

AN UNOFFICIAL COMPANION

Melissa Ford Lucken

For more information contact:
Riverdale Avenue Books
5676 Riverdale Avenue
Riverdale, NY 10471.

www.riverdaleavebooks.com
Design by www.formatting4U.com
Cover by Scott Carpenter

Digital ISBN: 9781626015807
Trade Paperback 9781626015791
First Edition, April 2021

Dedication

For Isabelle Drake.

You drew the fire.

And so now we know—
I know—
who is who
and who is not.

Table of Contents

Introduction

Riverdale 101

Creator and Showrunner
Roberto Aguirre-Sacasa

Executive Producers
    Warner Bros. Television & CBS Television Studios
    with Berlanti Productions & Archie Comics
    Greg Berlanti
    Sarah Schechter
    Jon Goldwater
    Roberto Aguirre-Sacasa

Studio
    The CW. Filming takes place primarily in Vancouver, British Columbia, with other locations throughout British Columbia. *Riverdale's* opening aerial image is from Harbor Springs, Michigan, USA.

Stars & Characters Appearing in 10+ Episodes
    K.J. Apa as *Archie Andrews*
    Lili Reinhart as *Betty Cooper*
    Camila Mendes as *Veronica Lodge*
    Cole Sprouse as *Jughead Jones*
    Casey Cott as *Kevin Kelle*r
    Madelaine Petsch as *Cheryl Blossom*
    Mädchen Amick as *Alice Cooper*
    Skeet Ulrich as *FP Jones*
    Marisol Nichols as *Hermione Lodge*
    Mark Consuelos as *Hiram Lodge*
    Vanessa Morgan as *Toni Topaz*

Luke Perry as *Fred Andrews*
Ross Butler (Season 1) Charles Melton (Seasons 2-4)
    as *Reggie Mantle*
Martin Cummins as *Tom Keller*
Alvin Sanders as *Pop Tate*
Nathalie Boltt as *Penelope Blossom*
Ashleigh Murray as *Josie McCoy*
Drew Ray Tanner as *Fangs Fogarty*
Lochlyn Munro as *Hal Cooper*
Jordan Connor as *Sweet Pea*
Robin Givens as *Sierra McCoy*
Cody Kearsley as *Moose Mason*
Peter Bryant as *Principal Waldo Weatherbee*
Molly Ringwald as *Mary Andrews*
Tiera Skovbye as *Polly Cooper*
Barclay Hope as *Cliff Blossom*
Trinity Likins as *Jellybean Jones*
Barbara Wallace as *Rose Blossom*
Zoé De Grand Maison as *Evelyn Evernever*
Hayley Law as *Valerie Brown*
Sean Depner as *Bret Weston Wallis*
Sarah Desjardins as *Donna Sweett*
Asha Bromfield as *Melody Valentine*
Doralynn Mui as *Joan Berkeley*
Trevor Stines as *Jason Blossom*
Eli Goree as *Mad Dog*
Wyatt Nash as *Charles Smith*
Shannon Purser as *Ethel Muggs*
Hart Denton as *Chic*
Alex Barima as *Johnathan*
Marion Eisman as *Doris Bell*
Malcolm Stewart as *Francis Dupont*
Brit Morgan as *Penny Peabody*
Rob Raco as *Joaquin DeSantos*
Emilija Baranac as *Midge Klump*
Scott McNeil as *Tall Boy*
Bernadette Beck as *Peaches 'N Cream*
Nikolai Witschl as *Dr. Curdle Jr.*

Season Airdates

Season 1
January 26, 2017 – May 11, 2017
Season 2
October 11, 2017 – May 16, 2018
Season 3
October 10, 2018 – May 15, 2019
Season 4
October 9, 2019 – May 6, 2020

Number of episodes

76

Where and How to Binge

Netflix is your best bet for previous seasons, but you can also find it on Prime, VUDU, Google Play, iTunes and YouTube. For the current season, head over to CW. It will take about 57 hours to get through all 76 episodes.

Riverdale 201

In the midst of the 2020 Coronavirus Pandemic, binge-watching became an acceptable pastime. No longer did we bingers have to discuss our hours in front of the screen with a sheepish attitude; time spent "binging" was no longer considered "wasted." Now, that time represented a connection to others. However, the endless watching wasn't enough. We wanted the viewing of each show, episode after episode, to be more enlightened. More complicated.

This Binge Watcher's Guide will structure and intensify your *Riverdale* viewing. Meant to keep you company, inform you and sometimes make you laugh, it will connect you to the compelling and spirited piece of the Archieverse that is *Riverdale*. And lucky for us, I'm here to guide you—I've been here in the Archieverse for a long time.

One of my earliest memories is of a cereal box with an actual, playable, cardboard "flexi record" printed on the backside. At age four, I was already a music fan and pop-culture scholar in the making, so I was both fascinated and excited. As I was still a preschooler, and naturally not so great with scissors, I enlisted by big sister's help in cutting the record from the package. The small album—featuring brightly colored images of Archie and the gang—played at 33 1/3 speed and had four songs from the cartoon band, The Archies, including one of my favorites, *Sugar, Sugar*. That flexi-record stayed on my family's turntable for at least an entire day.

Which, in little kid time, is forever.

At the time, I didn't know that Archie and the gang had been living on the pages of comics for 30 years. What I did know was that there was a Saturday morning cartoon aptly named: *The Archies*. This half-hour show began in '68 and was expanded to a full hour in '69. Looking back now, the expansion of the show might have been the reason for the album showing up on my cereal box. But back then, I just accepted the album as part of my world—a world that included Archie, Jughead, Betty, Veronica, Josie and the Pussycats and the rest from Riverdale.

Throughout my childhood, the cartoon changed names and formats. Some better than others, but always a constant part of my consciousness. At some point, I started reading the Archie Comics, declaring the Betty & Veronica issues my favorite. Not yet in high school myself, I loved seeing into the future and imagining my own teenage years.

Fast forward about two decades, and I have a son who reads, collects and studies comics and comic culture. When we would stroll through garage sales, flea markets and used bookstores for old issues of *Batman* and other superhero comics, he would encourage me to find some for myself. And just like that, comics—specifically Betty and Veronica—were back in my life. At first, I had an experience that many people have when encountering an Archie comic after decades since reading them as a child; I was astonished. These things are *still around*? And they're *creating new ones*?

The Archie Comics business has been going strong for over 80 years. It all started in 1939 with John L. Goldwater and the creation of M.L.J. Magazines. While well known for his role as national commissioner of the Anti-Defamation League, Goldwater also served as president of the Comics Magazine Association of America—the organization that in 1954 created the Comics Code Seal that appears in the top right-hand corner of comics deemed safe and appropriate for kids. For decades, that seal was very influential. Both product advertisers and comic book distributors made business decisions based on its presence.

Simply put, no seal, no sale. No sale, no money. And comic publishing *is* a business.

Times do change, though, and most publishers abandoned the seal in the early 2000s. Unsurprisingly, Archie Comics—created by the seal's creator—was the last comic publisher to discontinue the use of the seal, ending use in January 2011.

And it's a good thing for us that Archie Comics discontinued the use of the Comic Code Seal, as the code criteria stated that within the storyline:

- Crimes shall never be presented in such a way as to create sympathy for the criminal, to promote distrust of the forces of law and justice, or to inspire others with a desire to imitate criminals.

- If crime is depicted, it shall be as a sordid and unpleasant activity.
- Policemen, judges, government officials and respected institutions shall never be presented in such a way as to create disrespect for established authority.
- Nudity in any form is prohibited, as is indecent or undue exposure.
- Suggestive and salacious illustration or suggestive posture is unacceptable.
- Females shall be drawn realistically, without exaggeration of any physical qualities.
- Illicit sex relations are neither to be hinted at nor portrayed.
- Seduction shall never be shown or suggested.

With limitations like these, the new version of Riverdale seen in the show would never have come to light. In a way, that list gives you a taste of what makes the show hum: crime, corruption and carnal acts.

Riverdale—the town from the original comic—is a clean, wholesome, anyplace USA. It's the kind of place where the parents are kind, teachers are supportive, and teens are encouraged about their futures. The simple, cheery and unsophisticated qualities of comic Riverdale certainly contributed to the comic's popularity. But the dark, menacing and generally ambiguous qualities of Riverdale in *Riverdale* contribute to the TV show's allure. Our Riverdale is a peculiar town with a mysterious, yet appealing, aesthetic; sinister and secretive parents; cunning and opportunistic authority figures; and teens fighting to survive.

Now back to me and the inspiration for this book.

Fast forward a few more years, and I've become a fiction writer and college professor. As I scroll through TV shows, waiting for something to catch my attention, I spot an ad for *Riverdale*. I'm intrigued. Curious about what's similar and what's different, I'm soon tuning in to the show on a regular basis and using my writing experience to analyze the storyline and the characters. What works? What doesn't? Why did the creators make the decisions they did? Eventually, I was so far down the *Riverdale* rabbit hole that I began to do more formal research.

In the summer of 2019, I participated in the Popular Culture Association's Popular Culture Summer Research Institute at Bowling

Green State University. I spent hours at the Ray & Pat Browne Library for Popular Culture Studies, scrutinizing comics, including stacks and stacks of *Archie*, *Betty and Veronica* and *Jughead*.

First, I read each title in consecutive order, oldest to newest. Then, I merged titles and read across them again, looking for patterns and themes. I looked for social change. I examined the art and the advertising. Ultimately, I wrote a paper: *Gothic Girls Gone Wild: Riverdale's Recrafting of Betty Cooper and Veronica Lodge.*

The research mentioned above, the research done for the paper, my work as a fiction writer, and my multiple binge-watching rounds of *Riverdale* influence and inform what you will find in these pages.

The Zeitgeist

Ask older people about comics, and there's a fair chance they have a story to tell. They collected them, their neighbor read them, or maybe they remember walking to the drugstore to buy the latest issue of their favorite title. Maybe that favorite was one of the Archie titles. "Young" people, whatever age you think that is, may have never cared much about comics. They might not have ever seen an Archie comic. But there's a fair chance they've seen, or at least heard of, the show *Riverdale*.

As noted earlier, Archie Comics abandoned the moral protections of the Comic Code Seal in early 2011, and in 2014, they appointed lifelong Archie fan, Roberto Aguirre-Sacasa, Chief Creative Officer. Prior to becoming the CCO of Archie Comics, Aguirre-Sacasa had experience in both television as a writer for *Big Love*, *Glee* and *Supergirl*, and comics with *Nightcrawler, The Stand, Archie Meets Glee* and *Afterlife with Archie*.

No doubt that background was something Archie Comics Publisher & Co-CEO Jon Goldwater wanted to use to the publisher's advantage. Marvel and DC Comics were expanding beyond printed pages, making live-action films and television shows, so why not Archie? Clearly, the publisher was itching to grow with the times.

In late 2014, Archie Comics announced the upcoming celebration of the comic's 75th anniversary by relaunching *Archie*. The comic relaunched with a kick-ass debut issue from Mark Waid and Fiona Staples. The vibe of this new *Archie Vol. 1* was edgier than the recent issues, but not yet simmering with Gothic wickedness like the show would. Around the same time *Archie* was relaunched, Archie Comics also announced the upcoming live-action show *Riverdale,* the development of which was already well underway.

Originally for FOX, the series started the planning stages in 2013 intending to capture audiences of The CW's *The Flash* and *Arrow*.

Aguirre-Sacasa initially referred to the show as "Archie meets Twin Peaks." In a 2014 interview with *Fast Company,* Aguirre-Sacasa remarked on the importance of setting in *Smallville* and the breadth of characters in *Gotham:* "It could be something like *American Beauty,* something like 'secrets of a small town,' [but] be a little darker." From the very early stages of creation, he acknowledged a hefty influence from David Lynch. His goal was to create a dark show with weird twists.

Remember, Aguirre-Sacasa wrote *Afterlife with Archie,* the comic that starts off with Sabrina bringing Hot Dog back to life, only to turn Jughead into a zombie that who spreads a contagion throughout Riverdale. At the time in 2013, when the first issue rolled off the presses, *The Walking Dead* was still going strong. In fact, according to AMC, the third season attracted more viewers aged 18-49 than any other cable or broadcast television series to date. Two thousand thirteen also saw the release of the *Evil Dead* remake, *Afflicted* and *The Conjuring.* Horror films were on the rise and Hollywood knows horror makes money.

And Archie Comics knew that *Archie Comics* make money.

From the beginning, there was always a similarity to the *Walking Dead.* Both follow a small group—in this case high-schoolers—fighting against an impossible force. Banding together, they deal with each new threat as it confronts them. There was also a similarity to *Pretty Little Liars.* There is a mystery, beautiful teens and a hometown that looks great but isn't.

But there's also so much more.

When speaking to Abraham Riesman for *Vulture,* Aguirre-Sacasa clarified that, while his new world is dark, it isn't completely. "People say, 'I hear you're doing dark Archie,'" he says. "We're not doing dark Archie. We're doing an Archie that mixes dark and light." Riesman also quotes Cole Sprouse, who he spoke with at the same time: "The archetypes of Archie are like a theater troupe that just kinda fits themselves into any sort of situation." Sprouse offers his analysis.

As *Riverdale* demonstrates, these simple, antiquated characters have improbably become among the most adaptable—and enduring—in American popular culture. The theme song to the beloved 1960s Archie cartoon declared, *Everything's Archie,* but the current Archie regime has set out to prove that Archie can be everything.

And Archie *is* everything. While also being nothing in particular.

Much like Don Draper in *Mad Men*, the show revolves around Archie Andrews without ever actually being about him. Whether a viewer does or doesn't like him—or even notices him—is irrelevant.

At the conclusion of Season 3, *Film Daily* notes, "Though it boasts all the hallmarks of any other popular teen show which came before it—most notably an extremely attractive cast—it does so while subverting many of those hallmarks with a shrewd, progressive and deliciously macabre scrutiny." Thus, the show, much like Archie himself, is both recognizable and unexpected.

And therein lies its beauty.

In the assessment of the first three seasons of the show, *Film Daily* considers that:

By obscuring what are considered regular teenage concerns (dating, pimples and popularity) with more serious issues (murder, prostitution and gang violence), *Riverdale* suggests the modern teenager may have a little more on their mind than simply finding a date for the dance.

That assessment is true. The teens of Riverdale are faced with the definitive dilemma of good vs. evil, a conflict that is classic and continual. Our world, especially today, reflects this same dichotomy, and the human need to understand and reconcile it.

Before You Watch

Riverdale Plot: Tropetastic

As you bingers know, plot creates the action of any story. Simply put, it's what the characters do and what gets in their way. The characters want something or someone, but something or someone stops them, creating conflict. This conflict creates tension, and that tension increases as new things or people get in the way. We viewers love tension and it's what keeps us firmly in front of our screens. Ergo, a good plot means good tension.

But how to make a good plot?

Overall plot is created through elements, or small pieces of action. One such element is called a trope—a piece of action that occurs so frequently, across so many plots, that it becomes familiar and encompassing. And each genre tends to have different tropes.

For example, popular romance tropes are friends to lovers, second chances and forbidden love. Familiar horror tropes are the end of the world as we know it, us against them, and unsafe haven. Now, some high-brow literary folks like to frown on tropes, claiming they are both unimaginative and droll. They allege that tropes are nothing more than clichés used by bad, lazy writers. But we aren't interested in what those sad individuals think. Here in the *Riverdale* branch of the Archieverse, we embrace our tropes. We love them, and we live for them.

You can find a full list of the tropes used on Riverdale on *TVTropes.org*. Here, pulled from that site, are some tropes to look for:

- Arch-Enemy
- Adults are useless
- Apathetic citizens
- Big Bad

- Broken pedestal
- Fanservice
- Feuding families
- Game plays you
- Mythology gag
- Parental abandonment
- Pop culture shout outs
- Reality ensues
- Wham shot
- Where the hell is Springfield [Riverdale]?

As you watch, keep an eye out for these and other recognizable pieces of action. Analyze why and how they're used, and whether you think they're effective.

Riverdale Setting: Gothic as All Get Out

Setting is where the action happens. And when a show is titled after the setting, viewers know the setting counts big time. In *Riverdale,* the place is everything.

Now that wasn't the case in the classic comic world of Riverdale. That pleasant anyplace served mainly as a background for the antics of Archie and his light-hearted high school gang. It was so unimportant that the writers could create an ever-changing town with museums, airports and other landmarks that came and went over the decades, as the stories needed. As a result, there was no reason for creating a local history—and the town of Riverdale did little to influence the actions of the characters. However, the Riverdale of *Riverdale* couldn't be more opposite.

The setting of Riverdale itself is the character most changed from the classic comics. This new place is more than a backdrop—it complicates the plotline and motivates the characters. A Gothic setting gives the show a dark edge. Broken families, hearts and spirits replace the humor and happiness of the past.

Riverdale's storyline is built around the misdeeds, lies and subversive connections of the adults. The teens struggle against the adults' actions, trying to return their town to normalcy and safety.

Intergenerational family dysfunction, secret societies and local superstitions are classic elements of Gothic fiction and all present in CW's Riverdale.

Fred Botting—one of the go-to academic folks on what exactly is Gothic—in his go-to book *Gothic*, describes how the otherworldly setting, such as the one seen in *Riverdale*, provides an effective backdrop for movement from and back to a rational present: "More than a flight of nostalgic retrospection or an escape from the dullness of a present without chivalry, magic or adventure, the movement does not long for terrifying and arbitrary aristocratic power, religious superstition or supernatural events but juxtaposes terrors of the negative with an order authorized by reason and morality."

Not sure what all that means? No worries. You will by the end of the first episode. Academics who study Gothics are intrigued by how this genre is transgressive in terms of social norms; they explore the world of vice. Botting observes that "Gothic texts are, overtly but ambiguously, not rational, depicting disturbances of sanity and security... displays of uncontrolled passion, violent emotion or flights of fancy to portrayals of perversion and obsession." All these characteristics are visible from the start of *Riverdale*.

When you watch the first episode, note that all these traits are encapsulated in unscrupulous teacher Ms. Grundy. The corrupt femme fatale, a sexual predator who represents the Gothic tropes of abuse of power and eroticism, coerces an underage student, Archie, into a sexual relationship. Her depiction sets the tone for this new version of Riverdale and paves the way for other disruptive and disturbing adult behavior.

The parents of Riverdale generate much of that screen-gluing tension mentioned before. Disruptions of sanity and security are visible in Betty Cooper's parents, Hal and Alice Cooper. No spoilers here, but keep an eye on these two and observe how they manipulate others—their children in particular. As you spot their controlling actions, examine the tension created, and observe how their control harms those around them.

Portrayals of perversion and obsession are accomplished through Veronica Lodge's parents, Hiram and Hermione Lodge. These unapologetic criminals take advantage of their wealth and power to manipulate Riverdale's citizens, including their own daughter. Again, watch how the parents' actions contribute to the plot and force those around them, specifically the teens, to struggle.

Collectively, the characteristics and actions of the parents, and other adults in *Riverdale* represent and create Gothic tropes, including aristocracy, corruption, isolation, madness and family secrets. The antagonists—the adults—generate story conflicts and produce tension; the teenagers—the protagonists—respond to the evil, chaos and threats created by the adults' attitudes and actions. This dynamic is the essence of the Gothic what shapes *Riverdale*.

The transgressions that influence the action of the plot come mostly from Gothic tropes. You can find lists of the Gothic tropes online, but for convenience I've pulled some tropes to look for from the *Culture Notebook*:

- Darkness
- Isolation
- Madness and confusion over what is real or unreal
- Frame Narratives, someone working to structure events
- Folklore, local history
- Diaries, letters, other documents that hold past folklore and local history
- Dreams and Nightmares
- Eroticism
- Corruption
- The Aristocracy and the control of the privileged class

While watching the show, think of the town itself as a character. Riverdale, as a collective, has wants, desires and needs. Also, look for those Gothic tropes and analyze why and how they're used, and whether you think they're effective. Tip: also look for times when the Gothic elements are absent and assess the impact on the plot.

Riverdale Characters: Everything Old is New Again

In his classic comic universe, Archie Andrews is a light-hearted trouble-maker who lives for antics and action. Many classic Archie comic stories feature him antagonizing Riverdale High's Principal Mr. Weatherbee, trying to best Reggie in a contest, or simply hanging out at the beach. Most of the storylines show him as this easy-going guy who just wants to have a good time. As you binge, look for ways when his spontaneous side is turned into an impulsive nature that causes him to get into trouble, or his protective side becomes an unhealthy obsession.

In his traditional role as Archie's best friend, Jughead Jones is witty, smart and places food above dating. Frequently, comic stories featured him helping Archie with some prank or silly plan, trying to dodge a chore or a date, or tricking others into supplying him with food. As you roll through the *Riverdale* episodes, look for how his wit has an edge, and how his smarts are used to uncover darkness rather than aid him in getting out of schoolwork.

In the previous comic Archieverse, Betty Cooper was a sweet, hard-working girl next door. Classic comic stories highlight her tomboy side—revealing her to be a talented athlete or skilled car mechanic—but often the circumstances show that she is a compassionate girl who puts the needs of others before her own. On *Riverdale,* look for how this caring side is exploited, transformed into a weakness, and used to cause her downfall.

In her earlier comic world, Veronica Lodge is an easy to anger, spoiled and competitive daddy's girl. Those comic stories highlighted her wealthy lifestyle, depicting her shopping compulsively and buying her way to success. Her wealth comes through her father, and she doesn't hesitate to use her charms to get material possessions or access to privilege. On *Riverdale,* watch for how this dependency on her father forces her to operate within his criminal world, and how she does or doesn't use her privilege to her advantage.

You can find a full list of the tropes used on Riverdale on the *TVTropes.org.* Here, pulled from that site, are some character-oriented tropes to look for:

- Abusive parents
- Actor allusions
- Confession Triggers Consummation
- Establishing character moment
- It runs in the family
- Love dodecahedron
- True companions
- Ship tease

The Socials

Like and Follow
- Twitter: Riverdale (@CW_Riverdale) & Riverdale Binge Watcher's Guide (@BingeRiverdale)
- Instagram: Riverdale (@thecwriverdale) & Riverdale BingeWatcher's Guide (@binge_riverdale_guide)
- Facebook: Riverdale (@CWRiverdale)
- YouTube: Riverdale (@channel/UCJyEY_Iwtg8-FLP3Gg5pL0Q)

Hashtags
- #riverdale
- #riverdalecast
- #riverdalefans
- #riverdaleedit
- #bingeriverdale
- #archie
- #jughead
- #betty
- #veronica
- #bettycooper
- #archieandrews
- #jugheadjones
- #bughead
- #veronicalodge
- #varchie
- #colesprouse
- #lilireinhart
- #cherylblossom
- #archieandrews
- #kjapa
- #choni
- #camilamendes
- #isadrake (to see what this particular binger is up to)

RIVERDALE

SEASON ONE

Chapter One:
"The River's Edge"

Original airdate: *January 26, 2017*
Writer: *Roberto Aguirre-Sacasa*
Director: *Lee Toland Krieger*

Top Quote: "Are you familiar with the works of Truman Capote? I'm *Breakfast at Tiffany's,* but this place is strictly *In Cold Blood.*" Veronica's assessment of her place in Riverdale.

Top Trivia: Note the Welcome to Riverdale sign, featuring the slogan "The Town with PEP." That's a nod to the past. Archie Andrews first appeared in *Pep Comics.*

Watch For: The first glimpse of Archie's Abs. The way Alice Cooper hovers and micromanages her daughter, Betty. Archie and Veronica's first kiss.

Wonder About: Did Jason, captain of the water polo team, drown? On a scale from one to five, how disturbing is Archie's relationship with *Geraldine?* And what's up with Betty digging her nails into her palms during the Vixens tryouts?

Summary + Commentary:

A voice-over by Jughead Jones introduces us to his hometown of Riverdale, hinting at dark secrets hidden within the town's history and culture. He reflects on July 4th, the day the very pretty—and very twisted—redheaded Blossom twins, Cheryl and Jason, set out on a boating trip. And only one of them came back—Cheryl.

    The episode moves into the first day of school. Jason Blossom is dead, Archie Andrews has fallen hard for his music teacher Ms. Grundy and Veronica Lodge has arrived in town. Yes, the people of Riverdale are shocked and saddened by Jason's untimely demise, but that doesn't stop them from longing and lusting.

Take, for example, fresh-faced girl next door Betty Cooper, wearing a sweet enough to give you a cavity pink lace bra, proclaiming her crush on Archie. Admire the lingerie, but don't think too much about Betty's crush on Archie. That's mostly a nod to the comic days when Betty was constantly—like for over 50 years—trying to win over Archie. When it comes to Betty, pay more attention to her mom. She makes the mom from *Carrie* look like a bad-mom wanna-be.

Archie wanders around, looking for a place to express his newly found musical side. He tries Josie and the Pussycats, who are sporting kitty ears—another nod to the comics—but they ice him out. Eventually, he coerces his music teacher into tutoring him in the mornings. Why the music teacher be hesitant to mentor him? Apparently, she's reconsidering the sexual relationship she had with him over the summer and is belatedly attempting to construct boundaries.

Cheryl gets her way, as usual, declaring that her brother would prefer school carry on with the back-to-school semi-formal, using it to celebrate his short life.

Hermione Lodge—Veronica's mom—however doesn't get her way. Showing up at Andrews Construction, asking Fred Andrews—Archie's dad—for a job, she's turned down because he can't have the wife of a man arrested for fraud and embezzlement working for him.

Meanwhile, in an attempt to get accepted onto Cheryl's Vixens cheer squad, Veronica and Betty kiss. It misses the mark, with Cheryl pointing out that the faux femme kiss is played out. We're not sure why Cheryl caves when Veronica declares that "she is ice," but Veronica's berating of Cheryl works. And so, Veronica pulls Betty onto the River Vixens cheer squad.

Afterward, Betty asks Veronica the question everyone is wondering: "Why are you being so nice to me?" Veronica reflects on the tough time she had, falling from socialite perfection. In case you were wondering, Veronica's character growth is the third nod to the comic's past. For decades, Veronica was spoiled and rich. In this new version, she is still rich and spoiled, but also vulnerable and empathetic. Also different, her dad is in prison.

Once their friendship is established, Veronica challenges Betty to ask Archie to the back-to-school dance, which she does. The twist however, is that she invites Veronica to join them. When Archie claims he isn't in the headspace for a dance, Veronica tells him that isn't acceptable. The three of them are going.

At the dance, Archie keeps after Ms. Grundy and makes it plain: if she gives him music lessons, he won't tell anyone about what they heard while having sex at the lake. Also, at the dance, Betty keeps after Archie. It's all so wonderfully awkward.

Later, Betty gets her heart crushed at Cheryl's after-party, when Veronica goes in the closet with Archie. Things go from sad to worse when Betty declares her lusty, non-friends only feelings to Archie, and he puts the brakes on. Archie tells Betty she is perfect and that he'll never be good enough for her. Oh, please.

Jughead, in a reflective post-back-to-school party voice-over, does his best to tie things up while also leaving the ends loose. He tells us that Jason's body has been found, and an arrest is coming.

Chapter Two:
"A Touch of Evil"

Original airdate: *February 2, 2017*
Writer: *Roberto Aguirre-Sacasa*
Director: *Lee Toland Krieger*

Top Quote: "I'm fine. In fact, I'm amazing."—Cheryl Blossom as she stabs into a dead frog during science class.

Top Trivia: The song *Candy Girl (Sugar, Sugar)*—performed by the Pussycats at the pep rally—was performed and recorded by The Archies band. The original version went to number one on the pop chart in 1969. You can find it on YouTube. Just search for the song title, *Sugar, Honey, Honey* by The Archies and enjoy the accompanying cartoon!

Watch For: More glimpses of Archie's Abs, thus establishing his abs as a defining characteristic to be loved and adored by fans. Betty's iconic sweaters and collar pins, with many more sweaters and collar embellishments to come. Jughead discovering Archie's secret.

Wonder About: How twisted is Archie's relationship with Ms. Grundy? Who's threatening whom? How amazing is it, that Madelaine Petsch's (aka Cheryl Bombshell) hair is naturally that vibrant red color? Does Betty agree to Veronica's second chance too easily?

Summary + Commentary:

Jughead's opening voice-over describes the twisted event that is Jason's demise. The beautiful boy didn't drown. We know that because he had a bullet-hole in his forehead—and someone in town is guilty.

Archie's love-life is seemingly complicated. He wants to stay friends with Betty, but she won't talk to him. Not to worry though, as she's going to be over that in a couple minutes. Meanwhile, bare-chested Archie barges into his music teacher's house to convince her they should tell the police about the gunshot they heard at the lake. Knowing full well that it would reveal she was having sex with her student, she balks at the notion.

And now, there's also Veronica.

Veronica, knowing she hurt Betty by kissing Archie at Cheryl's party, clears the air via yellow roses, cupcakes and mani-pedis. And Betty—being Betty—accepts the apology. Soon she and Veronica are dissecting a frog together in science class.

Lunch is filled with drama. Kevin is struggling with his attraction to Moose, Archie is still clinging to the guitar, and Betty is not okay. But who can blame her? Just that morning, her mom said some pretty nutty, cryptic stuff about Betty's mental health, and warned her away from both Archie *and* Veronica. And things get worse during Vixen's practice. Betty implies Veronica is putting on an act, but Veronica explains that it isn't her fault Archie doesn't like her like that. Ouch.

Principal Weatherbee puts pressure on Archie. *Is there anything you want to tell me?* he asks. And Archie does the one thing he should not—run to Ms. Grundy. She claims her feelings for him are real, although they are not right. Jughead spots their embrace and appears, understandably, disturbed.

Things get uncomfortable for viewers when Veronica's mom forgets that she's no longer a privileged socialite, getting cougarish with Archie, who's come into Pop's for takeout. Due to some lucky timing, Veronica is also there. She walks out with Archie and offers him some advice: give Betty time.

Betty and Cheryl are friends for a couple minutes, but then Betty threatens to kill Cheryl.

Meanwhile, Jughead is on to Archie and confronts him about the *situation* with the *music teacher*. Obviously, they fight. Jughead is the voice of reason, but Archie insists he needs to protect Ms. Grundy. Later, in the student lounge, Archie defends Jughead from Reggie. So yeah, they're still friends.

Betty approaches Veronica to tell her she was right about Archie. So yeah, that fight is over as well. At a pep rally in Jason's honor, Archie tells Ms. Grundy he's going to come clean' about what he knows, then apologizes to Jughead.

After the Pussycats sing and the Vixens dance, Cheryl hallucinates that Jason is standing out on the football field, sending her running to the locker rooms. Veronica goes to her, and while Betty follows, she doesn't make her presence known. Later, Betty tells Veronica that not many girls would have done what she did. This is a little weird because Betty herself was doing it, but whatever. The moment serves to reinforce that the two of them are still friends. They head to Pop's where, over milkshakes, they make a vow that no boy will ever come between them again. Put an X in an imaginary box if you believe that.

Jughead's concluding voice-over brings bad news—Cheryl has been arrested for Jason's murder. Don't start thinking there is going to be some *Orange is the New Black* type stuff in the next episode though. That's not going to happen. But something else is. Hit next episode and find out what.

Chapter Three:
"Body Double"

Original airdate: *February 9, 2017*
Writer: *Yolonda E. Lawrence*
Director: *Lee Toland Krieger*

Top Quote: "Why don't you come and work with your father and me? *The Riverdale Register* could really use a Lois Lane type like you."—Alice Cooper's subtly snide and mocking retort to Betty when Betty confronts Alice about the paper's coverage of the Blossom family's tragedy.

Top Trivia: Greendale, the home of the Archie Comics character, Sabrina Spellman, is mentioned as being on the other side of Sweetwater River.

Watch For: Veronica makes an indirect reference to *Full Dark, No Stars,* a Stephen King anthology of four novellas, all dealing with retribution. The first appearance of Ethel Muggs. You think you know what to expect from her, but you're wrong. This is the famed "Dark Betty" episode.

Wonder About: As a parent, how inconsistent and clueless is Fred, Archie's dad? Why *did* Jason want to fake his own death? Is everyone in Riverdale beautiful, chiseled and visually amazing?

Summary + Commentary:

Jughead's opening voice-over overlays the scene of Cheryl Blossom— who had prepared for her arrest by slicking on a darker shade of lip color—being escorted out of school by Sheriff Keller, Kevin's dad. And what exactly is the redhead guilty of? Lying of course. Apparently, Jason wanted to run away, so she helped him fake his own drowning.

But wait, there is more confusion. Betty can't understand why her mother—co-owner of *The Riverdale Register*—sensationalizes Jason's death/murder. Betty's distress is reasonable, as Jason was Betty's sister's boyfriend. Stay tuned for more manipulations by Alice.

That morning at school, Archie comes clean to Principal Wetherbee and Sheriff Keller, Veronica makes it public that she has a date with Chuck Clayton, Betty restarts the school newspaper, and Jughead accepts Betty's offer to write for it. Later, Fred grounds Archie for doing the right thing. The very thing Fred encouraged him to do. Um, okay, Fred.

Here is a reminder that you'll need. These people are high school *sophomores*. Keep that in mind as you watch Veronica's expression when she challenges, then subsequently kisses, Chuck in the front seat of his car.

Ms. Grundy is also unhappy that Archie did the right thing— revealed hearing the gunshot at the lake the day Jason died. Even as she complains, he vows to protect her. Her response to that is to cancel their lessons.

Veronica is made aware of Chuck's post about him giving her a "sticky-maple." Thankfully, exactly *what that is,* is left to our imagination. What is made clear however, is that Veronica is not going to let that slide.

Betty, now Veronica's bestie, is at her side and on the case. After talking to other girls, they uncover a pattern of slut-shaming amongst the football players. Ethel—one of the victims—tells of a secret playbook where points for sexual acts are tallied.

Is anyone happy about Archie's do-good actions? Cheryl is. She promises Archie whatever he wants—except her body. He takes her up on the offer and uses it to get an in with the Pussycats. Are they happy to see him? No, not really.

Meanwhile, Jughead is all over Dilton Doiley and the scouts, because they were in the woods on July 4th and came across the falsely distressed Cheryl. Jughead corners one of the scouts at Pop's, snatches a cherry from the guy's sundae, and pops it into his mouth in a date-worthy fashion, telling them *I saw the way you looked at me.* The two of them proceed to discuss who apparently fired "the single shot."

28

After Betty, Veronica, Cheryl and Ethel find the football teams' Slut-Shaming Playbook, Betty invites Chuck to Ethel's. Hate to be a downer, but I need to remind you again that these are high school sophomores. Right after "dark Betty" enters the scene of the revenge date, we cut to The Taste of Riverdale to see Cheryl's mom punch Betty's mom. Keep Alice's actions and attitudes in mind for the next scene, in case you're wondering why a nice girl like Betty does what she does.

Also, at The Taste of Riverdale, the Pussycats perform. It's good, but let's face it—we're all waiting for the awkwardness that is Betty and Veronica preparing to shame and punish Chuck. Things get more than awkward when Betty steps on Chuck's head while calling him Jason, telling him to apologize for what he did to Polly. Next day, the book of shame exposé is out, published in *The Blue and Gold*, and Betty shrugs off Veronica's concern for her Dr. Jekyll-Mistress Hyde routine.

Jughead's concluding voice-over declares Betty and Veronica two sides of the same coin and reveals that the football coach saved his job—and the school's reputation—by cutting his son and the other players involved in the scandal. As Betty and Cheryl burn the playbook, Cheryl tells Betty she's sorry if her brother hurt Polly. Dilton tells Jughead he saw Ms. Grundy's car parked at the river's edge.

Chapter Four:
"The Last Picture Show"

Original airdate: *February 16, 2017*
Writer: *Michael Grassi*
Director: *Mark Piznarski*

Top Quote: "Oh, Archiekins. You're in it deep this time."—Veronica, to Archie, about his affair with Ms. Grundy.

Top Trivia: Betty Cooper, along with Jughead, first appeared in Archie's comic life in *Pep Comics* #22. The Betty Cooper of the Archie Comics also kept a diary, and panels of her writing in it were often the comic story's start.

Watch For: The cringe-worthy dinner with Fred, Archie and Ms. Grundy. While talking about her relationship with the Southside Serpents, Hermione says to Veronica, "When have I ever lied to you?" That's your cue to start counting those lies. The first appearance of Seaside Serpent, Joaquin.

Wonder About: Do you believe that Geraldine's—aka Jennifer—past drove her to have sex with a high school boy? Is Veronica too naïve about her parents? Have people forgotten about poor, dead Jason?

Summary + Commentary:

Jughead's opening voice-over notes that a week has passed since the discovery of Jason's body, and his home away from home and place of employment, The Twilight Drive-In, will be closing soon.

We get started with the main action inside Pop's. Jughead laments the closing of the drive-in and invites Kevin, Veronica and Betty to closing night. Outside of Pop's, Betty confronts Archie about Ms. Grundy. Veronica arrives just as Archie is coming clean and the three of them proceed to struggle to define their so-called relationship.

Alice Cooper pulls up and demands that Betty get in the car. This impromptu departure gives Betty the chance to cyber-stalk the line-crossing teacher. The next day, pretending that *The Blue and Gold* is doing a series spotlighting teachers, Betty grills the woman and discovers that the music teacher did an independent study with—wait for it—Jason Blossom.

Now Cheryl is all about the drama. At the parking lot of Pop's, she snaps a pic of Hermione arguing with a Southside Serpent, then taunts Veronica with the photo. Naturally, Veronica grills her mom, but she claims it was nothing more than putting a man in his place. Later, when Hermione drops off a bag of cash at the mayor's office, new questions arise.

Worked up about the closing of the Drive-In, Jughead asks Mayor McCoy to save it. For the mayor—an elegant woman who clearly appreciates up-scaling—keeping the trashy spot that's frequently a hangout for drug dealers and transients open, is not on-brand for her.

Even though Archie insists that he and Grundy are *together*, Betty continues to dig into the layer of lies around her. One of them being that she graduated from the world-renowned music school, Juilliard. Know who else is doing something unethical? Betty and Veronica. They break into Ms. Grundy's car and find a metal box, containing a Minnesota driver's license with a different name and a handgun.

After they tell Archie what they found, he mistakes himself for an actual boyfriend and asks Ms. Grundy about her past. She tells him of an abusive ex-husband. He believes her, but Betty later points out that Archie is in over his head, in an isolating—aka abusive—relationship.

After Alice finds Ms. Grundy's handgun stashed under a stack of Betty's T-shirts, she invades her daughter's privacy some more by digging out Betty's diary, and confronting her.

At the closing night of the drive-in, Kevin and Veronica are joined by Cheryl. Meanwhile Fred Andrews is dragged off by Alice Cooper, and everyone is annoyed by the noisy, bottle-throwing Southside Serpents. Archie isn't there, as he's again throwing himself at Ms. Grundy one last time.

Right after they declare their so-called relationship over, Betty, Alice and Fred bust into her house to break up that final embrace. Things get more twisted as Betty's mom just wants to make Archie look bad to Betty. Archie's dad doesn't want to face the truth that a teacher has abused his son, and Archie continues to protect his abuser. Still carrying the expensive gift Archie brought her—a bow for her cello—Ms. Grundy announces her impending departure.

Later that night, Kevin and his dad, Sheriff Keller, come home to find Jason's murder board destroyed. Hermione sums up the facts for Veronica. Her dad, although in prison, is still illegally manipulating others and still funding their lifestyle. Betty's mom switches gears and starts talking about Polly instead of Archie. No more secrets, she declares. But Betty reminds her mother that she is Betty—not Polly.

We conclude, not with Jughead this time, but with Betty as she writes in her diary about the possibility that Ms. Grundy was dangerous. *Maybe* she was dangerous?

Chapter Five:
"Heart of Darkness"

Original airdate: *February 23, 2017*
Writer: *Ross Maxwell*
Director: *Jesse Warn*

Top Quote: "The horror, the horror."—Jughead in Betty's ear when the two are interrupted by Cheryl's grandmother while searching Jason's bedroom.

Top Trivia: The top quote is a nod to Joseph Conrad's novella, *Heart of Darkness*. Despite receiving a lukewarm reception on publication, the 1899 novella inspired many adaptations, including *Apocalypse Now*. The placement of the quote, used often as a literary allusion, implies Nana Rose, Cheryl's grandmother, represents the evil deeds done by Cheryl's family.

Watch For: Backstory and character development for Cheryl. Backstory on the interconnection and longtime animosity of the Blossoms, the Coopers and the Lodges. Take notes. Betty and Jughead detectives. More, much more, to come on that front.

Wonder About: Was Fred's night out at the drive-in with Hermione a date, as he thought? How creepy is Hal, sitting in the dark alone, watching home videos of his shy daughter dancing in the grass? Where is Alice Cooper this whole time? Can you even believe she'd miss Jason's memorial?

Summary + Commentary:

Jughead's opening voice-over describes the town's creepy house, Thornhill—Cheryl Blossom's family home. You know you're dying to go inside.

Archie has set aside his guitar for the time being, hung up his punching bag, and buried his feelings for Ms. Grundy. Upon finding his son punching the daylights out of the bag, Fred slinks out of the room, leaving the real issue—Archie having been maltreated and manipulated by an authority figure—unaddressed.

Inside the school across town, Jughead, Betty and Kevin reconstruct Jason Blossom's murder board. While the crew at *The Blue and Gold* tries to figure out who killed the red-haired twin, Archie and Reggie start a battle over who gets to wear the dead guy's jersey. Over at Pop's, married Fred asks the married Hermione out on a date, and is shocked when Hermione shuts him down. His resentful attitude is cringe-worthy.

Archie still longs for his guitar, but now that Ms. Grundy is gone, he needs a new mentor. After football practice, Val stops by his house to help him out. Mr. Andrews pops into Archie's room and is cringe-worthy for the second time when he gushes all over Valerie, about how he is a huge fan of her group, the Pussycats.

Back at Pop's, Betty grills Trev about Jason and Polly. She learns nothing new, so afterward, she asks her dad some probing questions while they're working on a car engine. He tells her that Polly was sent away because she tried to commit suicide. Oh snap.

For those waiting for Veronica and Archie to get together, the writers offer a scene where she bandages his hurt wrist with the skill of an EMT. Later, Veronica has dinner with the Blossom family, where Cheryl's parents take the opportunity to dredge up Mr. Lodge's arrest and inform Veronica that Cheryl will not be participating in Jason's memorial.

Best sleepover ever. Ready for some weirdness? Of course you are.

While cleaning up at Pop's, Hermione finds a snake in a box. Betty finds her dad sitting in the dark, watching a home-video of the still mysteriously gone Polly. And everyone finds Jason's memorial twisted and disturbing, especially when Cheryl—who'd been told by her parents not to speak—enters the memorial wearing the same white outfit she wore on the day of her brother's murder.

Fred arrives at the memorial late and, not one to give up even when he should, tells Hermione that he's changed his mind about the position at his construction company. He asks her to come work for him. After she agrees, he gets what he really wants—an impulsive hug from the lovely, married lady.

Betty and Jughead pass on the light supper being served downstairs to search Jason's bedroom, but are interrupted by Cheryl's grandmother, Nana Rose. The old woman mistakes Betty for Polly and begins speaking to her, filling in a major blank—Jason and Polly were engaged. Later, when Betty confronts her father with this information, she discovers he already knew about the engagement. Then he drops his own bomb—great-grandfather Blossom murdered Clifford's grandfather. What? Wait? Why is he telling her this *now*? Oh, right—sins of past Riverdale stay in present Riverdale.

Jughead's concluding voice-over foreshadows a future poison, now that Jason is buried in the earth. Lies and secrets give life to pain. No kidding, Juggie. We noticed. We're left with a final quote from Jughead as he speaks to Betty, who's just pinned her own family name onto *The Blue and Gold*'s Jason murder board. "We need to talk to Polly." Yes. Please do.

Chapter Six:
"Faster, Pussycats! Kill! Kill!"

Original airdate: *March 2, 2017*
Writer: *Tessa Leigh Williams & Nicholas Zwart*
Director: *Steven A. Adelson*

Top Quote: "You have no integrity whatsoever [...] They're married. To other people."—Veronica to Archie on their parents hooking up.

Top Trivia: The logo on Melody's drum kit used at the variety show is a nod to the original Josie and the Pussycats from the Archie Comics.

Watch For: The first time Polly is visibly present in a scene. Jughead climbing into Betty's room, reminiscent of a scene in the 1996 horror film, *Scream*. First kiss for Betty & Jughead.

Wonder About: Would you be friends with Josie? How unsupportive and demanding are Josie's parents? Last episode, Hermione was all "We're both married," and now she's all "Dinner at my place." What's up with this Yo-Yo behavior?

Summary + Commentary:

Jughead's opening voice-over is a reminder that we're all afraid of something, and that monsters *do* exist. Meanwhile, Riverdale is getting ready for the annual variety show.

Having breakfast with Betty and her mom, an unfortunate Jughead is a demonstration in uncomfortable situations. Betty's mom is icy and clearly blames Jughead for Betty's obsession with Jason's death. Truth be told, the meal was just a ploy to distract Alice so that

Betty can dig through her mom's purse. So yeah, Betty's mom knows what's up, and now, thanks to finding a check made out to The Sisters of Quiet Mercy, so does Betty.

Despite his passion for music, Archie chokes at the variety show tryouts. Josie clarifies what happened—he had stage fright. But not to worry, Veronica saves him by pulling strings to get him a slot on the show with a bonus—she'll be joining him on stage.

Fred meanwhile hasn't given up on asking out the still-married Hermione. On her first day at work for Andrews Construction, he asks her to be his co-host at a dinner with Mayor McCoy. One of his goals (no need to clarify the *other* goal) for the dinner, is to get the contract for work to be done on the Twilight Drive-In's former site. She agrees to the meal prompting a kiss. The kiss prompts Fred to tell Archie that he is rekindling the flame with Hermione.

Archie says he's cool with that.

Apparently, everyone is also cool with ignoring the fact that both he and Hermione are still married. Everyone except Veronica, who calls her mom out on it, then tells Archie he has no integrity and kind of blames him for his father.

Then Veronica joins the Pussycats.

Betty and Jughead head to The Sisters of Quiet Mercy to see Polly, where Betty finds out that Polly is pregnant with Jason's baby—and Polly finds out that Jason is dead. Soon, Betty is interrogating her dad again, asking him if he killed Jason Blossom. Strangely, but not all that surprisingly, this makes Alice laugh. Betty turns away from both her parents, no longer trusting them. Can you blame her?

At a super awkward dinner party, hosted by him and Hermione, Fred Andrews makes a bid to Mayor McCoy. The mayor tells him The Twilight Drive-In's former landowner has selected someone else for the contract. Little does Fred know, the new owner is Hiram Lodge. (Secret #1). Long story short, Fred is so sad about not getting the contract. Hermione forges Veronica's signature on a contract so that he can get the work. (Secret #2—not that we're counting).

Betty's response to her first kiss from Jughead is not getting swept off her feet—it's remembering that Polly mentioned Jason's stashed car and realizing she wants to go find it. Instead of heading to the variety show, they head to Route 40.

Later at the variety show. Val and the Pussycats are on stage, magnificent and wearing skin-tight catsuits and thigh-high boots. The stunned looks of some of the parents in the audience are great. And Archie performs (very well) before he, impulsive as always, kisses Valerie.

Veronica doesn't find out about the kiss, but she does find out that her mom forged her signature to give the construction contract to Fred's company. She is not happy.

Jughead and Betty don't care about the kiss. They found Jason's varsity jacket.

Jughead's concluding voice-over, audible while we see Jason's car now in flames, reflects on fear. The fear that comes from monsters and danger close to home. He also tells viewers that Polly is on the run, alone.

Chapter Seven:
"In a Lonely Place"

Original airdate: *March 9, 2017*
Writer: *Aaron Allen*
Director: *Allison Anders*

Top Quote: "It's darkest before the dawn." But sometimes… There's just darkness."—Jughead in his concluding voice-over.

Top Trivia: Ginger Lopez, the green-sweatered girl eavesdropping in the student lounge, appeared in the Archie Comics in the early 2000s. She was originally created to replace Cheryl.

Watch For: The beanie Jughead is wearing in the opening scene is a nod to the one he wore in the early Archie Comics. FP appears to be drunk, even though they're at Pop's Diner. So awkward. Backstory on FP and Fred.

Wonder About: How weird is Polly? Is she mentally stable enough to raise a baby? Is Veronica's relationship with her mom a healthy one? What about Jughead and FP's?

Summary + Commentary:

Jughead's opening voice-over begins over a mid-century dream sequence showing him engaged to Betty, Jason Blossom alive, and Betty's parents being normal-ish and loving. Next, we see Jughead sleeping in a closet under the stairs at Riverdale High School. When Archie finds him in the locker room brushing his teeth, Jughead spills the truth—ever since Archie's dad fired Jughead's dad, things have been bad at home. Archie offers Jughead space at his house, but he declines and swears Archie to secrecy.

Polly is on the run, and Betty—who blames herself for Polly running away—aims to find her before the Blossoms do. Meanwhile Cheryl, who also wants to find the missing girl, is all over Twitter, seeking help from her minions. Sheriff Keller is feeling the pressure of the looming evil that is the Blossom family.

Fred, Archie and Jughead put together a plan to get Jughead's dad back on the sober wagon and back on the payroll of Andrews Construction. But Jughead's dad's plan is to stumble around his trailer, knocking over empty bottles and complaining about the sorry state of his life.

Later, while walking home with Jughead, Betty remembers where Polly hid the last time she ran away. Betty finds her in the attic, stressed and frankly being rather nutty. Maybe Alice and Hal are right about the girl needing help.

FP, wearing a flannel shirt, manages to sober up long enough to go to the Andrews Construction office to tell Fred—also wearing a flannel shirt—that he'll accept the offer to come back to work.

Alice and Hal lie about Polly to Betty's face, and when Cheryl insists that she wants to help Polly, Betty tells Cheryl what her sister needs most—money. Cheryl promises to talk with her parents.

Over food at Pop's, Archie and Jughead have a disconcerting conversation with their dads, who were apparently high school chums. Yes, more history forthcoming on those two flannel-wearing family men. Later, FP tells Archie that he and Fred started the construction business together, but when FP needed bailing out from some "hot water" Fred did so, but informed FP that the two of them needed to part ways. That's why Fred owns the company.

In response to her mother forging her signature on the contract giving Fred Andrews' construction company the big redevelopment job, Veronica goes clubbing with Josie, Kevin and Reggie. There is some fabulous, neon-drenched dancing and fun; it's all happiness until Veronica laments that her mother has taken away the last thing she had control over—her name. Moments later, she discovers that her mother has also taken away her credit card.

Betty talks with the Blossom trio about the still missing Polly, Archie talks with his dad about the past, and Veronica talks with her mom about her mom's affair with Fred. We get some answers, but of course, also a new set of questions.

Ignoring laws that require parents to be present while questioning minors, Sheriff Keller takes Jughead down to the station as he's now a suspect in Jason's murder. Jughead lawyers up. Good for him.

There's an ugly, then sad, scene outside the police station when FP shows up hung-over and apologetic before turning hung-over and angry. In the end, FP promises to get himself together. Fred, crossing yet another boundary, forges a timecard to create an alibi for Jughead.

At Pop's, Polly meets up with Cheryl who tells her to run, that the Blossom house isn't safe. No kidding. That place is a Gothic themed fun park with no exit. Polly listens to the voice of experience, changes her plans, and accepts Veronica's offer to stay with her.

Jughead's concluding voice-over reflects on hope and darkness, and implies that darkness trumps hope. Don't be ashamed to admit you're hoping for more darkness in Riverdale.

Chapter Eight:
"The Outsiders"

Original airdate: *March 30, 2017*
Writer: *Julia Cohen*
Director: *David Katzenberg*

Top Quote: "Hell is other people."—Jughead to Archie.

Top Trivia: The top quote is a nod to a line in No Exit, a play by French philosopher and writer Jean Paul Sartre. The 1944 play features three dead characters who are locked in a room, a symbolic hell, together. The often misunderstood quote refers not to the difficulty relationships present but to identity formation that results from judging ourselves based on the perceptions and interpretations of others..

Watch For: Archie and Valerie start their coupleship. Alice all over the place and kicking up dust. Betty and Jughead are officially identified as a couple.

Wonder About: Seriously, scale from one to five: how inconsistent is Fred's parenting? Check out the color of Alice's nails. What does that symbolize? Do Jughead and Archie have a magic Xbox that plays DC Universe Online?

Summary + Commentary:

Jughead's opening voice-over... he says the Coopers were The Stepfords of Riverdale until Jason Blossom happened. If the viewer understands that the perfect Stepfords of the seemingly idyllic Connecticut neighborhood were, in truth, mind-controlled by the community's men, that makes sense. What doesn't make sense is thinking that the Coopers were at one time suburban perfection. Families don't get this messed up overnight.

Polly—seated between Betty and Veronica—is questioned by Sheriff Keller and claims Jason planned to fake his own death, then do a one-time drug deal with the Southside Serpents.

The next morning at school, the gang plus Cheryl discuss Polly's situation. The Coopers want Polly, but not the baby. The Blossoms want the baby, but not Polly. Veronica's solution to this dilemma is to have a baby shower, hosted by her and her mom. As they begin to discuss things, however, Mrs. Cooper barges in and insists on talking with Betty and Veronica. Once alone, Betty tells her mom if she'd like to be loving and supportive, like a normal grandmother, then great—otherwise, stay away.

Things are getting bad for Fred as Clifford Blossom has lured his construction crew away. Ignoring that parent-child boundaries are there for a reason, Fred dumps his life troubles on his son, telling Archie that the business is in big trouble. But not to worry, though. Archie appears at the construction company with his high school friends, offering to be the new crew. Never mind school, homework or sports practice. They head off to work.

Which is fine until Moose gets beat up by a pair of thugs who've arrived to destroy Fred's equipment. Who is the cause, we wonder? The Serpents? Clifford Blossom?

Archie is worked up. He wants to take Moose to the Whyte Wyrm, a bar where the Serpents hang out. Why? To see if Moose can identify the guys who jumped him of course. But once there, they actually find Jughead's dad. Surprise, he's a Southside Serpent. Who isn't surprised about this? Archie's dad, thanks to FP's call, arrives to pick Archie up.

The next surprise is that Alice Cooper arrives at Polly's baby shower—followed by Cheryl, her mother and Nana Rose. We may be thinking that tensions are going to get worked out, but the shower takes a dreary turn when Archie arrives, stomping through the pastel-cardigan-wearing crowd. All to accuse Jughead of... something... that isn't quite clear.

Soon, Alice and Penelope forgo baby shower etiquette and go at it, throwing insults and ugliness until Polly breaks it up. Once the crowd is gone, Polly considers coming home as she tells her mom that had Hal arranged for Polly to "see a doctor" so she didn't have to "live with her mistake." This is news to Alice. Not good news.

At home, Alice confronts Hal, who won't allow Polly to move home because she's carrying a baby with *Blossom blood*. So Alice kicks Hal out. Polly is coming home, she says. But no, Polly decides to go to Thornhill to be with the Blossoms.

Archie has a heart-to-heart with his dad, where Fred feels bad about who he is. Betty has a heart-to-heart with Jughead, who also feels bad about who he is. Know who doesn't feel bad about who he is, but should? FP. He's drunk and rumpled, and full of excuses when Jughead shows up with Betty at the trailer, asking about Jason's one-time drug deal with the Serpents.

Jughead's concluding voice-over is absent, leaving us all bereft.

Chapter Nine:
"La Grande Illusion"

Original airdate: *April 6, 2017*
Writer: *James DeWille*
Director: *Lee Rose*

Top Quote: "Mr. Andrews. Nice haircut. Looking extremely DILF-y today."—Cheryl, assessing Archie's father.

Top Trivia: Cheryl Blossom first appears in the Archie Comics in 1982 as a love interest for Archie. Her overt sexuality caused controversy, and thus (unfortunately), her comic page appearances were few until the mid-90s.

Watch For: First kiss for Archie and Cheryl. Veronica yanking off that symbolic pearl necklace. The end of the truly short coupleship of Archie and Valerie.

Wonder About: Is Archie being honest about his involvement with Cheryl? Do we even care about Fred and Hermione's tryst being over? In the real world, maple trees are tapped late winter, mid-February to mid-March; Jughead's ending voice-over states that winter had come early to Riverdale. The Blossom family has just held their annual tree tapping ceremony. Ponder on that for a bit.

Summary + Commentary:

Jughead's opening voice-over talks of Maple syrup, its permanence in the town's history and economy, and the enigmatic family that holds the monopoly on the local trade—the Blossoms. With the heir to the family business, Jason, now dead, who will take over the reins of control when the time comes? Not Cheryl.

Reporter Alice is writing a tell-all exposé on the clan, cluelessly hoping to halt the decades' long feud that started when great-grandfather Blossom killed great-grandfather Cooper.

Distressed, Veronica is hoping to dodge questions about her felon father. Hermione confesses to her daughter, that her husband knows about the affair with Fred, and consequently, Veronica may need to shade the truth. Hello? Hermione? Your own daughter tried to warn you about the consequences of your behavior.

Cheryl invites Archie to an annual tree-topping ceremony, but he declines. She insists, and he declines again, sending her storming out, plaid skirt swishing. Later, Penelope corners Archie with a bribe—an in at the Brandenburg Music Academy. Suddenly he agrees to attend the tree-topping event. The gang understands his decision reversal, reluctantly acknowledging that networking is the way of the world. At the event, Archie tells Polly to talk with her sister, speaking up for Cheryl when some relatives make snide remarks about her. Polly doesn't appreciate Archie's words, but Cheryl does. Next thing he knows, he's been tricked into attending a Blossom banquet.

Ethel reads an emotional poem in class, and—hoping to correct some bad karma of her past—Veronica takes the girl under her wing. Later, at a luncheon at the Lodge house, Ethel tells everyone that her family may lose their home. Hermione lets her daughter know that Mr. Lodge is responsible for this misfortune. Later, Hermione lets Fred know he's in the middle of the mess that is her husband's business manipulations; she's attempting to use the connection to Andrews Construction to make Lodge Industries legitimate. Understandably, Fred is not happy.

Wearing a beautiful Blossom-red sweater, Archie relays his conversation with Polly to Betty and Alice, telling them both that she doesn't seem to want to come home. The next day at school, Betty confronts Cheryl, asking the queen vixen to pass on a message to Polly: please call mother. Cheryl agrees, but not before passing on the big news that Polly is carrying twins.

Valerie confronts Archie about his involvement with the Blossoms. Wouldn't he rather *earn* his spot at the exclusive summer program? Sadly, he doesn't seem to understand the ethical dilemma.

Later, at the banquet, Archie gets pulled deeper into Blossom manipulations, this time by Clifford. While on the dance floor, he finds out Polly is at Thornhill only to get closer to the Lodges, as she believes they had a hand in Jason's death.

Betty and Veronica, after hearing Ethel's dad attempted suicide, bring flowers to the hospital. Veronica comes clean to Ethel about who her father is and what he does to business partners. It does not go well. Ethel's mom fumes, and while Ethel tries to stand up for Veronica , in the end she hangs her head, falling silent. Veronica arrives home and informs her mother that she is done lying for her dad.

Back at Thornhill—sporting the tailor-made suit the Blossoms supplied him with—Archie strides through the snow, following Cheryl who's rushed out of the banquet. After kissing, Cheryl calls him on his BS that he only came to her house as a favor. He wanted something in return, just like everyone. Val also calls him on his BS. And that she's done with him. And Fred is done with Hermione.

Jughead's closing voice-over draws our attention to Cheryl and her storm of chaos.

Chapter Ten:
"The Lost Weekend"

Original airdate: *April 13, 2017*
Writer: *Britta Lundin & Brian E. Paterson*
Director: *Dawn Wilkinson*

Top Quote: "You catatonic bimbos didn't even vote. So, you stuttering sap-heads are too dim to exercise your own rights, and you've got the combined vocabulary of a baked potato. Consider this your last practice as River Vixens, and your last week as my social handmaidens. You're fired on all fronts. That's all. Shoo, bitches."— Cheryl, dumping two River Vixens, who didn't vote on the winner for the dance-off.

Top Trivia: At the start of Jughead's birthday, Veronica calls Jughead "Torombolo." This is a nod to the cap-wearing fellow called Torombolo in the Spanish version of the Archie Comics.

Watch For: The dance-off between Cheryl and Veronica. Jughead's ruthless berating of Betty. First appearance of Mary Andrews.

Wonder About: Is Chuck sincere in apologizing to Ethel? What is the point of the cherry-on-top dance-off between Cheryl and Veronica? How awkward is it when Betty sings *Happy Birthday* to Jughead?

Summary + Commentary:

Jughead's opening voice-over reminds us that, while everything in our lives seems orderly, Jason's death makes us realize there is no control or order. There is only chaos.

Fred is headed out of town, off to see Mary to finalize the divorce papers. Despite recently encouraging his dad to date Hermione, Archie tries to talk him out of ending the marriage. Fred explains, "sometimes, you just gotta rip the band-aid off."

Veronica is headed to her father's hearing, being asked to speak to his character, to make him look more human. But the raven-haired beauty isn't interested in helping the man and explains, "Dad made his bed, and I'm late for school." If you think the relationship between father and daughter is filled with mixed-messages and manipulations at present, just wait.

Archie is talking. He tells Veronica he overheard Clifford's claim to be the reason Hiram is in jail. He tells Betty that Jughead's birthday is the next day.

Betty tries to put together a birthday event at lunch, but Archie insists the guy hates his birthday. Veronica, looking for a reason to wear a cute dress, insists Betty move ahead. After Chuck shows up, claiming to apologize to Ethel, Archie reverses his position and offers his house for the birthday event. Betty, being her usual I-want-everything-to-be-perfect-self invites… Jughead's dad.

Veronica relays Archie's information about Clifford to Hermione, telling her that she's been digging into her father's files and discovered that Blossom Maple Farms had been making monthly payments to Lodge Industries for over 75 years. The catch? The payments halted as soon as Hiram was imprisoned. Veronica thinks they should tell Hiram's attorney both pieces of information. Hermione thinks they shouldn't. The resulting tension leads to a dance-off River Vixen-style.

In preparation for the upcoming party at Archie's house, Cheryl pairs up with Chuck. Who better to help her ruin Jughead's birthday bash party? When Betty and Jughead arrive at Archie's, they're welcomed by the rest of the gang, plus Kevin's boyfriend, Joaquin. Jughead is not happy about Betty's happy birthday party surprise.

Things go from bad to worse when Cheryl and Chuck arrive with a crowd—some sporting kegs on shoulders—and Archie is too pre-gamed to kick them out. It seems like Jughead seriously lashing out at Betty is the worst thing that can happen, until a game of Sins and Secrets reveals all the very personal messes everyone has been trying to keep hidden. Before you can sort out who is the worst person in Riverdale, FP—having just broken up a fight between Jughead and Chuck—declares the party done and over.

As the crowd disperses, FP—of all people—gives Jughead some good advice. He tells Jughead to apologize to Betty, which he does. Following his declaration of his own weirdness, Betty tells him there is darkness inside her, that it makes her do crazy things. So, having a party for your boyfriend is a *dark, crazy thing*? Meanwhile, Archie and Veronica agree that they are both messed up and seal the connection with a kiss.

The next morning, Veronica testifies on her father's behalf, but she's still conflicted, worried that her father may have been involved in Jason's murder. As such, she wants to help Betty with the investigation.

Jughead's concluding voice-over returns to the theme of order and chaos, stating that they are one and the same. Sure they are.

Chapter Eleven:
"To Riverdale and Back Again"

Original airdate: *April 27, 2017*
Writer: *Roberto Aguirre-Sacasa*
Director: *Kevin Sullivan*

Top Quote: "Nothing's lost forever. Everything comes back."—Penelope to Polly, talking about the ring Jason gave to Polly when he proposed.

Top Trivia: The title of this episode comes from a 1990 comedy film of the same name. In the movie, Archie is engaged, but not to Betty, or Veronica, or any other Archie Comics character. The plot centers around Archie's conflicted feelings because, after not seeing either Betty or Veronica for 15 years, he's suddenly forgetting his fiancé and pining after both of his old friends. The film was a pilot for a possible series, but the series never happened due to low ratings.

Watch For: Sober, clean, FP. The song Archie and Veronica sing at the homecoming dance, *We're the Kids in America,* was originally recorded in the early 1980s by Kim Wilde, written for her by her younger brother Adam. He wrote it hoping to give her a life-changing song to make her famous. It worked. You can find it on YouTube by searching for Kim Wilde—Kids in America (1981). Penelope's 'kindness' to Polly.

Wonder About: At whose family dinner table would you rather be a guest: The Coopers' or the Blossoms'? How weird is it that Fred takes both Mary and Hermione to the dance? Cheryl makes a comment to Polly about the babies, "If you think those babies will guarantee you safety, you're in for a rude awakening." What does she mean?

Summary + Commentary:

Jughead's opening voice-over comes from the bleachers of Riverdale's gym. There, with his keyboard on his knees, he writes about tradition. Despite Jason's death, the Bulldogs will battle their archrivals—the Baxter High Ravens—while the River Vixens cheer them on.

Archie has a tender moment with his mom, who has suddenly appeared in Riverdale. He tells her he's okay with being in Riverdale and invites her to come hear him sing at homecoming.

Hermione is elated to find out that Hiram may be released sooner than expected, thanks to a break from the judge. Veronica, still suspicious that her father had something to do with Jason's death, doesn't share her mom's joy. Jughead, in a surprising moment with his dad, arrives at his trailer to find it tidy and free of bottles. That's good. What isn't good though? FP encourages Jughead to move on and away from the Jason Blossom story.

Still on the mad-wagon from the exchange with her mother, Veronica tells Archie they're going to have to pretend those kisses and confessions after Jughead's party never happened. Veronica declares Archie boyfriend material, and thus not for her. Although there is little evidence for this statement. Take the way he treated Val, for example.

Polly catches Clifford without his red wig. That's unnerving, but also a bit of a relief for viewers because many have been aching to snatch that fake-looking mop off his head.

Veronica wants to search FP's trailer, and she's trying to swindle Archie into doing it. Her offer? He'll help her with the search, then she'll sing an upbeat, homecoming appropriate cover song with him at the dance. Kind of a win-win for her, isn't it?

Betty intuits that something is up with Alice and questions her mom about the sudden dinner invitation her mom extended to the Jones', but comes up empty. Except for the lingering aftereffects of having been lied to and manipulated.

At the homecoming dance, Betty catches on that Veronica and Archie are in cahoots. When she questions them about it, Archie cuts it short because it's time for him to go on stage. Betty corners the two of them afterwards, but just as they come clean, Jughead arrives—the whole story about Veronica and Archie going to FP's trailer on Alice's prompting coming out.

As Jughead reels from the discovery that his friends went behind his back, Kevin appears. Fred has been arrested for Jason's murder. This news sends Jughead over the edge, trashing the trailer, before fleeing in tears. Betty goes to look for him.

At the Pembrooke, Veronica and Hermione commiserate about their situation. If FP confesses… if Hiram did hire FP to kill Jason… they plan to cut ties with him. At Archie's house, Mary tries to talk him into living with her in Chicago. He promises to think about it, but we know he'll never leave Riverdale.

At Thornhill, Cheryl checks in on Polly to be certain the mom-to-be isn't dead. We get one last look at that knockout red dress Cheryl is wearing. At Pop's, Betty meets up with Archie and Veronica, who tell Betty that there was no lockbox when they searched the trailer. They know FP is being framed.

Jughead's concluding voice-over is as absent he is.

Chapter Twelve:
"Anatomy of a Murder"

Original airdate: *May 4, 2017*
Writer: *Michael Grassi*
Director: *Rob Seidenglanz*

Top Quote: "It's not like they were brother and sister. They're, what, third cousins?"—Clifford creating a non-incest stance on Polly and Jason's baby.

Top Trivia: Pop's Chok'Lit Shoppe existed in the comic world of Archie and was the gang's favorite hangout. The location you see in the show is a real place, and you can really eat there. It's called Rocko's Diner of British Columbia, but its interior is where the pilot was filmed. The diner used in later episodes is built to match Rocko's.

Watch For: Secrets exposed for Joaquin, Hal and FP. Jason's murderer is finally revealed. Cheryl's response to the intense information about her father, as well as his response to being called on it.

Wonder About: Why does Cheryl react as she does when Jughead apologizes to her? Penelope's sarcasm and cruelty. Where is her anger coming from? How complicated is the Blossom family tree?

Summary + Commentary:

Jughead's opening voice-over is absent because so is he.

Betty, Archie and Veronica tell their parents their theory about the gun being planted in FP's trailer. The parents are not on board, but Betty and Archie aren't content to do nothing. They head to the bus station to look for Jughead, joined by Veronica, and find their very distraught friend at Pop's. Together, they tell him they believe his father was framed.

At the Riverdale Police Station, FP recaps Jason's one-time drug deal and fake death story, confessing to Jason's murder. Meanwhile At Betty's house, she and her mom find Hal, who you'll recall was kicked out of the house, rummaging through a desk.

Here's where things get interesting. To explain his midnight cat-burglar act, Hal admits to stealing evidence from Sheriff Keller and whips up some really fake-sounding reasons why. Then he drops a bomb—Betty's great grandfather wasn't just murdered by a Blossom. He *was* a Blossom. Betty is shocked to discover that *she* is a Blossom and queasy over the fact that her sister Polly is pregnant with her *third cousin's* baby. At least now Alice gets some answers about why Hal did what he did, wanting to make that appointment. The three of them charge over to Thornhill to get Polly back, and after a philosophical discussion on incest, Polly—who's just got the rude awakening that she carries incestual babies—leaves with the Coopers.

Mary slides into the role of FP's lawyer and informs Jughead that, because FP won't budge from his confession story, Jughead should go see him in jail. Jughead goes and, through the bars, throws speculations and pain at his dad. His dad takes it, telling his son to never come back. Jughead leaves but knows his dad is hiding something.

Kevin, Archie and Veronica grill Joaquin, who tells them that on July 11, he helped clean the basement of the White Wyrm. The mess? Jason's dead body. There's more. Joaquin overheard FP and Mustang talking about a rich guy. You want to know which rich guy? So do Kevin, Archie and Veronica. They insist Joaquin take them to see Mustang. He takes them, but Mustang can't tell them who. He's overdosed at a seedy hotel. When a bag of money is found, Veronica tells Sheriff Keller that her father was doing business with the Serpents. Joaquin, knowing its past time to dip, accepts a goodbye kiss from Kevin, gives him a vital piece of information, and boards a bus to San Junipero.

Who is FP protecting? Not Hal. Not Alice. Not Hermione. Who's left? Hold on to the edge of your couch, bingers. A lot is about to happen.

Using the information he received from Joaquin, Kevin leads Jughead and Betty to the edge of town, where they find a backpack with Jason's varsity jacket under a Blossom Maple Farms sign. Betty puts the coat on Archie, digs around in the lining, and finds a flash drive. Oh yes! Something concrete. After the gang watches the video surveillance footage revealing Jason's killer, Betty calls Cheryl. Instead of doing what Betty suggests—leaving her home immediately—Cheryl interrupts her father's dinner to tell him, "You did a bad thing, Daddy. And now everyone knows."

Jughead's concluding voice-over is jam-packed. He lets viewers know Sheriff Keller and Mayor McCoy saw the video footage, that Jughead found out his father confessed to the murder to keep him from suffering the same fate as Jason, and that Hiram Lodge is on his way home.

Yet a new mystery lingers. Why did Clifford kill his own son? The police arrive at Thornhill, hoping to make an arrest that might eventually lead to the answer, but arrive to find Clifford hanging in his barn, body swinging over barrels of Maple syrup and drug packages.

Chapter Thirteen:
"The Sweet Hereafter"

Original airdate: *May 11, 2017*
Writer: *Roberto Aguirre-Sacasa*
Director: *Lee Toland Krieger*

Top Quote: "It's positively Dickensian. I love a long-lost brother."—
Veronica, responding to Betty, who has just shared the news that
she has a secret brother out in the world.

Top Trivia: The Jughead of Archie Comics has a shaggy, long-haired
pet dog named Hot Dog. At the end of this episode, it's revealed
that the Southside Serpents have a shaggy, long-haired pet dog
named Hot Dog.

Watch For: Signs that Betty is still fighting the manipulations of her
family. Archie pounding against the ice. Reportedly, he broke his
hand while filming that scene. Cheryl getting revenge.

Wonder About: What actual, concrete steps has Polly taken, by
herself, to prepare for the birth of her babies? Is Archie's song
good? How do you feel when Jughead puts on *the* jacket?

Summary + Commentary:

Jughead's opening voice-over, along with reporter Alice, summarizes
what is now believed to be the truth: Jason's discovery of his father's
heroin trafficking business, led to his abduction by Mustang and
subsequent murder by his own father. Clifford then overdosed Mustang
to cover his tracks. In the end, Jason's murder revealed dark truths of
Riverdale.

Right after Veronica tells Archie she plans to come clean about their semi-dating situation, Mayor McCoy calls Betty and Archie into Principal Weatherbee's office. She'd like to honor them at the town's upcoming 75th Anniversary Jubilee. After the mayor rejects the suggestion that Jughead also be honored, Betty and Archie decline. At lunch, Betty tells the gang she intends to write a story covering the recently revealed truths. Veronica takes the mention of truth as her cue, revealing her and Archie's status. Betty gives them her best wishes.

Archie, ego on his sleeve, hunts Betty down at *The Blue and Gold* office to make sure she is truly okay. She is. Enough said. Well apparently not, because soon Veronica is also asking Betty if she is sincerely okay. Again, yes, she is.

Cheryl ducks away from Thornhill long enough to give Veronica her River Vixens T-shirt. Next surprise, she then apologizes to Jughead and gives him her iconic spider broach. Those who have taken their suicide awareness training will not be surprised by a later scene when Veronica receives a text from Cheryl, stating that she's gone to be with Jason.

Somehow Betty has managed to write the aforementioned story about the town's dark secrets in a matter of hours, and publishes it in *The Blue and Gold*. What happens as a result? Someone uses pig's blood to write "GO TO HELL SERPENT SLUT!" on her locker. Later at home, Alice reveals a secret she has been keeping. She tells Betty that she herself was sent away to The Sisters of Quiet Mercy. Surprise Betty! You have a secret brother!

Betty, Archie and Veronica head to Southside High to rescue Jughead from his rough new school. After Veronica receives a chilling text from Cheryl, the four of them rush to rescue her, who, while trying to be with Jason, falls beneath the ice.

After depositing Cheryl at her house, Veronica—instead of getting Cheryl some mental health assistance—heads to the jubilee. Backstage, Archie and Veronica declare themselves soul mates. Onstage, Archie performs with Josie and the Pussycats who are upbeat and fun. Then Betty speaks, and all the fun is sucked out of the auditorium. She challenges Riverdale to stop lying and keeping secrets. To do better. The folks of the town are stunned silent until Jughead starts clapping. They must be shamed or accept their faults, so they all begin clapping too.

Penelope arrives home to find Cheryl lingering near the fireplace, gasoline poured all around her. Claiming it's the only way they can be purified, she drops the candelabra she's holding. Outside, on the lawn, she smiles as the place burns. We don't know if this is the first house in Riverdale to burn, but I can tell you it won't be the last.

Betty and Jughead exchange "I love yous," while Veronica and Archie sneak into Veronica's bedroom. Don't remember that these couples are high school sophomores. Doing so may make you feel bad about what you're watching.

The Serpents arrive to give Jughead his very own Serpent leather, breaking up his steamy scene with Betty. Him putting the symbolic jacket on puts a solid, powerful stop to the night. Archie and Veronica, however, make it through the night uninterrupted.

Things take a quick and brutal turn as Archie, still grinning from his night between Veronica's sheets, meets his dad at Pop's, and watches as his father is shot by a masked gunman.

Jughead's concluding voice-over narrates the image of the armed stranger dashing out of Pop's. Jughead declares that the last moment of Riverdale's innocence, a moment of violence that was anything but random.

Season 1 Pop Quiz

1) In this clip of dialogue, who speaks first?

"For the record, I'm not gay."

"Obviously not. You're on the football team. But if you were gay, what would you like to do?"

"Everything but kiss."

"I love a good closet case."

2) In this clip of dialogue, who speaks first?

"Can we make a vow?"

"Sure."

"That no matter what, no boy will ever come between us again. Deal?"

"Deal."

3) Who said it?

"I don't follow rules, I make them. And when necessary, I break them. You wanna help me get revenge on Chuck? Awesome. But you better be willing to go full dark, no stars."

4) In this clip of dialogue, which two characters are speaking?

"They'll tear that booth down, too. Raze the whole place. Send it to the junkyard. And us with it."

"Yeah. Maybe they'll save it. All the pieces. Store it in the town hall attic and rebuild it in a hundred years. Wonder who the hell we were."

"So, where you gonna live now?"

"I'll figure it out... I always do."

5) **Where are Kevin, Betty and Jughead when this conversation takes place?**

"Going on a date with Trev? Does Mama Cooper know about that?"

"Kev, I'm not on house arrest. Okay, she's out of town at a Women in Journalism spa retreat. Anyway, I mean—it's not a 'date' date."

"You just called it a date. You literally said, 'It's a date.'"

6) **Who said it?**

"So can't we just be friends? Or at least, frenemies?"

7) **Veronica and Reggie and talking. Fill in the blank.**

Veronica: "When my dad got arrested, the police, the lawyers, the judge, the courts... They took everything from us. Our houses, our cars, our club memberships, our yacht. Even, I'm not kidding, the clothes off our backs. Anyway. My mom sat me down at the edge of my canopy bed, and she told me not to cry... because there was one thing in this world that nobody could take away from me, not ever."

Reggie: "Your trust fund?"

Veronica: "_____, Reggie. Which, after telling me nobody would ever take it, that is exactly what she did. Like it meant nothing. Like it was nothing. Like I was nothing."

8) **At Polly's baby shower, Rose Blossom predicts that Polly will have twins. Who makes this comment in response?**

"This is occultism at its most ludicrous."

9) **Who said it?**

"It's like you know how in a time of crisis, people either come together or fall apart? It feels like we're falling apart."

10) **Who said it?**

"Who will the Grim Reaper take next? You? Me? Maybe your father had the right idea. Just end it. Better the sweet hereafter... than this awful limbo."

RIVERDALE

SEASON
TWO

Chapter Fourteen:
"A Kiss Before Dying"

Original airdate: *October 11, 2017*
Writer: *Roberto Aguirre-Sacasa*
Director: *Rob Seidenglanz*

Top Quote: "Oh. Betty. If that beanie-wearing cad defiled you, at least, please tell me that you were safe."—Alice to her daughter on Betty's evening with Jughead.

Top Trivia: The dream-like sequence when Fred imagines Archie, Veronica, Betty and Jughead telling him he "didn't live to see this day" became true when Luke Perry died from a stroke.

Watch For: The very fake looking backdrop when Veronica and Archie walk Vegas. Cheryl's confrontation with her mother; you've been waiting for that. Archie tells the gang he's ashamed about what he didn't do that morning at Pop's. Does he have reason to be?

Wonder About: Who do you think shot Fred? How does Jughead truly feel about his connection to the Southside Serpents? Are you surprised by Ms. Grundy's continuing behavior?

Summary + Commentary:

Jughead's opening voice-over picks right up where things left off last season. Despite the Mayor's Jubilee, Riverdale is still, at its heart, a haunted town.

It's an anxious morning. Archie delivers his wounded father to Riverdale General Hospital. Betty, Veronica and Jughead arrive just as he's taken into surgery. Betty's parents also come. Ever tactful, Alice takes the opportunity to ask Jughead if his associates, the Serpents, have anything to do with Fred being shot. When the sheriff arrives, Archie describes the shooting, including the black hood the shooter was sporting.

Cheryl arrives at the hospital with her mother; there is little fanfare as they whisk Penelope away to the burn unit. Cheryl cooks up a lie for Betty and Kevin, claiming that her mom risked her life to save her.

Veronica struggles with her new self, the considerate, supportive person she's working to become. At Betty's insistence, Veronica accompanies Archie—who needs to get out of his bloody clothes—home. This leads to a steamy—pun-intended—shower scene. Then, minutes later, Archie is yelling at Veronica, telling her to get out. She refuses to leave, however, and he breaks down and cries.

Jughead checks in with Tall Boy—another Southside Serpent—and enlists help, asking them to find out what they can about the shooting.

At Sheriff Keller's request, Archie views a line-up of guys wearing black hoods. Meanwhile, Veronica is on a mission to find Fred's wallet. Betty—taking her first motorcycle ride—heads to Pop's with Jughead to help look for the wallet. Pop tells them the man took no money and that the man wasn't a thief—he was an angel of death.

Veronica finally gets a clue and approaches her mom, telling Hermione that she believes the woman to be acting on Hiram's behalf, put a hit on Fred. Hermione retaliates with a threat of her own: get back in line or else. End result—Hermione gaining headway as the worst mom in Riverdale.

Jughead declares he is not a Serpent, but wants to be close to his dad. Concerned, Betty supports him anyway. Supporting him is her only choice, given that we all know he's not being truthful with himself. We know where he's headed.

In a classic power play, Cheryl informs her mother that if she tells anyone what really happened at Thornhill, she'll reveal what really happened in the barn with Clifford. She also declares things are going to be different—better. After the vindictive delivery, we believe her.

At the hospital café, Archie confesses that he feels like a coward. Instead of rushing to help his dad, he became paralyzed. Blaming himself, he says if he'd acted sooner, the gunman would have fled sooner. Fred is conscious with Archie at his bedside and tells him, *I came back to protect you.*

Stagger back bingers, Hiram is home. Veronica declares that she has changed, but she still does her father's bidding and kisses him hello. That's going to be the pattern for a while.

Jughead's concluding voice-over alerts us to Archie's new vow—he intends to keep his father safe from the man in the black hood. He also tells of an event in Greendale, a neighboring town, where a certain music teacher—who has taken on another underage mentee—is strangled by a certain angel of death.

Chapter Fifteen:
"Nighthawks"

Original airdate: *October 18, 2017*
Writer: *Michael Grassi*
Director: *Allison Anders*

Top Quote: "The answer is a double-cherry-on-top no."—Cheryl to Betty, when Betty asks if the Vixens will help save Pop's.

Top Trivia: Jingle-Jangle, the potent drug introduced in this episode, got its name from the 1969 song of the same name. You can find the original song, ironically light-hearted and filled with happiness, on YouTube, sung by the band The Archies, by searching for The Archies-Jungle Jangle (1969 Full Album).

Watch For: Alice reveals the murder weapon to Archie. Also, Midge Klump makes her debut appearance in this episode. The Pussycats performing on the roof of Pop's. We should have gotten more!

Wonder About: Veronica has zero interest in reconnecting with her father. Should she give him a chance? Is Cheryl's attitude toward FP justified? Is it reasonable to use a lawyer whose office is in the back of a tattoo shop?

Summary + Commentary:

Jughead's opening voice-over notes that Pop's Chock'lit Shoppe is the most recent casualty. The shop may be forced into going out of business.

Betty and Veronica band together to help save Pop's, agreeing that it's a place where memories are made and worth saving. Archie and Jughead pass, as they both have their hands full.

On legal matters, Archie corners the sheriff, telling him everything he's been doing to find the killer. He asks to go out with the cops, but the sheriff rejects the idea. Elsewhere, Jughead sits in with his dad and his dad's attorney. Things don't look good for FP—he's facing 20 years, and that's if he accepts a deal.

Filled with fear, hallucinating, and obsessed with finding the shooter, Archie is acting as though he's read a pamphlet on how to have PTSD. Veronica sends him to the school counselor, but that doesn't offer relief. Running into Reggie, he asks for *something* to keep him awake.

Betty and Jughead approach Mayor McCoy about both Pop's and FP. Things don't go the way they hope, however, and Jughead reprimands her, telling her to remember that day as the one when she turned her back on both Pop's and FP.

Hiram tries to get back on Veronica's good side but she gives him the cold shoulder. Can you blame her? The guy has all the warmth of an ice cube.

Jughead knows FP is innocent. When he seeks help from Tall Boy, the Serpent sends him to Penny Peabody, a seedy lawyer he refers to as a snake handler. Her office—being in the back of a tattoo shop—should have been a tip not to trade favors with her, but he does. His next mission? Get the Blossoms to speak up on FP's behalf. Given that injured Penelope can't utter a single word, and Cheryl is on an emotional rampage, how likely is that?

Veronica struggles to put the pieces of the who-shot-Fred puzzle together when she discovers that an anonymous buyer is buying Pop's. She accuses her dad, who denies it. Across the candle-lit dinner table, she shows her mother a threatening letter written by Hiram. Hermione, taking the opportunity to wound her daughter yet again, shrugs it off.

Jughead and Betty seek mercy from Cheryl and Penelope, but are solidly rejected. Later, Betty gets in touch with her dark side and blackmails Cheryl. They make a Riverdale style win-win deal. If Cheryl testifies on FP's behalf—and gets the River Vixens for Retro Night—Betty will give Cheryl the video of Jason's murder.

Retro Night gets off to a slow start. After The Pussycats are talked into performing, things pick up. Hiram and Hermione appear, and after Veronica buries the constantly swinging Lodge hatchet, Hiram declares Lodge Industries will make a charitable contribution to Pop's. Kind of like he's buying Veronica's approval, just like she accused him when she thought he'd bought the place. Never mind that though. The night is a success. Never mind that Hiram is a liar either; he did buy the diner.

Ever calculating, Cheryl shows her mom the video of Clifford killing Jason.

Ever observant, Alice tells Betty several drug deals took place in Pop's parking lot.

Ever vigilant, Archie meets up with Dilton, who's gotten him a handgun.

Jughead's concluding voice-over tells us that Archie slept well that night for the first time in weeks. If he'd been awake, he might've heard the two guns shots coming from the woods. Midge and Moose, who'd gone there to take Jingle-Jangle, were shot.

Chapter Sixteen:
"The Watcher in the Woods"

Original airdate: *October 25, 2017*
Writer: *Ross Maxwell*
Director: *Kevin Sullivan*

Top Quote:
"I self-identify as a loner."—Jughead to Toni on why he wants to sit alone in the cafeteria.

Top Trivia: The Red Circle comic book lying on top of Archie's handgun is a major literary Easter Egg. The Black Hood, first appearing in *Top Notch Comics* #9, was one of the Red Circle's characters. The comic version of the Black Hood has some similar characteristics, such as the desire to battle evil and the need to keep his identity hidden.

Watch For: Toni Topaz makes her first appearance as Jughead's Southside High mentor and a Southside Serpent. Sweet Pea, another Serpent, also makes a first appearance. The mysterious Jingle-Jangle and the gang feud at Southside High. Stay tuned.

Wonder About: Veronica is now getting along with her parents and wants her friends to meet her dad. What happened to that feud? Is Betty over-stepping in her advice to Kevin? Is Archie in over his head with Hiram? In over his head with his quest to protect Riverdale?

Summary + Commentary:

Jughead's opening voice-over reminds us that many fairy tales come with the same warning—children should never go into the woods alone. Bad things happen there. Now that we have a heads up, watch the woods folks.

The morning starts with Reggie informing the team that football practice has been canceled. Moose and Midge have been shot. The gang meets up in the student lounge, where Kevin recounts his "full-on Carrie" experience of how he found Midge covered in blood. Veronica invites them all over to her house later that night to meet her dad. Once Betty is alone with Kevin, she chooses not to mind her business and chastises him about cruising to hook up with random guys.

Moose tells Archie that the shooter was wearing a black hood. Okay so, by now, we understand it's not a black hood—it's *the* Black Hood. Archie is in full PTSD, over-protection mode. He tells his dad they should have a gun in the house, then continues to brood, even at Veronica's gathering. The only person who agrees with his take-matters-into-our-own-hands stance is Hiram, who declares the police aren't always the best protection. Ahh, it's the beginning of Archie and Hiram's relationship. Much more to come on this. You may want to start a point tally now.

The next morning, Archie shows his maturity by taking inspiration from a comic book and creates a watch group called The Red Circle—no weapons, no violence. That's ironic, considering he's hiding a gun. Over on the Southside, where students reject learning and hope, Jughead approaches teacher Mr. Phillips about restarting the school newspaper. One guy digging in while the other tries to dig out.

Alice Cooper receives a letter from *the* Black Hood. The shooter wants the paper to publish his message. He seeks to expose the town's secrets and punish the town's sinners. Yes, of course she prints it in her paper the next day.

Tension builds between Jughead and the Serpents. They want him to hang, but he wants to be a loner. What about that jacket he accepted?

After seeing the Black Hood's condemning letter in her parents' paper, Polly—an unwed mother carrying her cousin's babies—declares she needs to leave Riverdale. We viewers struggle to care that she's leaving.

Hermione tries to warn Veronica about Hiram. When Veronica calls her out, insisting that she admit Hiram is merciless, Hermione does what she does best—nothing. Not that we blame her. If she tried to do something, anything, Hiram probably would kill her or, at minimum, amp up his emotional abuse.

Betty visits Jughead at the Southside newspaper office, where he shares his discovery that the Ghoulies are the source of the Jingle Jangle. There's an awkward hello from Toni, who interrupts Jughead and Betty kissing, but the two girls end up bonding over the fact that they both brought coffee pots for the office.

Why, oh why, is Ethel Muggs walking alone on a dark, isolated street? I bet she wonders that too when a van slowly passes her, then circles back three times. She calls Archie's hotline, and he races to her assistance.

Betty, and of all people Cheryl, follow Kevin into Fox Forest. Betty confronts Kevin, where he finally points out that she lives in a pretty privileged world, while he does not. Maybe... just maybe... she'll respect that.

Elsewhere, Jughead gets a warning via beat down in the school hallway. He lies to Betty, telling her the scrapes and bruises are from a motorcycle accident. Toni reminds him he ought to take the earlier warning about the Ghoulies, from the Serpents seriously.

The long-awaited dinner at the Lodges concludes, with a so-called man-to-man chat in Hiram's off-limits-to-Veronica-study. Hermione throws Hiram's power play in her daughter's face; Veronica is stuck eavesdropping from the other side of the door. Hiram gives the high schooler some nutty how-to-be a vigilante advice.

Still out in Fox Forest, Kevin rejects a ride. When he gets home, his dad opens the door to talk about the things they haven't been talking about, making the night a real turning point for Kevin.

Jughead's concluding voice-over acknowledges that fairy tales rarely have a happy ending. But Archie doesn't believe that. He's making a video warning the Black Hood that he and his beefcakes in red are the Red Circle, and they are coming for him.

Chapter Seventeen:
"The Town That Dreaded Sundown"

Original airdate: *November 1, 2017*
Writer: *Amanda Lasher*
Director: *Allison Anders*

Top Quote: "You're Betty Cooper. Like *Nancy Drew* meets *Girl with the Dragon Tattoo*."—Jughead to Betty, on whether she should accept the blame the Black Hood is laying on her.

Top Trivia: This episode gets its title from a horror film written by Roberto Aguirre-Sacasa. The 2014 film features a serial killer on the loose in a small town.

Watch For: The name on Archie's fake ID. It's a nod to *Wilbur Comics*, which is a part of the Archie Comics Group. The scene where Betty ignores Kevin, telling her that she needs to back off about his private life. This one-sided friendship continues. The Lodges pull together as a family and declare a truce. Oh yeah, like that will last.

Wonder About: Remember the pastel nail polish Alice wore last season? It's gone now, being replaced by a basic red. Is there a reason why? Is Archie's Red Circle video actually such a big deal? Should he have to apologize? Also, where is Archie and Hiram's relationship headed and what does it mean?

Summary + Commentary:

Jughead's opening voice-over declares there is a serial killer in Riverdale; fear and suspicion seep through the streets.

The town is buzzing about the video Archie's Red Circle posted. Veronica's parents tell her she can no longer date him. Fred insists Archie delete it, but it's too late—the video has been shared. The Serpents share it with Jughead, and announce that they're going after the group leader. Principal Weatherbee takes Archie off the football team, insisting he apologize to the entire school community, whatever that means, or he'll be suspended.

Kevin attempts to have a close moment with Betty, but she's reeling from a letter she received in *The Blue and Gold* mail. The letter applauds her Jubilee speech and gives her a cipher, which details where the next victim will be punished. She refuses to share the letter with the sheriff, but shares it with her mom, who, of course, publishes it ASAP.

Reggie is steaming that Archie won't do as the principal says. Instead of backing off, Archie wants the Red Circle to go to the Southside. Dilton, who is loitering around, is on Archie's side and offers connections to get "supplies." Check the box *Dilton is up to something*.

Veronica enters her father's sanctuary and accuses him of manipulating her boyfriend. But he claims to have no memory of his conversation with Archie. Thank you, Hiram, for that classic example of gaslighting. How about some mixed messages? After a quick chat with Veronica to tell her the Red Circle is disbanded, Archie heads to the US Army & Navy surplus to illegally purchase some ammo, a holster and a Kevlar vest.

Betty gets a surprise when she finds out that Jughead and Toni have been working on the cipher. Archie gets a surprise when Veronica and the Vixens pass out Red Circle T-shirts.

Jughead has a crime-solving party at his trailer where he, Betty, Kevin and Toni stew over the Black Hood's identity. Somehow this leads to Toni telling Betty that Jughead has been lying about sitting with the Serpents at lunch. Even though Toni and Kevin immediately vacate, giving the couple some space, Betty doesn't care. She just wants to focus on the cipher.

While tagging red circles on the Southside, Archie gets threatened by Sweet Pea, but pulls out his gun. The Serpents run off. The next day, the principal and the sheriff call Archie out into the hall because they want to search his locker. No gun, but they do find a

Black Hood. At home, Archie explains it to his dad—that hood belonged to Reggie. Fred is having none of it. Good thing he doesn't know about the gun.

Here's to more secrets. Jughead finds out that Betty hid her letter from the Black Hood. As Jughead confronts her—hurt that she didn't confide in him—she realizes she may know how to decode it.

Veronica wrestles with the fact that Archie is, in fact, acting as a vigilante—he's putting himself in danger. Reggie, thankful that Archie didn't rat him out to Weatherbee, shows up with the team and a stack of pizzas in hand. Soon after, Sweet Pea shows up on Archie's doorstep. They agree on a fistfight to sort things out, duking it out all sexy tough in a rainstorm.

It's disturbing that Jughead and the Black Hood think alike. Using what Jughead said, Betty hunts down a Nancy Drew book and solves the puzzle. Just in time, as the next site for harm is the Town Hall, where the adults are gathered. Betty bursts in and pulls the fire alarm, sending them out into the street. Soon, she hands her mom the solved cipher.

Jughead's concluding voice-over declares that Riverdale is no longer the town with pep, but is now the town that dreaded sundown. Then, as though to prove that true, Betty gets a call from the Black Hood.

Chapter Eighteen:
"When a Stranger Calls"

Original airdate: *November 8, 2017*
Writer: *Aaron Allen*
Director: *Ellen Pressman*

Top Quote: "Don't take this the wrong way, but you are an epic buzzkill."—Nick, to Archie, when Archie says no one wants Nick's Jingle Jangle.

Top Trivia: Betty's ringtone, heard when the Black Hood calls, is the song *Lollipop* recorded in 1958 by the Chordettes. You can find a video of them singing on YouTube. Search for Chordettes—Lollipop.

Watch For: Nick St. Clair makes his first appearance. *The Good Wife* fans will recognize Graham Phillips from his portrayal of Zach Florrick. Alice's entrance into the SoDale open house. Cole Sprouse's (Jughead) performance is spot-on throughout.

Wonder About: In the scene when Hiram addresses the crowd, just before inviting The Pussycats onto the stage, it's dusk. And yet, when the Pussycats are singing only minutes later, it's already night. Hmmm. Who! Who exactly is the Black Hood? Did Betty do the right thing with Jughead?

Summary + Commentary:

Instead of a voice-over from Jughead, we instead begin with Betty on the phone. "I will strike next, where it all began... Tonight is all about you." So says the Black Hood. He also tells her to keep the call to herself. She does, except she tells Archie and swears him to secrecy.

The Serpents are building a pipe bomb for *The Riverdale Register* office. When Jughead tries to stop them, they challenge his loyalty. His response is to don his gang leather and declare himself a Serpent. The only thing in his way—the initiation. But if he wasn't already a Serpent, why did they give him the leather?

When the Black Hood sends Betty an email, he offers her a deal. She publishes what he sent, and he'll answer one question from her. She isn't planning to publish the email containing Alice's mugshot from when she was arrested as a teen, that is until her mother tells Sheriff Keller that she thinks Betty faked the cipher.

Jughead's Serpent initiation starts off nicely enough. The gang delivers Hot Dog, telling Juggie he must care for the beast. Next, he yells out the Serpent laws and retrieves a knife from a rattlesnake tank. Won't Betty be surprised when he gets around to telling her?

Alice is not happy to see her teenage bad-girl face on the cover of *The Blue and Gold*. Her doing the Hood's bidding earns Betty a piece of information—he confirms that she would recognize him if she saw him without the mask. Soon, the Black Hood makes a demand—cut off your friendship with Veronica.

The St. Clair family is visiting the Lodges. Veronica and Archie turn away from Nick St. Clair. But he keeps pushing and invites the Pussycats, Cheryl and Betty to his Five Seasons hotel party later that night. His party kicks off with a round of Jingle Jangle. Everyone— including Archie, who apparently thinks taking drugs equals being macho—partakes, except Betty, who is soon having a terrible time and telling everyone off, especially Veronica. Remember the Black Hood's threat?

Meanwhile, over at the trailer, Toni warns Jughead that if he's having any second thoughts about becoming a Serpent, he better turn back now. He brushes the warning aside.

Back at The Five Seasons, Veronica must throw Nick off her. Her punishment for not accepting his sexual advance is an abusive verbal lashing that she responds to with a slap. He finally gets a clue and leaves.

The Black Hood is on a power roll, and we're about to have a serious chain of events. He requires that Betty cut Jughead out of her life. She proceeds to break down and tells Archie about the threats, before asking him to give Jughead the breakup news. Archie arrives at the trailer—probably about to tell Jughead the whole truth—but when he discovers Jughead is with the Serpents now, he tells his friend to stay away from Betty. This news pushes Jughead closer to the Serpents, who welcome him with a traditional beat-in.

There is more excitement going on around Riverdale. Alice stirs things up with her entrance at Hiram's open house, celebrating the closing of the drive-in and the forthcoming building of condos. What is she celebrating? Her bad-girl past of course. After the dust settles on Alice's bold entrance, nasty Nick drugs Cheryl just as the Pussycats perform. Fortunately, they conclude in time to rescue Cheryl from Nick's planned sexual assault.

The Black Hood next sends Betty to an abandoned house across town where she finds a Black Hood. At his request, she slides it on and looks at herself in a mirror. She flees when she hears sounds come from somewhere in the house. He calls her again once she's home, insisting she give him the name of one guilty person. Her reply is the perfect choice—Nick St. Clair.

Chapter Nineteen:
"Death Proof"

Original airdate: *November 15, 2017*
Writer: *Tessa Leigh Williams & Arabella Anderson*
Director: *Maggie Kiley*

Top Quote: "Dear God, Betty, is there no memory, however traumatic, you won't defile?"—Cheryl to Betty when asked if the Sugar Man had something to do with Clifford's drug business.

Top Trivia: The book Betty is reading in the final scene is Thomas Harris' *Silence of the Lambs*. First published in 1988 and made into a popular film in 1991, this psychological thriller tells the story of a young woman who takes down a notorious and elusive serial killer.

Watch For: Toni and Jughead waking up together. Some viewers were so disturbed by this hook-up they harassed actor Vanessa Morgan (Toni) on social media. Books being read. Cheryl, Betty and Veronica each read a book that informs the plot.

Wonder About: Remember the *Lollipop* song ringtone Betty's phone had? It's gone. Why the change? Penelope states that nothing really happened to Cheryl. Later, she rejects Cheryl's plea for help. On a parenting skills scale, how terrible is this? Come to think of it, there is a lot of bad parenting going on. Who is the worst parent?

Summary + Commentary:

Jughead writes his opening voice-over from the couch, interrupted briefly by Toni, who is—surprise—wearing his clothes.

The Black Hood continues to call Betty, praising her for her dark side and implying that the two of them will be working together. Needless to say, she's not happy.

Penelope Blossom wants the incident with Nick and Cheryl handled *discreetly*. No pressing charges because, after all, nothing really happened. This icy, dismissive action offers some fresh insight as to why Cheryl is *Cheryl*.

Alice Cooper calls the gang—plus Josie and Reggie—and their parents to her house. She wants to know who acquired the Jingle Jangle. The parents quarrel, resulting in the mayor and sheriff deciding to raid Southside High. Archie races to the school to extract Jughead.

When Betty runs into Kevin and Veronica in the hall, they snub her. Right after, the Black Hood calls and, despite her promise to herself that she wouldn't answer his calls, she does. He has another task for her—bring him the identity of the Sugar Man. She jumps right on it by heading over to Thistlehouse, where Cheryl tells her that yes, she *has* heard of the Sugar Man, but *no*, he is not connected to her deceased father's drug business.

Things are heating up on the gang front as Tall Boy tells Jughead that the Serpents and Ghoulies must unite, because times are hard and chaos rules. Things are changing, he's told. Change with the times or suffer the consequences. It's just that simple.

At Pop's, Betty comes clean to Veronica. Veronica insists she break up with the toxic serial killer, but Betty won't. She wants to turn the tables on him. They clink glasses in collusion.

Archie and Jughead zip over to the jail for a father-son chat about gang life. FP's sage advice is to avoid bloodshed and have a street race instead. Why didn't they think of that?

Here's the offer: Serpents win, they don't join the Ghoulies. Whoever wins gets control of Southside High. During the negotiation with the Ghoulies, Jughead sweetens the deal by adding in the Whyte Worm *and* the trailer park. The stakes are high!

Intrigued by Betty's question and her own resulting poking around, Cheryl asks her mom about the Sugar Man. Her mom denies telling any stories about a potential child killer. Gothic style gaslighting anyone? Cheryl gets more torment when she runs into Nick, who scoffs at her recalling of the sexual assault, then throws her mother's acceptance of hush money in her face.

Later, Cheryl—no doubt aching for some shred of emotional support—holds the hush money check, begging her mom to care about her for once. When her mom refuses, she in turn refuses to hand over the check. Then she calls Veronica and tells her about the money.

Time to switch gears. Fans of the Archie Comics will understand why Jughead turns to Betty for street race-prep. Comic Betty was well renowned for her mechanical abilities. She fixes the car up, and it's race-ready. However, Betty's mechanic skills are wasted as Archie pulls the break mid-race, stopping Jughead before going over the bridge. Turns out, Archie tipped off the cops and the Ghoulies get arrested. Thanks Archie, but this resolves nothing.

After the race, Penelope dishes on the Sugar Man and how he led to Jason's death. Cheryl hands over the check, and, in a moment of humanity, Penelope tosses it into the fire. Cheryl wants to know who the Sugar Man is now, passing the intel on to Betty.

Remember Penelope wanting things with Nick handled discreetly? That's her style. What is the Lodge's style? Veronica finds out when her parents mention the terrible car accident the St. Clair's were in. Nick's recovery will take months.

Jughead's concluding voice-over considers Betty's Danse Macabre with the Black Hood as we see Mr. Phillips, in his jail cell, having his own Danse Macabre.

Chapter Twenty:
"Tales from the Darkside"

Original airdate: *November 29, 2017*
Writer: *James DeWille*
Director: *Dawn Wilkinson*

Top Quote: "Two boys on a country road, a crate full of God-knows-what. You're sinners, both of you. Careful, or you'll taste the Reaper's blade next."—Farmer McGinty's parting words to Jughead and Archie.

Top Trivia: Tony Todd, aka Farmer McGinty, aka Mr. American Gothic, portrayed Candyman in the 1992 cult classic horror film of the same name. He returns to the role in the 2020 sequel.

Watch For: The reference to Greendale, a place where nobody wants to be after midnight, home of Sabrina Spellman. Cheryl trying to be nice to Josie. Veronica's walking in on bare-chested, hot dad Tom. So wonderfully awkward.

Wonder About: The narrative is broken into three stories. Why? And is this effective? How does this choice impact the overall vibe of the episode? Is Josie wrong to sing without the other Pussycats? Is Sheriff Keller, as Betty suspects, the Black Hood? Or, as Veronica presumes, having an affair?

Summary + Commentary:

The opening narrative comes, not from Jughead, but from a found footage style narrator summarizing events and preparing viewers for the discovery of a letter from the Black Hood.

As the town reacts to the threatening letter, Betty ponders the possibility that the Hood got access to the sheriff's station. Meanwhile, Jughead meets with Penny Peabody, who is calling in the favor he owes her for legal work on FP's case.

Jughead in turn calls in a favor from Archie, who owes him for tipping off the cops on the drag race. He needs Fred's truck to transport *a crate*. Not bothered by the sound of that, Archie agrees. All is going as well as possible until they get a flat tire. A good Samaritan, Farmer McGinty, stops to takes Jughead and the crate. It's a creepy, but successful ride.

Over an impromptu stop at a diner, the old farmer tells the tale of the Riverdale Reaper, before leaving Jughead with the check. Not wanting to desert Jughead and *the crate,* Archie arrives, pays the bill, and the two of them load *it* back into Fred's truck.

Back at Pop's, they plan to research the Riverdale Reaper, seeking information as a way out of the sinister shadow caused by the Black Hood. What they should've been thinking about was what was in *the crate*. Because Jughead is about to get some bad news. Thanks to what was in *the crate*, Penny is just getting started using the newest member of the Serpents.

Josie isn't too worried about the serial killer on the loose—she's at school practicing her jams. Her mom is worried, though. Josie's mom confronts her upon late-night arrival at the Five Seasons where the two are staying—for security reasons. Josie is stressed. Not only is her mom all over her to be safe, but she's also going behind the other Pussycats' back, working on songs without them.

All the stress is making her vocal cords act up, so she heads to the steam room where the other two Pussycats call her on betraying them and dump her. Spooked, she races out of the locker room and literally runs into Chuck Clayton, who aims to convince her that he's no longer a misogynistic jerk. So, he takes her to Pop's and gets her to dance with him.

Her mom interrupts their stylistic twist to drag Josie home and tell the girl that she's been getting death threat letters. Sheriff Keller is there, and asks if she's received any odd packages. Josie lies. Cheryl gets in Josie's ear, and soon enough, she and Cheryl accuse Chuck of being the one sending the threats. Later, after a Black Hood nightmare, Josie loses her voice. Across town, Cheryl draws another picture of Josie like the one she claimed Chuck drew.

Kevin's dad is acting weird and Betty has a theory—he's the Black Hood. Veronica has her own theory—he's having an affair. Each has a plan to dig into their theory. Betty interviews the sheriff and Veronica invites herself to a sleepover at Kevin's house. While Veronica is snooping through the house, they join forces via the phone. Things get difficult when Veronica interrupts the sheriff's bare-chested workout, but she discovers nothing.

Determined, Betty—invading Kevin's world in a new way—breaks into the Keller's house, and into the sheriff's study. Things get more difficult when the sheriff walks in on her, while she's holding a Black Hood. But getting caught doesn't discourage Betty. Veronica isn't discouraged either. The two friends stake out the Keller house, then follow the sheriff to a hotel where Mayor McCoy is waiting for him. Vee wins this round—the man *is* having an affair.

Archie, Jughead, Cheryl, Josie, Betty and Veronica are now settled into the booths at Pop's when the Black Hood calls. They've all failed the test, they're all sinners, and the reckoning is upon them.

Chapter Twenty-One:
"House of the Devil"

Original airdate: *December 6, 2017*
Writer: *Yolonda Lawrence*
Director: *Kevin Sullivan*

Top Quote: "I am not going gently into the night!"—FP declaring he won't retire.

Top Trivia: Actress Lili Reinhart (Betty) notes that the scene when she performs her Serpent dance was one of the most difficult to shoot.

Watch For: Betty's Serpent dance: awkward, beautiful and sexy. Veronica's realization while speaking to Hermione about the L-word. Both Alice and FP see their children going down paths they themselves took.

Wonder About: Archie's reaction to Veronica *not* returning his declaration of love. Jughead's reaction to Betty's Serpent dance. Hmmm… Where is Kevin this whole time?

Summary + Commentary:

Jughead's voice-over declares how "Varchie" defies the threat of the Black Hood.

Here's something you should've seen coming—Archie telling Veronica, "I love you." What does she say? Nothing. Thus, prompting a round of jitters and excuses.

The next morning at Pop's, Jughead tells Betty about the

murderous Riverdale Reaper. When he shows her an old copy of *The Riverdale Register* she tells Jughead something he must have already known—she's been to the house where the Reaper murdered an entire family, because the Black Hood sent her there.

Big news. FP is out of jail, so Betty and Jughead ask Archie and Veronica to investigate the murder house, dubbed at the time, the "Devil's House." Creeping around old houses is really off-brand for those two. What is on brand? Not talking about real emotions, like love.

Cheryl's uncomfortable attempt to start something with Josie gets interrupted by the awkward janitor who took it upon himself just to burst into the girls' locker room.

Outside of the jail, Alice drops a bomb by asking FP if he's sexually frustrated. Worse, she asks it in front of Jughead and Betty. Later at Pop's, he drops his own bomb—he's pulling away from the Serpents, and he's in AA.

Later, while father and son are looking roguishly cool with their bikes, they have a serious talk about gang life. Jughead says he did a job for Penny. His dad tells him he wants Jug to go to college, not have the gang life he's had. Jughead promises to keep writing and FP gives his blessing.

Those who hang around with Serpents lead twisted lives. When Cheryl drops a milkshake on Pop's floor and insists that FP clean it up, Betty suggests to Jughead that they throw a retirement party for FP instead, and then tells Toni that she wants to be a Serpent. Even if it means learning the outdated, sexist Serpent Dance. When Jughead tells Penny he's out, she threatens Betty, who, as we noted, is trying to get in.

While Betty is learning the dance moves, Archie and Veronica ramble around the Devil's House, retracing the pattern of the Reaper's murders. They do figure something out though. There's a kid in the family who wasn't murdered.

The four of them meet up, with Jughead suggesting that kid is the Black Hood. Betty suggests maybe he could tell who the Black Hood is. They then self-consciously invite Archie and Veronica to FP's Serpent retirement party. But they only half-heartedly acknowledge the invite—they're on a mission. While flipping through old yearbooks, they find Mr. Svenson, aka Joseph Convey. He tells them that the killer was killed, but never reported. Archie pulls Veronica away when she accuses the man of being the Black Hood. Archie declares he looked into the Black Hood eyes, so he knows. The janitor isn't the man.

People struggle with things. Betty struggles with what is to come—her Serpent Dance. Archie struggles with the four-letter word, the one Veronica didn't say back. Won't say back. Alice struggles to be appropriate. She accepts a compliment from Jughead, aimed at Betty.

FP's retirement party is everything you expect and more. When Veronica bails on the sad, sappy song she and Archie are singing together, he dashes off the stage, calling her name. Betty takes the opportunity to take her place at the mic and continue the lyrics. She peels off her denim top and pink skirt, and does her Serpent Dance in black lace. When she concludes, there is stunned silence until FP takes the stage to thank her and announce that he won't be resigning from the Serpents after all. No, not because of Betty's dance, but because of Penny's pressure on Jughead. FP is in. He tells Jughead he's out.

Here's some proof that putting yourself out there isn't always best. Veronica tells Archie, "we can be friends, but that's it." And Jughead tells Betty, "we can be friends, but that's it."

Jughead's concluding voice-over proclaims that they'd been playing a game, and all had slid off the board. The final scene, Archie watching Betty from across the street, implies there is a new game about to start.

Chapter Twenty-Two:
"Silent Night, Deadly Night"

Original airdate: *December 13, 2017*
Writer: *Shepard Boucher*
Director: *Rob Seidenglanz*

Top Quote: "You should've drowned them at birth, like a basket of kittens."—Nana Rose to Penelope after Cheryl establishes that her mother's only skill is being a terrible mother.

Top Trivia: The opening scene with Santa dressed as the Black Hood is a direct nod to a similar scene from *Twin Peaks*, one of the show's influences.

Watch For: Archie wearing that red sweater. The identity of the Black Hood revealed! Best friends kiss!

Wonder About: Is Archie's gift to Betty, a read-along edition of the book, *Swiss Family Robinson*, a hint at what's to come? What plotline similarities exist? Cheryl challenges Penelope to get a job. What sort of employment might the woman seek? Is the Black Hood plotline over?

Summary + Commentary:

Jughead writes from Pop's, contemplating on the Feast of Fools. Even though this year's Lord of Misrule is the Black Hood, Christmas is still on.

Well, for some more than others. Penelope proclaims the Blossoms are broke. Fred is also broke, telling Archie about the huge hospital bill from his extended hospital stay.

Not to worry though, not all is gloom. FP is doing his best to act like a dad. He tells Jughead the problem with Penny is his—not Jughead's. He then tells Jughead to mind his business about some mysterious bags that were just delivered, and go to school.

What's new at school? Mr. Svenson is gone. Archie and Betty think they may have led him to the Black Hood, and gotten him killed. Oh, the guilt! Jughead and Betty exchange Christmas gifts. When he apologizes to Betty for dumping her—to keep her safe—she tells him it's her choice who she takes risks for. Archie and Veronica also exchange gifts. When she asks why he isn't excited about the expensive, sweetly engraved watch she's just given him, he tells her things are bad at home.

While digging in her father's desk for… what, we don't know, Veronica discovers her father bought Pop's Chock'lit Shoppe. That's disorienting. Soon resolved though, when Veronica uses one of her mother's credit cards to pay off Fred's giant hospital bill.

Jughead is disoriented, his father showing up with bags of wrapped Christmas gifts. Instead of being happy about that, Jughead confronts his dad who makes it plain—they have no leverage with Penny. FP must dance to the woman's cruel tune. Jughead has a resolution too—take out Penny. Tall Boy, Toni, and Sweet Pea, along with some other Serpents, are in.

Instead of enjoying the holiday season, Betty—still consumed with fear over the Black Hood—gets Archie to go with her to check on Mr. Svenson. After they find his house empty, they confront Sister Woodhouse at The Sisters of Quiet Mercy, where the janitor lived after his family was massacred. There, they discover Mr. Svenson's sin. He accused the wrong man. What's more—Nana Rose was one of those who executed the wrong man.

Holy crap. Jughead shaves off Penny's Serpent tattoo. Thus, proving to his dad and to the rest of us, Juggie is a true Serpent. Enough said on that.

Hot on the heels of the truth about Nana Rose, Archie and Betty head over to the Thistlehouse. There they find that, due to a no-girls-allowed-while-killing-others rule, Betty's grandfather was one of those who buried the innocent man alive. For some reason, all the excitement makes Archie and Betty kiss. Betty's response? We have to hurry.

Meanwhile, Hiram and Hermione pull Veronica into their secret plan. She's in. She's in on the truth—aka secrets—and the town-wide manipulations, but she refuses to do anything illegal. Stay tuned, bingers, see if that sticks.

Betty and Archie head to the burial site. They dig and it's empty. The Black Hood arrives, telling Archie to get in the empty hole! OMG! He does. OMG! At the Hood's insistence, Betty starts to bury him alive. OMG! Thank goodness they called Sheriff Keller while on their way to the site. Off in the distance, as police sirens wail, Betty finally does what we've all wanted her to do—hit the Black Hood on the head with the shovel. The Sheriff shoots, whips off the hood, and the man is revealed. It's Mr. Svenson.

Jughead's concluding foreboding voice-over begins, as Betty burns her Black Hood articles, clues and notes. She then declares that she had seen a darker reflection and delved into dark truth that whispered, "This isn't over."

Chapter Twenty-Three:
"The Blackboard Jungle"

Original airdate: *January 17, 2018*
Writer: *Britta Lundin & Brian E. Paterson*
Director: *Tim Hunter*

Top Quote: "No, you know what I think? I think you're a small-town hick who's beginning to realize how deep into the shark-infested waters he really is."—Nick, to Archie, sharing his thoughts on why Archie really came to see him.

Top Trivia: Madelaine Petsch was originally brought in to play Betty Cooper. This episode is one of the many that shows why the casting directors made the right choice in having her be Cheryl Blossom instead.

Watch For: The entrance of the FBI. More intrigue! Bring it on. Cheryl and Toni truly interacting for the first time. (There was that moment before the drag race... but we aren't counting that.) Archie and Veronica's kiss at Pop's. The camera angle shifts. Whoops.

Wonder About: How questionable is Veronica's choice to aid her parents with the secret about the closing of Southside High? Scale from one to five: The dysfunction that is Cheryl and Penelope's relationship. Archie beats up a guy who is in bed with two broken legs. Too much? Or did the guy deserve it?

Summary + Commentary:

Jughead's opening lets us know that the Christmas decorations and the dead janitor are put away, and it's business as usual in Riverdale.

Principal Weatherbee announces, effective immediately, that the Southside High is shut down. Many Riverdale students are stunned. Some, like Cheryl, are dismayed. Who isn't surprised? Veronica, because getting that school closed is part of her parents' backdoor dealings. They want the land beneath the school and the mayor wants a big donation to her campaign.

After school, Betty almost pepper sprays Polly, who has suddenly returned home. Not home to stay, just home to get some things. Things being non-maternity clothes because—surprise—the babies have been born. Juniper and Dagwood. And the three of them are staying at the Farm.

A man claiming to be an FBI special agent stops Archie on his way to school, offering a detailed summary of the bad goings-on with the Lodges. But Archie isn't interested in uncovering what really happened to Nick St. Clair—that is until the guy reminds him that Fred is in business with the Lodges.

At Pop's, Betty goes to Jughead for help, to find the baby her mother left up for adoption many years ago. As though having the kid back in her mother's life will fill the gap left by Polly. Defying reality, Betty meets with a social worker who tells her what really happened. Then Betty drops two, or to be more accurate three, bombs on her parents. 1) Polly had the twins and 2) she has the address of Charles, her formerly secret brother.

Betty and her mom go to the address and knock on the door. No warning for the poor guy. Alice is genuinely surprised when he's hostile. Now she's been rejected by her daughter, Polly and her son, Chic. Good work, Betty.

So, you know how Archie wasn't interested in helping the agent find out what happened to Nick? After hearing how Nick tried to hurt Veronica, Archie does a 180. He pops in to see Nick, who has two broken legs and asks for a replacement check for Cheryl. Nick calls him a small-town hick, so Archie pummels him. Nick wastes no time snitching to Veronica, who, at school the next morning, calls Archie out on his behind-her-back actions. Cheryl appears, magically, and covers for Archie, claiming that it was her idea. Soon, Veronica is telling Archie she can tell something is wrong, and he's telling her about kissing Betty.

Jughead, now stuck between two loyalties—Southside and

Northside—refuses to follow the "no Serpent leathers at school" rule. He turns to his dad for advice on how to fit in at Riverdale. This leads him to 1) decide not to wear the leather and 2) establish the Sword and Serpent club.

Betty delivers a bloody and beaten Chic to the Cooper home. They clean him up.

Cheryl delivers the new blood money check to her mom. But Penelope wants to continue getting dirty.

Jughead's concluding voice-over taunts that Archie, who suspects they may not have actually stopped the real Black Hood, is trying to do the right thing, but is actually getting deeper into the bad.

Chapter Twenty-Four:
"The Wrestler"

Original airdate: *January 24, 2018*
Writer: *Greg Murray & Devon Turner*
Director: *Gregg Araki*

Top Quote: "I'm just trying to plan my life, Alice."—Hal, to Alice, while they discuss Chic's living arrangements.

Top Trivia: The plaque on General Pickens' statue indicates that he is the "Founding Father of the Sweetwater River Valley" not the town of Riverdale. This prevents a timing conflict with the massacre of the Uktena, which occurred prior to the 1940s founding of Riverdale.

Watch For: Jughead's reference to the *Snowpiercer* train. The train is the setting for the science fiction film featuring a train that carries humanity's final remnants. New character appearances: Mrs. Haggly and Coach Kleats, both from the original Archie Comics. Archie wrestling as though he'd been on the mat for years instead of a few days.

Wonder About: How weird is it that Hiram is so involved in Riverdale's wrestling team? Betty's statement that performing online via webcam is fascinating. Chic. Trustworthy? Honest? Wolf in sheep's clothing?

Summary + Commentary:

Jughead's opening voice-over is characteristically contradictory. Everything is the same, yet nothing is the same. Take Archie—he looks the same, but is hiding the chaos that is his life.

At the Andrews home, H & H Lodge, Fred Andrews, Mayor McCoy and Sheriff Keller fret about the Southsiders who are now getting schooled in rudeness at Riverdale High. As is the Riverdale way, they'd like to plan yet another community event to pull the town together, and let the new kids, the Southsiders, feel welcome.

Over at the Cooper house, while Hal interrogates Chic, Chic and Betty bond over the scars they've given themselves by digging their fingernails into their palms. Note, Hal is not a fan of this bond or of Chic in general. Let the needling begin.

Archie meets up with Agent Adams, who offers some obvious advice—get close to Hiram. This leads to Archie tossing in the basketball and heading to the wrestling mat, apparently one of Hiram's favorite places. This leads to some sweaty scenes featuring sexy singlet-wearing studs tussling on the mats.

Jughead is digging into the past. He says? for a *Blue and Gold* article, interviews Riverdale's oldest living Serpent, and learns that General Pickens slaughtered hundreds of Uktena on the land Hiram is planning to build on. The Serpents are the last remnants of the tribe. Jughead contacts Hiram, who later takes his frustration out on Archie—on and off the mat.

Kevin, by stewing on the image of the boy's pretty face, figures out that Chic is a webcam boy and passes that intel on to Betty. Not sure why she's surprised, because he pretty much said it when they first met. That and she saw his apartment with the webcam and accessories. Once she shakes off the surprise, and after a quarrel, Betty gives him an old laptop to get back to business.

Things get heated. Toni rants at Jughead, saying she doesn't like what he wrote about her grandfather. Josie bails on Veronica, taking back her offer to perform with her at the Pickens Day event, because she doesn't like the Lodges' backhanded business ways. Chic needles Betty; he wants to know why she came back for him.

After shaming Archie on the wrestling mat, Hiram is open and honest for once. He comes right out with it, telling Archie he'll never be good enough for Veronica. They go at it until Veronica breaks that round up, but Hiram comes to Archie's house the next morning and pulls him out for a run, followed by a pep talk over breakfast. Hiram offers to tolerate Archie. I hope you don't believe that. I hope you're waiting to see why the offer is snatched away.

At the final wrestling try-outs, Archie—using the move Hiram used on him—beats Chuck. The wrestle-off is not nearly as awesome as Cheryl and Veronica's incredible dance-off from Season 1. Although the other that had more visual appeal, this one seems to serve a plot function. Hiram begrudgingly applauds Archie's win, then invites Archie to the Pembrooke.

The Pickens Day event starts off with some low-level tensions. Hiram continues to pick at Archie, Hal argues with Alice, and Veronica sings with the Pussycats while Josie watches. As Veronica sings, the Serpents make their way into the park, duct tape covering their mouths. Hiram does his best to turn the protest to his advantage by calling for a round of applause.

Hal's resentment for, and suspicion of, Chic continues to rise. Next thing you know, Penelope Blossom is propositioning openly unhappy Hal. Who's on a slippery slope now, *Dad*?

Chic, probably knowing he needs an ally, tells Betty he understands her. Next, instead of bonding over darkness, they're bonding over webcamming.

Jughead's concluding voice-over tells of the dark education of Betty Cooper, delivered by Chic, and the dark education of Archie, delivered by Hiram.

Season 2 Pop Quiz 1

1) **In this dialogue exchange, who speaks first?**
   "Are you threatening me?"
   "This? No. No, this is... fun girl talk."

2) **Archie, while staring at his gun, says the quote below. To whom does he say it?**
   "I'm not crazy. The guy's still out there. It's just for protection."

3) **Who said it?**
   "That's the common misconception about fairy tales. They very rarely... have a happy ending."

4) **Who said it?**
   "Betty's ponytail is iconic and beyond reproach."

5) **Who said it?**
   "So, what is it that you country mice do for fun up here? Catch lightning bugs with mason jars?"

6) **Who said it? And to whom?**
   "You're sinners, both of you. Careful, or you'll taste the Reaper's blade next."

7) **Who said it? And to whom?**
   "This is about territory... If there's one thing Ghoulies love, it's their crazy souped-up retro cars and hearses. You catch my Riverdale drift, boys? Challenge them to a street race, one on one."

8) Fill in the blank:

Sister Woodhouse: "After his family was massacred, young Conway, young Svenson, identified the man responsible. Then, a small group of Riverdale's citizens took matters into their own hands and, well, _____."

9) Which two characters are speaking?

"You're having a sleepover at Kevin's? Without me? In the middle of an investigation?"

"This isn't an investigation, okay? This is me helping a friend deal with his father's infidelities."

"So you're there snooping to prove that Sheriff Keller's having an affair?"

10) Who said it?

"The snake, the laws, all based on Uktena tradition… Uktena is a serpent, a horned serpent or a water serpent. Before there was Riverdale, all this land belonged to the Uktena."

Chapter Twenty-Five:
"The Wicked and the Divine"

Original airdate: *January 31, 2018*
Writer: *Roberto Aguirre-Sacasa*
Director: *Rachel Talalay*

Top Quote: "Beating up on a kid, even a filthy animal like Nick St. Clair, while his legs are in casts... I'm... impressed."—Hiram, to Archie, when he questions the teen about Archie's visit to the battered St. Clair kid.

Top Trivia: The Jughead of Archie Comics days had such wit and humor he eventually earned his own comic series. Cole Sprouse, the actor who ultimately brought this entertaining friend to life, was originally brought in to play Archie. The veteran actor, who initially wasn't interested in the show at all, connected with the 'outsider' vibe of the *Riverdale* depiction of the character. This episode proves he is the man for the role.

Watch For: The variety of family members from crime gangs that surround the Lodges. The excruciating mother-daughter chat with Veronica & Hermione and Sierra & Josie. Betty and Jughead, finally.

Wonder About: Again, is Archie in over his head with Hiram? Betty, aka Dark Betty, on the webcam. Where is this going? Chic. What's up with the guy? What does he want?

Summary + Commentary:

Jughead's opening voice-over shines a light on Archie's current situation—wealthy and corrupt Hiram Lodge has taken the small-town kid under his wing.

Remember how Hiram pretended to care about the Serpent's Pickens Day protest? You know that wasn't sincere. Principal Weatherbee suspends Jughead and Betty from *The Blue and Gold*, because Hiram threatened to sue the school. This shake-up leads to Jughead telling Betty that he "did some stuff with Toni." Forgetting that kiss with Archie, as well as her new sexy Dark Betty online persona, she declares to Jug that she hasn't done anything with anyone.

Also, relating back to that so-called celebration, someone chopped off General Pickens' head. No, not his actual head. The one on the statue. Who did it? The sheriff wants to know, the principal wants to know, and even the Serpents want to know. It's Jughead's turn to ask Betty for help. As punishment for the decapitated statue, the mayor demands that the Serpents vacate the trailer park. So... Betty joins the mission to find who beheaded General Pickens.

Later, Hal pops up with an ultimatum. If Chic doesn't leave the house, he will.

As Veronica's confirmation day draws close, Hiram pulls Archie deeper into his sticky web, letting the teen into the inner, inner circle. Veronica fears she's leading Archie down an unrighteous path. She seeks advice at the church, but her confessor blows her off and shuts the confession door in her face.

The night before the ceremony, while Veronica listens to the wives' dismal talk over wine, Archie listens to the husbands talk crap over poker. Then, when the toilet backs up, Archie gets to plunge some actual crap. That works to his advantage, as he is in the right place to overhear two of the gangsters declaring that Hiram is weak, and that they plan to "take him out" before leaving town.

After the ceremony, Mayor McCoy presents the Lodges with the deed to the land where Southside High now stands. Minutes later, Archie and Veronica's dance is interrupted by Hiram, of course. On the dance floor, Veronica tells her father she doesn't want Archie to be part of their life. Little late for that now, though, isn't it, Veronica? As though to prove that point, Archie tells Hiram what he overheard.

Jughead and Betty meet up with a junkyard man who found the general's head in a refrigerator. Next thing you know, Jughead is calling out Tall Boy, getting *him* kicked out of the Serpents, and securing his own spot in. Once Jughead's Serpent membership is secured, he and Betty go to the trailer. And bam—they're back together. Oh, wait—Betty needs to tell him something. Oh, wait—never mind.

Meanwhile, in the Andrews' garage, Agent Adams tells Archie that Poppa Poutine was found dead in his hotel room. Over at the Lodge house, a package arrives with the general's head inside. At the Cooper house, Betty arrives home to find a dead guy in her living room, with her mom bent over him, cleaning up the blood. Keep tabs on this dead guy. He's going to cause some trouble. Jughead, busy with his freshly secured role as a Serpent, offers no concluding voice-over.

Chapter Twenty-Six:
"The Tell-Tale Heart"

Original airdate: *February 7, 2018*
Writer: *Michael Grassi*
Director: *Julie Plec*

Top Quote: "Mom, we're in way over our heads here."—Betty, in her understatement of the year, while speaking to her mother about their disposal of the Shady Man's body.

Top Trivia: In the classic Archie Comics, Hiram Lodge and Archie Andrews' relationship is like the one depicted in the show. Comic Archie, like *Riverdale* Archie, continually tries to prove himself worthy to Hiram and mostly falls short.

Watch For: In an early scene, when Betty drops her bowl of cereal, she creates a milky mess on the floor. Seconds later, as Betty moves to the door, the floor is clear of any mess. Anything having to do with the Shady Man's body. Dead men don't tell tales, but they continue to cause problems.
General Pickens' head. That thing gets around.

Wonder About: Scale from one to five: How interesting is the FBI storyline? Archie states that Hiram is, at heart, a good guy. Truth or delusion? Who lies to the other more frequently: Hiram to Veronica, or Veronica to Hiram?

Summary + Commentary:

We pick up right where we left off, with a dead man on the floor of the Cooper's house. Betty wants to call the police, but her mom won't let her. So, they clean up the mess.

Next door, the FBI agent gives Archie a Mob Life lesson, including a new vocab word: Capo—a man who does the boss' dirty work.

In usual Cooper style, the morning after dumping a body in a sewer pipe, Alice and Chic are seated at the breakfast table eating chocolate-chip pancakes. Betty is having blood clean-up flashbacks, but her mom is fine. Chic is blank-faced and as useless as he was the night before.

FP wants to take the general's head to the mayor, but as you know, it's too late for that. Hiram has it and the threat that goes with it. Veronica suggests Hiram negotiate, and invites Jughead to invite his dad to talk to her dad about the trailer park. Sure, that's rather convoluted, but hey, it works.

When Kevin drops the bomb that a bloody scene was found at the hotel, Veronica freaks. Archie stands up for Hiram, saying he's a good guy. Then he has a sit down with Agent Adams. All of a sudden, Archie is telling Hiram how to handle his relationship with Veronica. Embarrassing for them both.

Betty goes to check on the dead guy she and her mom tossed in the sewer. When the guy's phone rings, she takes it and returns home, to find her mom and Chic, once again, acting as though everything is better than fine. It's perfect. Betty blows them off, goes to her room, and scours the phone. She confronts Chic about the shady guy being his drug dealer, and Chic responds with crocodile tears.

Hiram and Veronica show up at FP's trailer. Hiram offers to pay all the back rent that is due, in exchange for peace. FP shakes, but Hiram adds to the deal—asking Jughead to keep quiet about Hiram's dealings. Jughead refuses, so the deal is off. Things get worse for Hiram when the mayor threatens to expose the Lodges. But H & H Lodge have her followed and subsequently threaten to expose her affair with the sheriff.

Who else has been cheating? The shady guy. We know this, because his partner calls Betty back and accuses her of being the other woman. For some reason, this makes Betty tell Jughead about the dead guy.

Veronica goes behind her parents' back and tells the mayor that her parents know about the affair, and plan to use the info against her. The mayor's response? Resign. Daddykins catches on to Veronica's betrayal. Her response? Lie.

The other adulterous affair, Hal and Penelope, has also been noticed. Cheryl is distraught and angry with her mother, but her mom shrugs it off. So, she threatens Hal instead. She doesn't get anywhere there, so she tells Betty. Betty throws it in her dad's face, demanding he leave Chic alone. This means that Hal cheating on Alice helped Chic, the one person Hal most wanted to hurt. Gotta love that irony.

It's good to know a gang member, because they can help you get rid of bodies like FP does for Alice and Betty. He moves the body, then heads to Pop's to join them all for coffee, where he assures them it's over.

When Agent Adams puts pressure on Fred for some semi-shifty dealing Fred took part in, Archie confesses to Hiram about the FBI and how the agent has been threatening him. Hiram assures Archie everything will be fine. And it is, because it turns out the man was a fake FBI agent hired by H & H Lodge to test Archie. He passes. Hermione welcoming him to the family.

Chapter Twenty-Seven:
"The Hills Have Eyes"

Original airdate: *March 7, 2018*
Writer: *Ross Maxwell*
Director: *David Katzenberg*

Top Quote: "It's like the four of us are in a powder keg. All it would take is one match, and we'd all blow up."—Jughead to Archie on how close the four of them are.

Top Trivia: KJ Apa (Archie) was the last actor to be cast among the main characters. They offered him the role only three days before the show's test read. Immediately after accepting, he was sent to have his naturally dark brown hair dyed red. During filming, he has his hair touched up every other week.

Watch For: Toni approaching Cheryl and offering something Cheryl probably doesn't recognize—compassion. Veronica and Jughead kiss. Josie tells Kevin something intense about their parents.

Wonder About: Remember back when Jughead asked Betty if she'd done anything since they broke up and she lied? Should Jughead be angrier when he discovers her lie? Are these teenagers too sexually sophisticated? Is the argument between Varchie and Bughead over Hiram's actions too quickly resolved?

Summary + Commentary:

Jughead's opening voice-over describes Betty, waiting for her secret, the dead body, to be revealed. That does sound darn stressful.

Hiram sends Archie and Veronica to the lake house. He suggests Betty and Jughead go too. That sounds fun, right? No. Hiram is involved, so of course it is not. Why does Jughead want to go? So he can investigate the Lodges. Why does Betty need to go? She wants an escape from clingy, creepy Chic. The four of them arrive at the lake house all smiles. Minutes later, Cheryl—freshly motivated to be cruel by some vicious treatment by her mother—calls Jughead to tell him that Betty and Archie kissed in front of her house. Toni, who's in the girls' room and overhears Cheryl's cellular nasty gram, calls her out on it, telling her it's obvious she's in a lot of pain. No doubt.

Who isn't in pain? Veronica and Archie. Because remember, he already told her about *the kiss*. Who didn't tell? Betty. Jughead isn't happy, but he isn't intimidated either. Soon, the four of them are having jalapeno margaritas. After a few sips, Jughead starts in with his investigative questions, trying to uncover some Lodge secrets. Veronica breaks it off by inviting everyone to get into swimsuits. Then, she suggests that she and Jughead kissing would clear the air. So they do. Um, okay. Betty's response to her insecurities is to don the Dark Betty wig and climb on top of Jughead. Archie's response to it is to do push-ups and give Veronica the cold shoulder. Things seem pretty resolved until the next morning when Veronica catches Archie in the woods with Andre.

Back in Riverdale, Josie walks in on her mom and the sheriff. For an unknown reason, that's the moment Josie's mom decides to tell her that she's getting a divorce. Later, Josie meets up with Kevin at Pop's and tells him about their parents' affair. Kevin completes the circle by confronting his dad, calling him out on his hypocrisy.

Up at the lake house, Jughead gets a call from FP, who reports that Hiram bought the Southside trailer park, so now all the Serpents can stay. FP is thrilled, but Jughead sees a bigger picture. The man is buying up the Southside. Betty, Archie and Veronica all tell Jughead to chill on the idea, but he's bitten into it with both fangs.

Back in Riverdale, Josie's mom is not happy that Josie told Kevin. And Kevin isn't happy either. Moose and Midge invite Kevin to sit with them at Pop's. Midge is clueless to the fact that her boyfriend and Kevin had moments, proving that Moose lied to Kevin about Midge being cool with them. Josie runs into Kevin. Cheryl runs into Toni.

Up at the lake house, Betty gets a call from her mom. Hiram bought *The Riverdale Register*. Now things get tense. Jughead and Betty vs. Veronica and Archie. Their brutal verbal exchange is broken up by ax-wielding guys wearing black ski masks. While in the bedroom, Veronica hits the panic button. Andre appears. Archie runs after the bandits. There's a gunshot.

Back in Riverdale at Pop's, Kevin—who has been jacked around by Moose these past few days—and Josie, who is sorry about what she told Kevin, have a sit down with their parents. Over milkshakes, Cheryl pours her heart out to Toni. Toni declares Cheryl *Sensational*. Yes, it is the start of fan-fave, perfect couple, Choni.

Jughead's concluding voice-over tells how Archie kept the truth from his friends but talks, instead, with Hiram. Did what happen bother you, Hiram asks Archie. Archie's response, to hand Hiram Veronica's necklace, the one he recovered from the intruder.

Chapter Twenty-Eight:
"There Will Be Blood"

Original airdate: *March 14, 2018*
Writer: *Aaron Allen*
Director: *Mark Piznarski*

Top Quote: "Shut your face, you half-melted, 10-cent trollop."—Alice to Penelope at the reading of Clifford's will after Penelope asks her to leave.

Top Trivia: Smithers uses the code name, "Deep Throat." "Deep Throat" is the name of the secret informant, Mark Felt, who provided information during the Watergate scandal. It's also the code name of a character who leaks information in the TV series X-Files, but it was first the title of an X-rated film made in 1972.

Watch For: Hal unloads on Alice and Betty then makes an announcement. Anything having to do with Chic and the Blossom will reading. The plotlines get a bit twisted. Penelope's cruel need for control. It's building up to something.

Wonder About: Is Betty a good friend to Kevin? Is Veronica trying to manipulate Archie and Fred? Does Fred throw in the towel on his mayoral campaign too easily?

Summary + Commentary:

Jughead's voice-over is reflective, speculating about Hiram's plans for Riverdale.

The Lodges have plans. After a cozy family dinner at the Pembrooke, Hiram suggests to Fred that he run for mayor. What do you know? Fred has been dreaming about being Riverdale Mayor ever since he was a little kid.

Fred isn't the only one who wants something though. Hal wants a divorce, stating that he treated Alice like a goddess. Now he'll pay her off fairly if she agrees to the divorce immediately. Betty wants to know more about her brother, so she gets Kevin to catfish Chic. She is sure the guy is hiding something. And Jughead wants to know what Hiram is up to—the man is buying properties all over the city.

Now on to some surprises. Surprise, Coopers! Polly is home with the twins. Surprise, Polly! Meet brother Chic. Surprise, Betty and Alice! There is a Blossom will reading the following day.

Cheryl, on the other hand, is not surprised—her father having a secret will is no shock at all. So, she speaks at the reading, calling for an end to the blood, madness and horror. We know that is simply asking for more. Cue up Uncle Claudius, Clifford's twin, who shows up only to tell the tale of how he ran away to avoid the Blossom curse of one twin killing the other. Now, we have the Blossom surprise.

Kevin bails on catfish duty, leaving Betty on her own to uncover whatever Chic is hiding. Of course, Chic isn't the only one with secrets. Mayor McCoy is also hiding something. Archie wants the woman to talk to Fred and discourage him from running for mayor. She does, telling him what she learned in office—everyone will turn their backs on him, and the money isn't worth it.

Archie isn't the only guy who's unhappy with his dad. When FP confesses to Jughead about working for Hiram Lodge, trashing the drive-in so Hiram could buy it at a cheaper price, he's more determined than ever to uncover whatever plan the Lodges are working on. At the Riverdale Bus Station, Jughead meets up with a mysterious driver, Mr. Smithers, who reveals Hiram's connection to Shankshaw prison. Jughead is on it, now knowing *the plan* has something to do with the prison.

Stealing directly from Jughead's earlier anti-Hiram rant, Archie calls Hiram Dracula before showing the man his journal—the one where he kept detailed notes on Hiram's actions. Instead of snatching the book and tossing it into the fire, Hiram assures Archie that everyone will benefit from *the plan*. Archie, the teenager, declares he'll hold Hiram to it. He's also holding on to the journal.

The Lodges spill *the plan* to Fred, but he's not on board with a for-profit prison. Fred storms out while Archie stays behind to hear what Hiram has to say. Later, Archie, approving of *the plan*, declares his loyalty to the Lodges via a very dramatic blood exchange with Hiram. He then decides not to hold on to the super-threatening journal after all, tossing it into Hiram's fireplace. Now, Hermione is running for mayor. Prosperity for everyone!

Polly is over the whole weird Chic thing, packing the babies and leaving. Bye—again. Again—not sorry, boring Polly, you're leaving. Betty is over it, too. She snagged a strand of Chic's used dental floss and had the DNA tested. The discovery is more of a confirmation, really. The guy is a liar.

Jughead's concluding voice-over: Time has run out for Riverdale.

Chapter Twenty-Nine:
"Primary Colors"

Original airdate: *March 21, 2018*
Writer: *James DeWille*
Director: *Sherwin Shilati*

Top Quote: "I'm gonna bring you down. Because I catch bad men."—Betty, warning Chic that he isn't the only one who can scare people with crazy.

Top Trivia: Lili Reinhart auditioned for the role of Betty Cooper from her North Carolina home. Her mother helped her make her audition tape and she moved to LA while waiting to hear back.

Watch For: The sticky pink lunchroom scene when the truth of Veronica's involvement with her parents' plots bubbles to the surface. More to follow. Toni's solo dance at cheer practice. It's a warm-up for later. The reveal of what Penelope is planning for Cheryl.

Wonder About: Why does Veronica go against her parents' wishes? Is Mary right when she blasts Archie? Who is Chic's father?

Summary + Commentary:

Jughead's opening voice-over tells us something we already know— Betty let a dangerous stranger into her house.

Here's where we're at with Chic. He isn't a Blossom, Hal isn't his dad, but wait—there's more. Alice is still his mom, and Alice being Alice isn't about to reveal who Chic's father is.

Here's where we're at with *the plan*. The prison will fund a brand-new wing at Riverdale High, and the Lodges, who know the people of Riverdale don't want the prison, are determined to not draw attention to themselves.

Here's where we are with the gang. Ethel, whose family was screwed over by *the plan*, throws a milkshake in Veronica's face. Veronica plays it cool until Reggie asks if her own father will be the first inmate at the new prison. This confrontation spurs Veronica into running for Student Body President. Not to be left out of the excitement, Toni teases the Vixens with a show of hot moves. Fans will be left wishing the scene was as long as the pointless dance-off in Season 1. Rest assured though, aside from the excellent eye candy, it's still, plot-wise, pointless.

Now things get into motion. We start in Hiram's always-dark study, where he spends a lot of time seeking assistance from a high school kid. This time, he's talked Archie into helping him ease the community pain of knocking down Southside High sooner than he'd announced.

That was a warm-up. Now the motion turns into a frenzy. Over at Thistlehouse, Cheryl gathers the inner circle Vixens for a sleep-over, where she confesses that she's terrified of being alone in her own house. She's afraid of being poisoned.

The next day, at the Swords and Serpents meeting, Jughead rallies the Serpents and gets them to fight the demolition of Southside High. Their plan? Chain themselves to the school building in protest.

After school, Betty arrives home to find Kevin in her kitchen, the date of Chic. She kicks Kevin out, warning Chic off, implying she is even darker than he is. And... the frenzy spins into some circles.

Josie, who has been promised a spot on a celebrity show, now seemingly endorses Veronica. While they are singing about feminism, Ethel distributes flyers revealing Veronica's knowledge of her parents' backhanded dealings. Where did Ethel get the inside scoop? Josie. Who also bails on Vee? Betty. Veronica is weary of fighting her parents' fight and being treated like a criminal. She really should have seen this coming.

Chic turns the tables on Betty, by giving Alice her Dark Betty wig. For some reason, Alice is shocked that Betty is sexually active. Chic is smug that he drove a wedge between Betty and her mom, but seriously, that's the best you can do, Chic? Not to be outdone in the weird sex story category, Alice uses the safe sex talk with Betty, to let her daughter know that she had sex with Jughead's dad. Betty sidesteps that disturbing mess and tries to get her mom to see that Chic is dangerous. Alice is clueless.

Now we discover why Cheryl had that fear of being poisoned. It certainly happens at the Blossom house. Nana Rose was poisoned with Tannis root. When Cheryl calls her mom on it, her mother declares she no longer has a choice. No choice about what?

When Archie rejects Hiram's request to stop the Serpents' protest, Hiram reminds him of the oath. So, Archie says he'll do it, but only if Hiram releases Fred from the contracts. Archie arrives at Southside High, bolt cutters in hand, and cuts the Serpents from the school, ending the protest and clearing the way for Hiram. Now Jughead plans to run for Student Body President. Speaking of running for office, Fred runs for mayor again, this time against the Lodges. Some viewers may wonder, who was he going to be running against before?

Toni arrives at Thistlehouse to be told Cheryl has been sent to boarding school in Switzerland. An all-girls school, Penelope tells her. But the irony is, all girls is the problem Penelope aims to fix. Cheryl has been sent off for conversion therapy.

Chapter Thirty:
"The Noose Tightens"

Original airdate: *March 28, 2018*
Writer: *Britta Lundin & Brian E. Paterson*
Director: *Alexis Ostrander*

Top Quote: "God and Gucci willing, Cheryl's safe, wherever she is."—Veronica to Archie while walking home.

Top Trivia: Conversion therapy is a therapy that attempts to alter an individual's sexual orientation or gender identity. The use of this cruel and outdated practice is a nod to the ambiguous time period where Riverdale exists.

Watch For: Shocking blast from the past that is bad news for Alice and Betty, FP and Jughead. Betty and Alice seem to be having a retro-sweater battle. A kiss that starts off a new couple.

Wonder About: The Dark Circle, replacing the Red Circle. Is it at all realistic that Hiram would have high schoolers protecting him? On that note, should Archie accept the gift? Given that Archie proclaims loyalty and family are his top values, why is he siding with the Lodges against his own parents? Given that Cheryl lit her own home on fire, will she make good on that closing threat?

Summary + Commentary:

Jughead's opening voice-over lets us know that while Cheryl, now at The Sisters of Quiet Mercy, withers, while her friends, deep into the electoral debate, are squaring off.

Jughead and Betty are not getting the Serpent vote. Jughead, doing something as wholesome as running for Student Body President, is not acting gangster enough. Oh, wait, it's Betty who isn't gangster enough. Archie and Reggie both want the Bulldog vote, so they arm-wrestle. Fueled by a slam against his dad, Archie wins the contest, and thus, all the Bulldog votes. The mayoral candidate list is simpler, but the run isn't.

Hermione's campaign makes Hiram's associates anxious, so Hiram accepts Archie's suggestion that he come to dinner with Lenny and Carl. Because bringing along a teenager, when you're plotting something underhanded, is always the best idea. Still, even with Archie there, the dinner is a bust. Hiram rejects Lenny and Carls' offer—they want 25% of the profit Hiram will get from the prison, in exchange for Hermione being allowed to continue her campaign. Apparently, gangsters don't think wives should be in the public eye. They mock Hiram and Archie, who embarrasses himself by threatening the mobsters.

Oh geez. Dead Dwayne's car has been found. That is bad news. Alice, FP, Jughead and Betty meet at Pop's to discuss the tricky situation. The plan? Go on with life as usual. Betty and Jughead decide to do what FP says—act normal. Their normal is to investigate and the first person they talk to is Kevin. Now they know the car is stolen, but so does Chic. Alice puts her foot down and insists Betty move back home. 'Cause that's normal.

Toni wants to find Cheryl, who is undergoing "therapy" meant to make her see the flaws within herself. So, yeah, she wants Toni to find her too. Toni, Veronica and Josie pop by Thistlehouse to demand the truth from Penelope, who informs them that Cheryl has been sent to a wellness institute where they will help her. When Penelope hands Josie a hand-drawn picture that Cheryl drew, Josie is out. Now Josie knows Cheryl is the one who threatened her.

Meanwhile, Archie and Veronica walk into the Pembrooke to find Adams beating up Andre. Archie breaks it up, delivering a message to Hiram. Lenny and Carl want their 25% as requested and, given the circumstances, the Lodges are unprotected. Hiram's solution is that Hermione must do all her campaigning from home, and Archie must be Veronica's guard dog. That's circling the wagons Lodge style. Hiram has no idea long-term.

Ever the manipulative idiot, Chic gets in touch with Darla and brings her to the Cooper house. What does she want? The 10 grand he owes her. The Serpents, baring box cutters, chase off Darla and Marcel. Darla got to keep her 10K—Chic doesn't get to keep the cushy digs.

Nana Rose has been left at home. Instead of watching the Bob Ross show Penelope put on, she throws herself out of her chair and crawls to the phone to call Toni. Before the phone is disconnected by Claudius, she tells Toni that Cheryl is close and with the sisters. Toni and Veronica put two and two together and turn to Kevin, who confirms that The Sisters of Quiet Mercy is one of the few places that still does conversion therapy. Veronica and Toni bust into The Sisters of Quiet Mercy via a tunnel Kevin led them to, Where Toni finds Cheryl The two take plenty of time to kiss, before fleeing through the tunnel and out into safety.

Hiram confides in Archie, telling him he's going to accept Lenny and Carls' offer, but Archie stops him. Wait for it—you'll never guess—Archie stops him because he has an idea. What plan would a teenager come up with? Blow up their car. What reward does said teenager get for being so brilliant? A car of his own.

Enough about that. Cheryl is back, and she's claiming the lead role in the school's upcoming musical, *Carrie.*

Chapter Thirty-One:
"A Night to Remember"

Original airdate: *April 18, 2018*
Writer: *Arabella Anderson & Tessa Leigh Williams*
Director: *Jason Stone*

Top Quote: "I will not succumb to thespian terrorism and allow myself to be ousted from this production."—Cheryl, to Kevin, when he insists he take her out of the role Carrie.

Top Trivia: The first of the now annual musical episodes. These episodes prove that the right song fixes everything.

Watch For: Bare-chested Archie reading his lines while doing push-ups. The car Archie bought to fix up with his dad is a nod to the beat-up one the Archie of the comics drove. The next dead body!

Wonder About: Given the ages of those playing high school Riverdale's high schoolers, the irony of Kevin's statement that age-inappropriate casting is amateurish. Regular fans have complained about this episode, saying it was hard to watch due to the singing throughout and the documentary being filmed. Agree? The song, "A Night We'll Never Forget," shades of ick, like the football journal from Season 1.

Summary + Commentary:

Kevin is filming a behind-the-scenes documentary of the making of the school musical, *Carrie*. This footage gets us into the action.

The first day of rehearsals holds some bombshells. Alice is doing the part of Carrie's mom—to what, reinforce her personality?

Chuck is playing the villain—to change his reputation as an asshole. And Cheryl is playing Carrie to do what she does—take the spotlight.

The first day of rehearsals is also a hint of danger to come. Cheryl has a brush with death when a heavy sandbag falls from above, nearly taking her out. Next, Kevin gets a letter from the Black Hood, telling him to take Cheryl out of the lead role. Betty and Jughead try to find out who crafted it. The first person they question is Ethel, who they believe would have been a natural for the part of Carrie. Hello? Bughead? Not a compliment.

Rehearsals continue. While Josie and Cheryl rehearse a song about friendship, Cheryl apologizes to Josie. Speaking of friends, what is up with Betty being so mean to Veronica? Archie shakes her down. So Betty sings to her, Veronica joins in, and they are besties once more. Ahh... the right song does fix everything.

Hiram, who is giddy about the growing distance between Archie and Fred, takes it upon himself to tell Fred about the gift—the Firebird—thus expanding that distance between the two of them. A guy who doesn't get to give his son his first car is bummed. Hiram did not give Archie the car to be nice though. He gave it to him, because a guy running a campaign with his own family divided isn't much of a threat.

But a threat is still out there. Kevin gets another letter from the Black Hood. This one promises that next time the sandbag won't miss. Kevin gets lucky—he doesn't have to talk Cheryl into stepping aside, because Penelope refuses to sign the permission slip. Midge—not Ethel—is moved into the role.

More drama during rehearsals. While singing as Margaret White, Alice makes it personal by suddenly singing to Betty. Then the poor lady breaks down in front of everyone and runs into the hall. Betty follows her, consoling her the best she can. Archie is also feeling the feels. He realizes that he's gone down a dark path, leading him away from his dad. No kidding, Red. He returns the Firebird to Hiram.

The morning of opening night, Hal arrives with a bouquet. He also brings his desire to come back home. Guess it's a good thing FP turned down Alice's invite to come see the show. Alice half-heartedly concedes, but demands that there be no more secrets. Then she unloads a secret—Chic isn't his son. But Hal doesn't care, he just wants to come home.

Viewers finally get a hearts and rainbows moment with Archie and Fred. Archie bought an old jalopy from Junkyard Steve and tells his dad he hopes they can fix it up together.

It's *Carrie* night, so you know there must be a bucket of blood. Cheryl doesn't wait for it. She gets her own, dumps it on herself, then enters Thistlehouse carrying a candelabra and informing her mother that she wants Thistlehouse to herself. Nana can stay too. Penelope has been warned.

The night of the opening performance, Jughead digs through Ethel's trash and finds magazine cut-outs like the ones used to make the Black Hood letters. Veronica declares Chuck's pariahship over, Chic arrives to shake Betty up, and Alice gets even more shook when she finds herself onstage with Midge, who has been stabbed to death with scissors and knives.

No concluding voice-over from Jughead, but can you blame him for staying quiet right now?

Chapter Thirty-Two:
"Prisoners"

Original airdate: *April 25, 2018*
Writer: *Cristine Chambers*
Director: *Jennifer Phang*

Top Quote: "With crisis comes opportunity."—Hiram speaking of Midge's murder and the town's fearful reactions.

Top Trivia: Veronica Lodge was the last of the gang to arrive in the comic Archieverse world. She first appeared in *Pep Comics* # 26. Camila Mendes' casting journey to the role of Veronica Lodge included two studio tests and having to wait out an extended national search even after she'd done the second studio test. Aside from an IKEA commercial, *Riverdale* is her first acting gig.

Watch For: The black pompons of the River Vixens. Just too splendid to miss. The Lollipop ring tone is back. And so are the calls from the Black Hood. Two big reveals about Alice's son.

Wonder About: How many times has Sheriff Keller been blamed for everything going wrong? Do you think Chic is telling the truth about what happened to Betty's brother? Do you think Alice sincerely believes Betty took Chic to the bus station?

Summary + Commentary:

Jughead's opening voice-over declares that Midge's sudden death brought the town together—in grief.

The gang gets together to discuss whether Mr. Svenson was, in fact, the Black Hood. Jughead suggests it's a copycat killer, maybe Chic. After reminding us all yet again that he looked into the Black Hood's eyes, Archie asserts that the real Black Hood could still be alive.

The sheriff has his hands full interviewing the teens, as he tries to answer the burning question—who killed Midge? He arrives at the Coopers, asking for Chic. Hal, no doubt happily reports that Chic doesn't live there any longer. Betty wonders if there is a connection between Chic and Mr. Svenson, since they both spent time at The Sisters of Quiet Mercy. So, she and Jughead head over to speak with Sister Woodhouse. Only after being threatened by Betty does the sister break some laws, turning over Chic's file. Wow, the boy in the institution files is *not Chic*. Betty and Jughead race to the Cooper house to confront him, again. Chic grabs a knife and slices Alice, while trying to attack Jughead. Betty knocks him out with a rolling pin.

Chic, who finds himself tied to a chair in the Cooper's basement, calls Alice on her rejection of Charles when he came to the door years ago. Chic tells them the guy overdosed on Jingle Jangle that night. Alice goes to FP, telling him what we've already been supposin'—the baby she gave up for adoption was his.

The Black Hood calls Betty and admits to killing Midge. Her response is to tell Jughead that they need to go back to the hostel where she found Chic. There, they get lucky and meet a woman who gives them intel that leads them to believe Chic killed the real brother, Charles.

Archie is scouting around town, looking for the Black Hood, who he thinks is following him. Turns out, he is being followed by Nick St. Clair, who kidnaps Archie and calls Veronica for the ransom. Hiram and Hermione refuse to pay. Hey, they're probably glad he's been whisked away. Archie, tied to a chair in a warehouse, pleads with Nick—the guy he pummeled while in bed with two broken legs. Nick, filled with resentment because Archie and the others made him look bad to his father, won't hear it. Veronica and Nick meet at Pop's, where she gives him part of the money and tells him if he lets Archie go, she'll get the rest. Nick makes his plan clear: he wants to kill Archie to "make his bones" and prove to his dad he's worth something.

Veronica, who has agreed to pay off the second half of Archie's ransom via a good time for Nick, arrives at the Five Seasons for her date. Lucky Archie gets to watch via a webcam that Nick has set up in the suite. So distraught at what he sees, he breaks free from the chair and escapes the warehouse where he is being kept, running to the hotel. Viewers will wonder why, if he could get out of the chair, why did he wait so long? Never mind that.

Jughead and Betty are in Chic's face, and we see a tougher, rougher side of Jughead. Who else is seriously worked up about Chic? Hal. He wants to call the cops. Alice spills the beans about the Shady Guy. While the two of them argue, Betty goes down to the basement and cuts Chic loose. She takes him to the Black Hood, who suggests she deliver him for justice.

Archie breaks through the hotel door to find Nick unconscious from a drug Veronica slipped into his drink. He and Veronica tie him up, then call his dad. What will he pay to get him back? A million dollars. While Veronica counts her stack of cash, Archie and Hiram meet in the dark study, where Archie informs Hiram that he wants to bring down the Black Hood. Not to keep people safe, but to impress Hiram. Ugh.

Jughead's concluding voice-over looks into the future, seeing how Archie is imprisoned by ambition and rage, and Hiram holds the keys to the cell.

Chapter Thirty-Three:
"Shadow of a Doubt"

Original airdate: *May 2, 2018*
Writer: *Yolanda E. Lawrence*
Director: *Gregory Smith*

Top Quote: "I think there's a chance that my dad… That somehow… He might be the Black Hood."—Betty, to Cheryl, as they discuss their fathers.

Top Trivia: The character Sweet Pea is not from the original Archie Comics. Jordan Connor (Sweet Pea) was originally signed for only four episodes of *Riverdale*. We can see, he is so excellent, they had to invite him to stay longer than originally planned.

Watch For: The undying loyalty of the Serpents. Hiram's continuing controlling measures. Veronica toying with the family "princes."

Wonder About: Considering how he responds upon discovering Midge cheated on him, is Moose a hypocrite? Is Hal the Black Hood? Will Hiram ever stop trying to manipulate Archie?

Summary + Commentary:

Jughead's voice-over confirms that it is the eve of the mayoral debate, and Archie is going door to door campaigning for his dad. But really, he's searching for the Black Hood.

Veronica is benefitting from kidnapping Nick. Well, in all honesty, her parents are. She now must spend time entertaining a bunch of so-called princes with business proposals. Hiram is loving all the offers and interest from the other mobsters. All full of confidence, Hiram encourages Archie to regather the Dark Circle and use them to find the Black Hood.

Hiram says, Archie does. The Dark Circle is back. Moose reveals to the Dark Circle that Midge was going behind his back, hooking up with a Serpent. Reggie is disproportionately steamed. After some macho style tussling, Jughead and Archie work out the next steps—Archie will get Reggie to back off from threatening the Serpents. Then a visit to the new sheriff, Sheriff Minetta.

Betty is also looking for the Black Hood, and thinks that he may be her dad. If true, that will make him easy to find, but she needs proof. At *The Register,* Hal and Alice step out to get some dinner, so Betty takes the opportunity to scan her father's calendar. OMG! The death dates match up! After a trip to the morgue—and a pep talk from Cheryl—Betty confesses her involvement with the Black Hood to her parents. Betty and Hal bond over their darkness. So cozy and sweet.

The mayoral debate begins. With lovely red, white and blue banners behind and beneath them, Fred and Hermione go at it, only to be interrupted by… wait for it… the Black Hood. In the aftermath, Hiram volunteers Archie's services, but for the first time in a while, Archie puts his own family first. Veronica is also unhappy with Hiram. When she tells him she's going ahead with the best of the prince's offers without his blessing, he shuts her down, informing her he put her million dollars in a trust.

Betty and Cheryl sneak into the room Hal was renting, and find a *Nancy Drew* book—the very book used by the Black Hood to make the cipher she solved. Betty questions her dad about the book, and tells him that she thinks he is the Black Hood. Now things aren't so cozy and sweet.

The video of Fangs in Midge's dressing room opening night goes viral. The cops arrive at school and arrest Fangs, prompting Reggie into leading the Dark Circle in a night of wilding. Archie, who's been coming unwound ever since the Black Hood left a threatening letter for his dad, tells them to disband. Reggie informs them that Hiram is now paying them, and that their loyalty has shifted. Now Hiram is meeting in dark rooms with Reggie. He pretty much tells the teen that they should have killed Fangs, because now the Serpent is being released and will be back out on the streets. That's all the encouragement Reggie needs.

Across town at the Andrews' house, Veronica tells Fred she'll back him for mayor, then she and Archie go upstairs to have sex. What the heck is Fred doing?

Jughead calls Archie, urging him to come to the sheriff station. The Dark Circle is out of control. The Serpents band together to guide Fangs out of the police station and Archie, seeing a gun in Reggie's hands, knocks the bulldog to the ground. The gun goes off, shooting Fangs in the stomach. Chaos ensues.

Betty calls her dad, asking him to meet where it all started. While Betty waits at the town hall, Cheryl answers a knock at her door. It's the Black Hood, wielding an ax.

Jughead is too busy fighting to offer a concluding voice-over.

Chapter Thirty-Four:
"Judgment Night"

Original airdate: *May 9, 2018*
Writer: *Shepard Boucher*
Director: *Cherie Nowlan*

Top Quote: "Shut the hell up, Alice, for once in your life."—Hal to Alice when she asks why they are watching his childhood trauma revealing family home movies.

Top Trivia: The final scene where FP brings Jughead out of the woods is a tribute to a *Batman* scene—Batman carrying Robin—in the critically acclaimed 1988 comic, *A Death in the Family*.

Watch For: An additional Batman tribute, this one from Veronica, when she references Gotham City. Cheryl taking a shot at the Black Hood. Editing goof: When Mr. Cooper shows Betty and Alice the home movie, the projector reel is not moving although the light is flickering

Wonder About: How ridiculous is Hermione offering a million-dollar bounty on the Black Hood? How ridiculous is Hermione's statement that Hiram has 'secret funds' to cover the bounty? Is Jughead dead?

Summary + Commentary:

Jughead, still busy with the riot, offers no opening voice-over.

Cheryl allows the ax-wielding Black Hood into her home, who comes at her. Not one to be in the right place with the wrong outfit, she dons a red cape before meeting him outside, armed with her bow and arrow. She threatens and he approaches. She shoots him in the right shoulder, then calls Betty, who is searching for her dad.

The streets of Riverdale are chaotic. Jughead and FP take Fangs to the hospital while the Serpents rage on the streets, hunting Reggie. Believing the Black Hood shot Fangs, Hermione offers a million-dollar bounty for whoever delivers the Black Hood, dead or alive.

This reward is good news for Veronica, who delivers the shooter—Mrs. Clump—to the sheriff's office. Now she wants her million dollars. Not one to wait on formality, she breaks into Hiram's desk and finds an "October Surprise" folder. It contains photos of Fred and Hermione, and a report on Fred. Veronica is stunned to find out that her mother already knows about the "October Surprise." Veronica tries to get her mom to see that Hiram is cruel, but Hermione is either so emotionally battered or corrupt herself that she can't see it.

Even after being told Mrs. Clump shot Fangs, not Reggie, Sweet Pea and the Serpents continue to riot. Meanwhile, Reggie—who is being blown off by Hiram—meets Archie at Pop's. The Ghoulies arrive and promptly begin destroying everything in their path. Just before Archie can solve all the problems by throwing a Molotov cocktail into the crowd, Fred, Tom and FP arrive, breaking things up with a shotgun blast.

It's a busy night for the Black Hood. He murders Dr. Masters and threatens to kill Alice, if Betty doesn't arrive home within 10 minutes. Hurry up, Betty! And a busy night for Jughead. Penny, who has kidnapped Toni, calls him. If he doesn't meet her at his hangout by the docks, she'll cut up Toni's face. Hurry up, Jughead!

At the Cooper's, Hal shows Alice and Betty a *Sinister* style home movie. The twist? The kid being told his father is noble for massacring the sinner Conway family is Hal. So yes, Hal's dad was the Riverdale Reaper and wants to clear the air. Great-Grandpappy Cooper wasn't murdered by his brother. He did, and he killed the Conways because they knew his secret, and took on the Cooper name. Wanting his wife and daughter to understand who he is, Hal admits to shooting Fred and killing Geraldine Grundy, the Sugarman, Midge and Dr. Masters.

At the Andrews' house, The Black Hood bursts in. He and

Archie fight before he shoots at Fred, but Fred is wearing his riot gear. Wait, isn't Hal still at the Cooper's?

Jughead walks into a trap, but he has archer Cheryl with him, so they get Toni back. Back at the Whyte Worm, after finding out Fangs is *gone*, the Serpents vote. Rumble with the Ghoulies, yes or no? Jughead votes no. He pleads with his father, but FP is way worked up and wants to honor the vote. Jughead calls the source of the problem, Hiram, and makes an offer.

At the Cooper house, Alice tells Hal he can't do anything right, including being a serial killer. This prompts Hal to choke her, so Betty smacks him with the fireplace shovel. Hal is taken away by the sheriff, and as the cop car pulls away from the curb, Archie and Betty puzzle over how the Black Hood could be in the Andrews house *and* her house at the same time. Hmmm.

No time to work that thought through. Veronica and her mom are in trouble. Small Fry Boucher, son of Poppa Poutine, arrives at the Pembrooke, ready to kill them both. Hermione kills him instead. That was the last straw for Veronica, who declares she's had enough dark surprises from her dad. Might she also want to start wondering about her mom, who just killed someone?

Jughead is also in trouble. We discover what his offer to Hiram is when he hands himself over to Penny and the Ghoulies, who begin to beat him thoroughly as Penny slides out her knife. Later, a tip from Betty aids FP, who finds Jughead barely alive in the woods.

Chapter Thirty-Five:
"Brave New World"

Original airdate: *May 16, 2018*
Writer: *Roberto Aguirre-Sacasa*
Director: *Steven A. Adelson*

Top Quote: "What about your daughter? And her meddlesome friends?"—Sheriff Minetta to Hiram, asking about Archie and the gang.

Top Trivia: The expression "make my bones" means "establishing my bona fides." In other words, the expression means to do something that will establish respect or status.

Watch For: Kevin and Moose kiss. The Silence of the Lambs style scene when Betty visits Hal in prison. FP retiring from the Serpents. Again. Jughead, Serpent King.

Wonder About: Is Betty truly cutting ties with her dad? Will she be back, as he says? Is Hermione's post-election visit to Fred sincere? How absurd is too absurd?

Summary + Commentary:

As Jughead recoups in his hospital bed, the gang ponders a new mystery: Who is the second Black Hood? Some quick discussion narrows the suspect list down to Hiram's newest man—Sheriff Minetta.

Meanwhile, over at Thistlehouse, Cheryl arrives at the barn where her mother and Claudius are now living, and spies them in a meeting with, you guessed it—Hiram. She reports this to Veronica, who questions her dad, but, as usual, he has a quick, vague reply.

The next morning, Kevin walks in on Moose crying over Midge in the boys' bathroom. A simple consolation hug quickly turns into a passionate kiss. Don't stay tuned on that because, sadly, we aren't getting more on that budding romance.

Jughead feels like his family, aka the gang, has been torn apart. He and Sweet Pea bury their antagonistic past and head over to the Whyte Worm, where some remaining Serpents are camping out. Then, Jughead heads over to the trailer and tells his dad the remaining Serpents need their help. FP, drinking again because Hiram has fired him from Pop's, wants to leave town. Jughead rejects that.

Alice, too, feels like her family has been torn apart. She is distraught over the picture-snapping mob gathered around her house, while being the daughter of a serial killer shames Betty. But Polly, being Polly, is ready to forgive Hal and encourages Alice and Betty to go visit him. Why is she even more bland and pliable than ever? The influence of her new family.

The moms are being helpful for once.

Penelope gives Cheryl a tip—the sheriff will be raiding the Whyte Worm. Jughead races over to clear the place out and head to Archie's house, where they all get a pancake breakfast in the morning. Soon, the Southside and the Northside unite against Principal Weatherbee, who seeks to punish the teens for the damage they did to the school during the riot.

Hermione gives Veronica a tip—Hiram wants to buy the Whyte Worm. Now, Veronica wants to buy the Whyte Worm. She pulls a Lodge move and blackmails her father into giving her back the money she earned by kidnapping Nick. After she buys the Whyte Worm, she offers it in trade for Pop's.

Now let's tie up the season's loose ends and set the stage for the next 22 episodes.

Betty goes to see her father after all. She tells him goodbye, claiming that he no longer has any power over her. He doesn't believe her. We don't either.

FP retires—again—and anoints Jughead Serpent King. Serpent King! More gangster style Jug upcoming.

Fred loses the mayoral race. Hermione wins. Mmmm... okay. We didn't really think Fred had a chance.

Archie confronts Hiram. Again.

Veronica learns that there used to be a speakeasy in the basement of Pop's. This news delights her, and she is ready to reopen the club and make it a place for world-class entertainment. We bingers are ready for that as well.

Polly tells Alice she should come to the Farm for healing. Interesting…

And Hiram? You know he's planning something. You don't have to wait long.

Jughead's concluding voice-over ends on a scene when Archie, instead of taking office as the Student Body President, is arrested for the murder of that guy at the Lodge lake house, Cassidy Bullock. Hiram nods his approval as Archie is led away.

Season 2 Pop Quiz 2

1) Who said it?

"I got nearly 10 acres of scrap out there, and I come across weird stuff all the time. But this is the first time I found a bronze head."

2) Who said it?

"What you're doing could destroy your family. That's why I'm not going to tell Betty. But I suggest you hurry home to your wife and daughter before I change my mind."

3) Who is Moose referring to when he says this to Kevin?

"You can come with us. She wouldn't mind... Yeah, she knows all about us."

4) Who said it?

"Yeah, that's right, I said inbred."

5) When Veronica says this to Betty, that activity is she referring to?

"As the Thelma to my Louise, I couldn't imagine doing this with anyone else."

6) What exciting moment happens right after Toni and Cheryl exchange these lines?

Toni: "Cheryl, are you in here?"
Cheryl: "Toni?"
Toni: "We came to rescue you."
Cheryl: "You did?"

7) **What two characters exchanged these lines?**

"No. This is a classic *Phantom of the Opera* tactic. Mystery man sends menacing note demanding a certain diva soprano gets recast or else…"

"Who's to say this letter came from a mystery *man* at all?"

"That's a good point."

8) **What two characters are Betty referring to when speaking to a woman and she replies:**

"I don't know about any drugs, but they fought, those two. Nasty fights. It was scary. And then, one day, there was only one."

9) **What two characters are speaking?**

"What are we looking for exactly? Trophies from his victims?"

"Just anything unusual or incriminating."

10) **Who asks this question of Betty?**

"If we don't go visit, how are we supposed to forgive him?"

RIVERDALE

SEASON THREE

Chapter Thirty-Six:
"Labor Day"

Original airdate: *October 10, 2018*
Writer: *Roberto Aguirre-Sacasa*
Director: *Kevin Sullivan*

Top Quote: "Okay, I'm listening to my soul. And what it's saying is: 'Get the hell away from your mother because she's been body snatched.'"—Betty to Alice when her mom advises her to slow down and listen to her soul.

Top Trivia: Although an attorney, Mary wouldn't have been allowed to defend Archie, her son, due to a conflict of interest. There are other ways the show took 'poetic license' with the depiction of juvenile court proceedings.

Watch For: Fred's response to Hiram's suggestion that Archie "have a terrific weekend." That really should have happened long ago. Cheryl's display of empathy. Hiram, on the other hand, displays yet even higher levels of cruel manipulation.

Wonder About: The gang is beginning their *junior* year. Consider what happened, what you watched them do, in Season 1 and 2. Feel a bit icky? Disturbed. Be glad the actual actors are years beyond high school. Is the Farm a cult? Aside from Betty's comments, what actual evidence is there that it could be a cult? Jughead suggests to Archie that he head north, close to Quebec. Where *is* Riverdale?

Summary + Commentary:

Jughead's opening voice-over mentions the calm before the storm that was the summer before their junior year, and the months the gang spent in the courtroom while Archie was on trial for a murder he didn't commit.

Mary offers her closing statements to the jury, then they begin deliberation. The jurors are sequestered, the court goes into recess, and Archie has Labor Day weekend to spend with this family. But first Fred punches Hiram in the face.

Immediately afterward at Pop's, Betty, Jughead, Veronica and Archie discuss next steps. Try to find the actual killer? Archie wants to follow the judge's advice to spend time with them. Cheryl, looking a-ma-zing, and fresh off a road trip with Toni, passes by and offers the perfect opportunity to do just that—her end-of-summer pool party.

The next day, Betty deals with her mom's weirdness, and Polly gives Fred props for punching Hiram. Veronica begs her dad to stop the frame up he's put in motion. Meanwhile, Archie is preparing for the worst. He preps for juvie by getting a Serpents tattoo.

Despite what Betty's therapist says, Alice wants to burn Betty's diaries. Why? Edgar from the Farm says it would be best. Remember this "should we burn the diaries" moment. We'll get back to it, but it's going to be a minute. Meanwhile, Polly and Alice pressure Betty about healing. They insist the Farm can help her.

Cheryl's pool party is a time for semi-thoughtful reflection and planning. One of Veronica's plans is to break the law and speak to one of the sequestered jurors. The other plan? Have Jughead rescue Hot Dog from the Ghoulies. Veronica is intercepted by Sheriff Minetta, while Jughead is intercepted by Penny.

Archie prepares for court by going to the Sweetwater Swimming Hole with Veronica, Jughead and Betty. He declares he's guilty, even though he didn't kill anyone. He needs to take responsibility for that. For what, viewers wonder? Also, at the swimming hole, Betty comes clean to Jughead about how she hasn't slowed down for a minute. She's been lying about going to the therapist and lying about taking Adderall. Jughead kisses her and assures her they'll get through it. Across the campfire, Archie tries to break up with Veronica, but she cuts him off.

Dilton stops by Jughead's house to tell him that the Gargoyle King is real. Jughead is on his way to court, so he suggests the anxious and excited kid wait there for him.

The jury is deadlocked—six to six. Impulsive Archie, not wanting to put his friends and family through another trial, pleads guilty to a lesser crime to accept a deal of two years in juvie. Mary heads back to Chicago, but Fred and the Serpents aren't giving up. Over at the Pembrooke, Hiram informs Veronica what happened to Archie is her punishment for betraying him. OMG!

Jughead, after watching his best friend being dragged off to a cell, arrives home to find a sketch and a map Dilton left for him. Eerie and intriguing. Archie is off to juvie. Riding in the prison bus, wearing his spiffy suit, he passes the Welcome to Riverdale sign. Later that night, Jughead follows the map to the woods where he finds Dilton and Ben unconscious, nearly naked, symbols carved into their backs. Yes, viewers, something is up.

Betty is also facing an eerie scene. Her mother, Polly and members of the Farm are holding Polly's twins over a fire, dangling them and suddenly letting go. Betty sees the twins floating over the fire, then collapses.

No voice-over tonight... Jughead, still in the woods, has his hands full.

Chapter Thirty-Seven:
"Fortune and Men's Eyes"

Original airdate: *October 17, 2018*
Writer: *Michael Grassi*
Director: *Jeff Woolnough*

Top Quote: "The moment you set foot in here, you lost your humanity. You're an animal in a cage now. An animal does whatever he has to do to live, to survive."—Mad Dog to Archie, telling him he's going to have to adjust to his new normal.

Top Trivia: All episodes of Riverdale are filmed in Vancouver, Canada. The exterior of Riverdale High School is Lord Byng Secondary School. The interior of Riverdale High is a combination of several schools.

Watch For: Dr. Curdle's son. Thank goodness he is just as creepy as his deceased father. Cheryl's mention of the Innocence Project. This organization really exists. The Vixens have new, sexier uniforms. We get to see them in the most unlikely cheer session ever.

Wonder About: Veronica applies to be *interim* school body president. Considering Archie never began his term, is that the correct term? Is Alice being sincere with Betty? Betty sincere with Alice? Are the actions taken by the guards at the end of the football game unnecessarily brutal?

Summary + Commentary:

Jughead describes Archie's distress as he gets "processed" at the Leopold and Loeb Juvenile Detention Center.

Fred, FP and Tom meet up at Pop's, which remember, Veronica now owns. From behind the counter, she insists that she'll keep things at school per usual as he will be, she's certain, back in time for Thanksgiving. Denial anyone?

Dilton is dead and Ben is barely hanging on. Jughead asks Betty if she'd like to investigate. As if she wouldn't? Their first step is to visit Dr. Curdle, who they ask some questions about Dilton's death. The doctor says they're looking at the true face of evil.

Archie meets his roommate, Mad Dog. The only advice the guy has to offer the new kid is to keep the laces of his nice shoes very tight. Archie's first move is to find the Serpents. Surprise, he finds Joaquin, who tells him he has to shiv a Ghoulie to earn their protection. Surprise again, a mob of unhappy Ghoulies steal Archie's shoes. He lies to Veronica about where they went, and she lies to him about being Student Body President. Great start.

At the Cooper house, Polly and Alice tell Betty that she hallucinated the floating twins. At the Blue & Gold office, Evelyn Evernever—daughter of the Farm's leaders—introduces herself to Betty. Yes bingers, the Farmies seem to be everywhere, and that Farm is creepy.

Jughead and Betty visit Ben in the hospital and have a convo with his mom. She tells them how he started sneaking out and acting peculiar—they also discover another kid associated with Dilton is missing.

After Archie gets his shoes stolen, Mad Dog tells Archie to be an animal. Archie dons a bright pair of new shoes—a gift from Veronica—then offers such a passionate impromptu speech that the Serpents and Ghoulies agree to a football game right there on the juvie grounds.

Jughead and Betty question Ethel and find out that Ben is her boyfriend, that there is a secret bunker in the woods and she agrees to take them there later. After assuring her mother that she's going to take care of herself, Betty does the opposite, sneaking out to meet Jughead. On their way to Fox Footbridge, they encounter *the* Gargoyle King—a huge tree-like beast. Back at Pop's, they look at Dilton's sketch of the beast, and the map of the beast's realm. The next day, they locate the secret bunker and find some game pieces, cyanide, and the missing scout who doesn't know that Dilton,

"Master Doiley," is dead. Jughead and Betty hunt down Ethel, find her at school, and grill her about the game. Her response? Get so freaked she has a seizure.

At the detention center, the football game starts as planned. What isn't planned, are the Vixens showing up and doing a super, sassy cheer dance to "Jailhouse Rock." The inmates love it. Hiram does not. He shows up, tells Veronica she'll no longer be allowed to visit her boyfriend, then watches as the guards viciously attack the inmates. Once back in his cell, a guard tells Archie that Mad Dog died in the riot. Not one to listen to her dad's warnings, Veronica creates a fake identity so she can continue to visit Archie. The warden also visits Archie to tell him he's been tapped. He's the warden's new Mad Dog.

Kevin and Moose hooked up over the summer, so naturally, Kevin thinks they are still a 'thing.' But Moose keeps giving him the cold shoulder at school, then blows him off again when he sees him at Pop's. So Kevin joins RROTC. Moose's dad is the RROTC instructor.

Hermione, Hiram, Sierra, Tom, Fred, FP, Alice and Penelope gather at the Pembrooke to discuss their decades' old secret pact. Their children are in danger, so maybe they need to break the pact and call the sheriff. Maybe. Jughead and Betty head to the hospital to talk to Ben. They arrive just in time to hear him say some creepy, cryptic stuff, then toss himself out the window.

Jughead, apparently too distraught over Ben's death, offers no concluding voice-over.

Chapter Thirty-Eight:
"As Above, So Below"

Original airdate: *October 24, 2018*
Writer: *Aaron Allen*
Director: *Jeff Hunt*

Top Quote: "Speak from your heart. From what your mother and Polly have told us, we know you've been through so much. Between your dark kinship with your father and the role you played in disposing of the dead body in your kitchen."—Evelyn, to Betty, among the Farmies.

Top Trivia: Ashleigh Murray (Josie) was super close to taking a break from acting when she got the role on *Riverdale*. She was living in New York and struggling to pay rent and meet everyday expenses. We're all thankful she hung in there and did just one last audition.

Watch For: Veronica looking amazing in a plain white T-shirt her reveal of La Bonne Nuit. Veronica, Toni and Cheryl sneaking into the basement of the Whyte Worm while the music playing is the original 1969 version of "Jingle Jangle" from The Archies. The sinister action of the Farmies. Take note, more to come.

Wonder About: The music from Season 1 was amazing. Music from Season 2… not amazing. Music so far this season… amazing. What does Alice know about Gryphons & Gargoyles? Can Hiram get even crueler than he already is?

Summary + Commentary:

We start, not with a voice-over from Jughead, but with Archie, still in solitary and still refusing to be the warden's new *Mad Dog*.

Alice and FP are in bed at FP's trailer. Their pillow talk is a celebration that it's been three weeks with no suicides or deaths. Jughead and Betty, also in bed but in Dilton's bunker, ruminate on Ben's death and ponder if it's ghoulish to be bunking in the dead kid's bunker.

Betty and Jughead begin connecting the dots between the Farm and the game. They start off by again questioning Ethel, who is now besties with Evelyn. Jughead gets approval to see the G&G rule book while Betty gets advised to go to Evelyn's peer support group.

At Pop's, Veronica tells Betty that the speakeasy is ready, but she's waiting for Archie's return. Betty pushes her to open, so she does. They will serve mocktails, and Josie will entertain while Kevin emcees. Penny offers Veronica *protection* for the speakeasy, but Veronica says she'll pass and continues promoting her opening night event. Penny puts on the pressure by shipping a box of Jingle Jangle to the speakeasy, then tipping off the sheriff that there are drugs on the premises. The sheriff puts on the pressure by letting Veronica know he's expecting a cash donation for Riverdale's under-funded sheriff's department.

Over at juvie, the warden introduces Archie to *the pit* and the underworld of fighting. Baby Teeth tells Archie the ropes, and Archie gets his first fight, making short work of winning. His prize is lunch from Pop's and a tip from Baby Teeth—don't win so fast next time.

Veronica hits Toni and Cheryl up for some dirt on her dad, which she can use against him. They take her to the basement of the Whyte Worm, where the Ghoulies are making Jingle Jangle. Toni snaps some pics for proof.

At school, Betty arrives at Evelyn's peer support group meeting to find the room empty, except for Evelyn. She uses the moment to ask the girl if her dad, the leader of the Farm, could help her with her daily convulsions. We all know she just wants to meet the guy. Jughead gets his first spin at G & G, playing with Ethel in the bunker. His first test—prove his worthiness by drinking from one of the Sacred Goblets. His second test—kiss her to earn the treasure, the scripture (aka rule book). Once Ethel passes the book over, she downs the contents of the other, poisoned, goblet. At Riverdale General Hospital, she thanks Jughead for helping..

Meanwhile, at her house, Betty gets to tell a bunch of Farmies all the bad things she's done in her life. Soon she finds out her mother has already told them her nasty secrets, including the Shady Man. Betty flips the script and questions Evelyn, finds out that her mother is holding a G&G secret, but soon feels woozy as she backs out of the room.

Opening night of La Bonne Nuit is off to a sparkling success until Hiram arrives, bringing Veronica's portrait as a gift. She takes him downstairs and asks Reggie to keep an eye on him. Josie puts on an amazing show, her singing the backdrop for Archie's bare-knuckle fight taking place. He puts on a great show and once back in his cell finds her reward—Mad Dog's hand-me-downs and a bottle of rum bearing Hiram's label. Archie's new plan is to escape.

Betty and Jughead arrive at his trailer to find FP and Alice, enraged and filled with questions about G&G. FP tells Jughead that no one will ever play that game again and then burns the only copy of The Scriptures. Betty tells Jughead what she's realized—Alice and FP played the game.

Jughead's concluding voice-over informs us that Ethel spread the King's gospel. Soon, everyone at Riverdale High will be playing the evil game.

Chapter Thirty-Nine:
"The Midnight Club"

Original airdate: *November 7, 2018*
Writer: *Tessa Leigh Williams*
Director: *Dawn Wilkinson*

Top Quote: "Cliques don't cross-pollinate."—Teenage Penelope quoting *Heathers* to explain why the group at Saturday detention knows nothing about each other.

Top Trivia: The entire episode is an homage to *The Breakfast Club*. Molly Ringwald, who plays Mary Andrews, was one of the stars of this 1985 teen comedy-drama.

Watch For: FP's flashback G&G costume includes a crown like the one Jughead of the original Archie Comics wore. Editing error: The flashback vending machine contains Cheddar Jalapeno Cheetos, which did not yet exist. Penelope, fighting. Then again.

Wonder About: Red-haired KJ Apa (Archie) vs. brown-haired KJ Apa (young Fred). Which of the cast does the best work portraying the young version of their parent?

Summary + Commentary:

Jughead's opening voice-over tells of a deadly virus, spreading like an epidemic. The illness—the sinister game of Gryphons and Gargoyles.

Hermione, as mayor, is banning the play of the game. Stay away from the game, she tells the teens of Riverdale High. Yeah, because grown-ups telling teens to not do something always works. Especially when the dangers are announced.

Dr. Curdle provides Betty with a case file that she shows to her mother. Her mother uses this moment to tell her of her past high school days when she found out she was pregnant. Back then, the discovery led to a fight between Penelope and Alice in the girls' bathroom. As the girls tussled, Fred and FP streaked (That's run naked for you younger bingers) through the school. The four of them—along with Sierra and Hermione—got Saturday detention. We are well into the flashback, and the fashion and music are most excellent.

The first detention, Josie kicks off a round of Secrets and Sins, and the bonding and verbal sparring are a go. They break the rules and get more detentions. Breaking into Mrs. Krabappel's desk, they find a box containing Gryphons and Gargoyles, and play the forbidden, dangerous game. The allure of the game is that it takes them away from their everyday pains and troubles. The Midnight Club grew, as more players joined, and took over their lives.

Ascension Night things change, becoming even more depraved and evil. Pregnant Alice is the only one who doesn't take the Fizzle Rocks Hiram brought. She escapes, racing past the Gargoyle King as she flees the school.

The next day she arrives at school to be told that Fred's dad died during the night while they partied, and Principal Featherhead is missing. They make a pact to keep quiet about Ascension Night. When the principal is discovered dead, the Midnight Club members realize someone was trying to kill one of them. They make another pact to get rid of the game materials and never talk about the game ever again. The club breaks up and each member, weighed by guilt, leave their dreams behind.

Back in the present, Alice tells Betty they never discovered who was trying to kill one of them. When Betty asks her mom more questions, Alice warns her and tells her that playing the game turns people into monsters. The Gargoyle King could be the same person from before, so the threat is still real. Betty swears to her mother not to play the game.

Betty discovers the chalices in the Riverdale High trophy case. She arrives in the bunker, ready to tell Jughead the story her mother told her, only to find Jughead—who will not be heeding any warnings not to play—and some other Serpents, deep in a game of G&G.

Jughead has no concluding voice-over. He's way too busy rolling the game dice.

Chapter Forty:
"The Great Escape"

Original airdate: *November 14, 2018*
Writer: *Greg Murray & Ace Hasan*
Director: *Pam Romanowsky*

Top Quote: "I saw Archie. He's caught up in some diabolical teen fight club."—Veronica, interrupting Betty, Kevin, Josie and Reggie discussing their parents' involvement with G&G, to tell them about her plan to free Archie.

Top Trivia: Munroe Moore (Mad Dog) is not a character from the original Archie Comics. Eli Goree, the actor who portrays him, began his acting career at six in *Sesame Park*, the Canadian version of *Sesame Street*

Watch For: As Cheryl prepares to take a shot, the can on Jughead's head already has a hole in it. Whoops. The warden asking a question that reveals the influence of Gryphons and Gargoyles and the Gargoyle King. Betty threatening to mace the warden while guards aim guns at her. And it works.

Wonder About: Veronica as a blonde. Does the disguise work? Has Jughead lost it? Or is his G&G obsession a ploy? Who killed Featherhead?

Summary + Commentary:

Jughead's opening voice-over describes the gameplay. You've planned an escape. But it is unsuccessful, and everyone dies.

Across the town, a real escape takes place. Archie, Joaquin and some other inmates try to scale the yard fence only to be shot down.

Over in Dilton's bunker, Jughead—now all-in on G&G—explains to Betty he now understands the game. Riverdale *is* the game—the events they have experienced were quests. Jug now plans to become a Game Master and prove he's at the Gargoyle King's level to ultimately come face to face with him. Betty realizes her boyfriend has lost it and leaves to investigate. She meets with Kevin, Reggie and Josie to tell them their parents played the game.

Upon returning from his morning run, sweaty Hiram gloats to coffee-sipping Veronica about Archie's failed escape. What Hiram doesn't mention is that Archie's attempt earns him a brand from the warden.

Veronica taps Elio for help to get in to see Archie. Once inside juvie, she watches Archie fight, then surprises him in the locker room. After a passionate interlude, they form another escape plan, one that will take place during his next fight.

The Game Master, aka Jughead, isn't taking any crap from the Serpents or his dad. He tells FP he knows about his time with G&G. Jughead starts to get really cryptic, and his clueless dad fails to notice.

Meanwhile, Josie and Kevin grill their parents to see if they will break the pact of silence. The grown-ups lie, claiming they never played the game, then for some kooky reason think that is the right time to tell the two kids they're planning to tie the knot.

Jughead is spiraling deeper into the game and his role as Game Master. When Betty asks him to help break Archie out, he babbles about the game and pretty much refuses to help his best friend so he can play.

The warden confirms Archie's suspicions, that Hiram paid witnesses to say they saw him pull the trigger. Minutes later, Joaquin stabs Archie in the stomach because the warden told him he'd ascend if he did. Archie, gash in his envious abs, goes into the pit to find himself face to face with... surprise, he's not dead... Mad Dog. Veronica, Betty, Reggie, Josie and Kevin put their plan in action. Soon, Archie is out and tucked safely in Dilton's bunker.

Veronica heads home to deal with her dad, who knows she broke Archie out. Betty and Jughead stay to watch over Archie. Hermione, for once, is also disgusted with Hiram. Why? His involvement with the crooked, G&G obsessed warden is making her look bad.

Jughead's concluding voice-over tells of the warden's suicide by cyanide, drunk from a G&G chalice.

Chapter Forty-One:
"Manhunter"

Original airdate: *November 28, 2019*
Writer: *Cristine Chambers*
Director: *Rachel Talalay*

Top Quote: "You're safe with The Sisters of Quiet Mercy. Nothing can hurt you in here."—Sister Woodhouse, to Betty, who knows that isn't true.

Top Trivia: The 1962 song *The Ballad of Paladin* sung by Johnny Western, as heard when Jughead and Archie head down the train tracks, was used in the 1986 film *Stand by Me*. In that film, four kids sing the song as they walk along train tracks.

Watch For: The scene when FP (Skeet Ulrich) climbs in Betty's window and hugs Alice. This is a nod to a similar scene in the 1996 horror film *Scream*, in which the same actor, Skeet Ulrich, portrayed Billy Loomis. Betty, cornering Sheriff Keller—again. Betty, back at The Sisters of Quiet Mercy, but under quite different circumstances.

Wonder About: Evelyn claims to know nothing about "this Archie person." Given that she seems to know all the Cooper family secrets, how likely is that? Who is the Gargoyle King? What's going on with Sheriff Minetta?

Summary + Commentary:

Jughead offers no voice-over, but instead arrives at the bunker to tell Betty that he has seen the Gargoyle King and his gang of gargoyles.

Through his injury-induced haze, Archie manages to tell them that Joaquin told Kevin about a new gang. The warden was playing the game, but he wasn't the Gargoyle King as Betty suspected. Later, Betty finds the warden's picture in an old yearbook, thus proving Alice and the rest of the parents are still lying.

Despite his desire to search for people who can clear his name, Veronica insists that Archie stay put, which he does. Good thing too, because his wound is infected.

Sheriff Minetta grills the kids of Riverdale High, sending Josie into a seizure. But that doesn't stop him—the guy is tearing up the town looking for the Red Paladin, aka Archie.

Betty gets the parents together, telling them something they already believe—one of them is a murderer. After a round of bickering, Fred asks Betty what they should do. Penelope tells the group Darryl Doiley is the one who put the poison in the chalices. The group concedes that may be possible, but it doesn't explain who the *current* Gargoyle King is.

After that little get together, FP goes straight to the trailer to handcuff Jughead to the refrigerator. Lucky for Jug, his girlfriend comes by and picks the cuffs, so he can go find Joaquin being beaten up by the Serpents. After some roughing up, Joaquin tells Jughead he saw Hiram meet with the warden. Jughead goes straight to Hiram to accuse him of being the Gargoyle King, and Hiram... wait for it... denies and deflects.

Meanwhile, Veronica, who's just determined that the sheriff's footage interviewing Shadow Lake murder witnesses proves Archie's innocence, tells her dad Archie will never be locked up again. Hiram understands the threat and calls Sheriff Minetta to tie up loose ends—aka kill the Shadow Lake *variables*. Veronica continues to dig, this time in her mother's office, where she finds the unedited video and emails it to herself. Now she has the proof she needs.

Betty digs into Mr. Doiley's death, thanks to Dr. Curdle Jr., and discovers that he was poisoned. Penelope, who grew poisonous herbs back then, is the prime suspect.

In Shadow Woods, Archie and Kevin find the Shadow Lake crew. One is still alive, so they take him to the hospital where he dies. Someone else who is also not alive—Joaquin. Jughead finds him under a plastic tarp with the sacrifice symbol carved into his forehead. Archie blames himself for both deaths. Plagued by guilt, he believes he must leave Riverdale.

Betty meets up with Auntie Penelope to ask her if she killed Darryl. The woman reminds Betty that her own mother wrote the article that covered up the murder. Has the woman been taking deflection tips from Hiram? Betty heads home to question her mom. While the two of them are having it out, the Gargoyle King appears in their home. FP also appears at the Cooper house. Good timing. He's there right in time to hug Alice.

Veronica gloats to her parents that Archie's conviction is being overturned, and Sheriff Minetta is going down. Her excitement is short-lived, though as Archie calls to tell her he'll always be Hiram's target, so he's hitting the road. But he's not alone, he's with Jughead.

The Cooper house is no longer safe. No kidding. Like it was safe before when the Black Hood lived there? Alice is going to the Farm. She's sending Betty off to The Sisters of Quiet Mercy where shades of the Gargoyle King shadow everything.

Jughead is on the road, so there is no concluding voice-over.

Chapter Forty-Two:
"The Man in Black"

Original airdate: *December 5, 2018*
Writer: *Janine Salinas Schoenberg*
Director: *Alex Pillai*

Top Quote: "Sometimes when you try to survive, it's easy to lose sight of who you are."—Opportunistic farm-girl Laurie Lake to Archie when he tells her he can't "do this right now."

Top Trivia: The yellow farmhouse in this episode is the same set as the Kent Farm in *Smallville*. The barn is the same one used as the Blossom's storage barn in *Riverdale* Season 1.

Watch For: Editorial error: bare-chested Archie stacking hay bales. There are no scars. When Hiram asks Veronica if she's angry about something. He's unbelievable! Ethel, also at The Sisters of Quiet Mercy, getting in Betty's face.

Wonder About: Is the run-in with Hiram just too, too much of a plotline coincidence? Is having Hiram at the center of literally everything bad just too, too much? Is Ethel the HBIC of Sisters of Quiet Mercy?

Summary + Commentary:

Jughead's opening voice-over describes two young men, fleeing from Hiram Lodge.

Archie, concerned that Betty continually does not answer the phone, tells Jughead he ought to go back. Jughead points out how tough Betty is while Archie is always in a mess. They come across a barn and decide to bunk for the night. Here's a tip: country people get tired of city people always thinking barns are ownerless. This resentment is demonstrated by the girls holding a shotgun on the two trespassing guys. They manage to charm the girls into giving them some stew. All of a sudden, they're being offered a place to sleep. In the morning, to repay their generosity, bare-chested Archie loads bales of hay onto a truck while Jughead investigates the nearby empty town covered in G&G symbols.

Back at the farm, Archie is getting a blade shave and kiss from Laurie. He puts the brakes on, and in a very Archiesque style, bares his soul. Next thing we know, she knocks him out with a cast iron skillet while he's eating the eggs she made in it. Jughead arrives just in time to rescue Archie from... yes... Hiram, who apparently has spies literally everywhere. Next plan, they'll go to Toledo to see Jughead's mom.

Back in Riverdale, Veronica is tired of people going missing or dying because of her father, and is packing to leave. She suggests Hermione leave too. Her new crash pad is La Bonne Nuit, which is barely making it despite her hard work. Why isn't she wondering where Betty is? Maybe because she's meeting with Elio to develop plans to host a casino night at the speakeasy.

Casino night is a sparkling, beautiful success. Except that Elio is winning, and winning big. Veronica advises him to cash out, but he refuses. So, she raises the stakes to one hand, winner takes all—and she is the winner, thanks to Johnny Goldwater, a dealer with nimble fingers. Veronica has stepped into her father's shoes, and Pop does not approve. More bad news, Sheriff Minetta's body was found, his hand sawed off.

Over at The Sisters of Quiet Mercy, Betty fakes her way through a Rorschach test given to her by Sister Woodhouse. She also fakes taking her dose of Fizzle Rocks, given to her for her good behavior. Ethel, also a resident at the cheerful institution, gives Betty the scoop on how Jughead is into her now and how she's been having conversations with the Gargoyle King. What's more, Ethel is the Queen Bee—not Betty. Claudius Blossom delivers something in a maple syrup truck, and Hiram, aka The Man in Black, helps the sisters with anything they need.

In one of the secluded, off-limits hallways, Betty finds the Gargoyle King's chamber. Before she can get inside, she's found by Ethel who insists Betty play G&G. Betty fakes a seizure to get what she wants—access to her evaluation report. There, she finds proof that Hiram is involved, using the residents as test cases. She tries to escape via the tunnel Cheryl used but is caught and forced to eat Fizzle Rocks, before being led to the chamber to meet the King. The following day she retakes the Rorschach test, this time broken and giving bleak answers that reveal her fractured state of mind.

Again, no voice-over from on-the-road Jughead.

Chapter Forty-Three:
"Outbreak"

Original airdate: *December 12, 2018*
Writer: *James DeWille*
Director: *John Kretchmer*

Top Quote: "You sinful girls. I will strap you to your beds, and electroshock the sin out of you."—Sister Woodhouse to Betty and Ethel when the two girls strap her into a chair inside the Gargoyle King chamber.

Top Trivia: This episode aired on Mädchen Amick's birthday. Prior to *Riverdale*, Ms. Amick was best known for her role as Shelly Johnson in *Twin Peaks,* the cult horror television series that inspired Riverdale. She had her Riverdale directing debut with Season 4's finale.

Watch For: All the Vixens collapsing to the floor. Very dramatic. Ethel, still so ready to get in Betty's face again. Hiram, finally admitting he is a king in search of his kingdom.

Wonder About: Jughead's still-brewing resentment toward his mother. Scale from one to five: How valid? Why's Veronica wearing the pearls her dad gave her? What will become of Archie?

Summary + Commentary:

Jughead's voice-over warns that despite how things look, there is no normal in Riverdale.

The morning starts with all the Vixens, except Cheryl, collapsing in the hall, while Betty throws up her Sisters of Quiet Mercy "candy." Meanwhile, Jughead and Archie arrive at the Jones Junkyard. Later, Cheryl asks Toni to move in. Veronica wakes to find herself back at home to discover her drug-dealing father is replacing Jingle Jangle with Fizzle Rocks.

At the Jones Junkyard, Jughead's mom thinks Jughead and Archie are a couple. Then she sort of apologizes for telling her son he couldn't come stay with her when he called and brags about getting her GED.

Alice is concerned about the mass seizures at school. Enough so that she visits Betty at The Sisters to assure Betty that she is safe there. Ethel is concerned about Betty's new relationship with the Gargoyle King, insisting that Betty is not worthy enough for him. Betty uses the girl's jealousy as bait and soon Ethel is unlocking the chamber door. Betty shoves her in, leaving her for some Betty-style aversion therapy. Betty clears the air to now-sober Ethel—the sisters run a scam with Hiram, using the girls as test subjects for his drugs.

Believing that the seizures are contagious, the school board wants to shut down the school. Reggie reports his findings to Veronica—Fizzle Rocks are coming out of Hiram's prison. Just as Mayor Hermione is announcing her shut down of the school, Veronica and Cheryl bust in and call Hermione and Hiram on their evil shenanigans. Hiram, as usual, denies.

Meanwhile, in Toledo, Jughead's mom is cringey to Archie, grilling Jughead on the G&G goings-on, and asks for news about the Serpents. Jug calls her on her illegal lifestyle and the weird criminal camp for kids she's running. Across the junkyard, Archie gets jumped by Penny, only to be saved by a sling-shot brandishing JB, aka Jellybean—Jughead's little sister. Gladys ties the woman to a chair, questions her, grabs a hunting knife and sends everyone inside.

Back in Riverdale, delusional Hiram tells his daughter he wants what every king wants—a kingdom and a legacy. He wants Veronica by his side. If you aren't creeped out enough, you will be. He reminds Veronica that she hasn't been wearing the pearls he gave her, and he hopes to see her wearing them again. Back in Toledo, Hiram is still the issue. Using the info she got from Penny, Gladys confirms that Hiram is trying to take over Riverdale. Soon, she tells Jughead that anyone who helps Archie is in danger. Archie declares he must leave and be on his own.

It's a rough night for the grown-ups. Over at The Sisters, Betty gets to a phone and tells Veronica where she is and what's going on with the Fizzle Rocks. She recruits Veronica and Cheryl for help, then hauls Sister Woodhouse to the chamber. Sister Woodhouse, sounding like a mid-century CIA researcher, summarizes all the pieces that attentive viewers have already put together. The girls leave her there, walking away as she screams for help. In Riverdale, Penelope is getting doused by maple syrup while Veronica and Cheryl question her about Hiram taking over the town. What are his plans for drugs and prostitution?

Veronica and Cheryl get the information they need, but Betty and Ethel hit a roadblock. The inmates don't want to escape The Sisters. Ethel suggests the Gryphon Queen is the answer. Betty puts together a stick and feathers arrangement, then leads the girls out from the asylum.

Fred takes Archie to the border and leaves him there. He puts up a little resistance, but ultimately lets his kid walk away to go live in Canada without food, clothing, shelter or a means of getting them. That's weird, right?

Veronica and her RROTC army arrive too late to stop Hermione from quarantining Riverdale. Hiram is giddy with excitement that his plan is in action, and the Gargoyle King is hanging out with him in his office.

Jughead's concluding voice-over lets us know Riverdale is doomed.

Chapter Forty-Four:
"No Exit"

Original airdate: *January 16, 2019*
Writer: *Arabella Anderson*
Director: *Jeff Hunt*

Top Quote: "Why would I care? I'm not a Serpent."—Cheryl, to Jughead, when he insists she return the Lodge's Glamergé egg, so the Serpents will get a protection job from Veronica.

Top Trivia: The above-ground, rules and control on Riverdale's streets—below ground, a haven of carefree fun at La Bonne Nuit, this dynamic is empathized by Josie's opening number, *Cabaret*, the title song for the pre-WW2 Berlin set musical that highlights the growing Nazi party.

Watch For: Time period ambiguity via the vintage delivery truck Reggie drives for the across-border delivery runs. While hallucinating, Archie sees Betty, Veronica and Jughead in the same clothing they wore in the very first *Riverdale* episode. Those crafty sisters of The Sisters of Quiet Mercy, doing anything to get out of accepting responsibility for their actions.

Wonder About: Does the Cheryl and Toni hot cat-burglars storyline make sense? Considering why he was told to give his jacket up, Fangs gets a second chance, is Jughead in the right when he takes Cheryl and Toni's jackets? Are you sick to death of Hiram?

Summary + Commentary:

Jughead's opening voice-over tells of Archie's self-imposed exile in the Canadian hinterlands, the string of cat burglaries in Riverdale, and how Riverdale was a former shell of itself—all except La Bonne Nuit, where life is beautiful.

Jughead is in bed with Betty, when one of the escapees from The Sisters of Quiet Mercy starts screaming in the middle of the night. The escapees are having a mass sleep-over at the Cooper house. Betty finds a pack of Fizzle Rocks—which appear to be all over town.

Reggie, on his way back from buying beer across the border, is ambushed and threatened. Who is behind it? Hiram, of course. What does he want? Protection money for La Bonne Nuit. Veronica's way around his threat for more money from La Bonne Nuit? Cooked books, of course. How very Lodge of her.

While out in the woods, a bear attacks Archie. He bandages himself up the best he can, then lies on the bed, waiting for help. While delirious from pain, Archie has visions of dead Cassidy, who lures him into a game of G&G. After taking down the Black Hood, he runs into the Warden. His marching orders? Kill the man in black. Dream-state Archie meets with Hiram, who mocks him for telling all his plans, then threatening him. Archie stabs Hiram, then comes face to face with Betty, Jughead and Veronica. Betty tells him he needs to come back to Riverdale. He returns to his bedroom to find himself asleep in bed. The message from his intense, complicated hallucination—he must destroy the troublesome, bad side of himself.

Betty meets with Sierra McCoy, who lets her know the nuns have taken a vow of silence, so there is no one to testify against Hiram. Veronica, dealing with the takeover king, gives him her cooked books and agrees to the 10%. Unfortunately, he figures out the books are cooked.

Jughead gathers the Serpents at the Southside Trailer Park in an attempt to find which one of them is dealing drugs. The ranks grumble about not having any money, but FP silences them with part of the Serpent code.

At the cozy Cooper house, Polly and Evelyn are recruiting from The Sisters of Quiet Mercy escapees. Polly tells Betty the escapees are afraid of her, because she's a Serpent. After some convo, the truth comes out—Fangs is the Serpent dealing Fizzle Rocks. Even though he should cut Fangs from the club, Jug lets its slide. Just this once, he says. Don't tell anyone, he commands. It's a busy time for Jughead and Veronica needs his help. Because of her dad's threats, she needs the egg back that Cheryl stole. He gets the genius idea for her to let the Serpents do the protecting, instead of Hiram. When he takes the deal back to the Serpents, they're excited about the protection deal because they need cash.

The escapee strays are unhappy and complaining to Betty that they've seen the Gargoyle King. They don't feel safe, and it's Betty's fault. Fred, Nana Rose, and Sierra agree to take in some of the kids, but before the kids can be relocated, Alice calls Edgar' he comes to get all of them and take them to the Farm.

On his way back from making another beer run, Reggie is ambushed. This time the back of the truck is filled with Serpents who pop out and chase off the attackers. Reggie returns to La Bonne Nuit to report the success of the protection ploy, and to share a kiss with Veronica.

Jughead plays favorites, kicking Cheryl and Toni out of the Serpents for stealing the Lodges' egg, but offers Fangs a chance at redemption. Fangs will go undercover and join the Gargoyles. This happens just as Archie is found by the park rangers; he appears to be dead.

Apparently, the so-called nuns would rather die than testify against Hiram, as Betty finds them all dead in the chamber, having killed themselves G&G style—blue lips and all.

Chapter Forty-Five:
"The Stranger"

Original airdate: *January 23, 2019*
Writer: *Brian E. Paterson*
Director: *Maggie Kiley*

Top Quote: "I'm in high school, how am I supposed to know that?"— Archie to Jughead when, during SAT prep, Jughead explains the meaning of iconoclast.

Top Trivia: Scott McNeil (Tall Boy) is well known for his voice acting. He has a long list of Japanese animation dubbing, Western animation and video game credits.

Watch For: Veronica's beautiful performance for Archie interrupted. The Gargoyle King unmasked! Hiram, finally, gets what's coming to him.

Wonder About: Why is Alice putting her makeup on at the dining room table? How and why is Archie so different? Who shot Hiram?

Summary + Commentary:

Jughead's opening voice-over tells of Archie's spiritual death. A new Archie is born, one with darker hair and scars.

Archie, back in Riverdale, surprises Veronica at La Bonne Nuit. Later, upstairs, they meet up with Betty and Jughead. They catch him up on everything he's missed so far in Season 3. Then Betty drops the bomb on him—SATs are coming up on Saturday. Then her mom drops a bomb on Betty—Alice donated all her college money to the Farm.

FP and Fred head over to Hiram's to announce that Archie is back in town and threaten him to let the kid alone. Mr. Weatherbee is also dealing with the returned redhead. He strongly suggests Archie repeat junior year, but Archie isn't feeling that.

While Veronica sings an amazing song in Spanish to Archie, he freaks out and runs. He's plagued by violent memories of the past and weighed down by guilt. The next day, Reggie calls him on his angsty behavior. Also, there's an awkward moment when Reggie accidentally tells Archie that he and Veronica kissed. Archie was actually asking about how to cheat on the SATs. LOL.

Betty visits her dad, who is in a *Silence of the Lambs* worthy cage, and asks for his signature on an affidavit. Hal tells Betty that if she gets him a copy of the G&G manual, he'll sign. She delivers it. He signs and talks about Ascension Night, telling her he was the one who poisoned the chalices and was the Gargoyle King.

Undercover Fangs meets the Gargoyle Gang in Fox Forest. Just before being branded, the Serpents rush in and reveal the identity of the King. It's Tall Boy. They drag him back to the bunker to beat answers out of him.

Betty finds out Penelope has been posing as Alice to meet with Hal. She also finds out that he only knew about Ascension Night due to Penelope. She calls him on his lies, and tells him she'll never come back. Yes, she already told him that. Yes, she will again.

Archie's gloom spreads. Saturday—the day of the SATs. In the boys' bathroom, the memories of what Hiram put him through flood his mind, and he smashes the mirror.

Betty arrives home to find out that her mother, wearing an amazing Joker worthy striped jacket, has gotten a job, and the Farm has bought The Sisters of Quiet Mercy building and grounds.

Hiram is shot and Veronica asks Archie if he did it. Does this mean their relationship is over? Reggie is ready to take advantage. He visits Veronica, who's sitting at her father's bedside.

Tall Boy has also been shot. We see Jughead is as excited as he ever gets. The Serpents throw a celebration party at the Southside Trailer Park. The shock of the evening is when the sheriff arrives and it's FP.

Jughead is too stunned to offer a concluding voice-over.

Chapter Forty-Six:
"The Red Dahlia"

Original airdate: *January 30, 2019*
Writer: *Devon Turner & Will Ewing*
Director: *Greg Smith*

Top Quote: "I don't need you to mob-splain what's best for my family."—Veronica to Leo right before she fires him and Nico.

Top Trivia: Kelly Ripa plays the role of Mrs. Mulwray, the possible mistress of Hiram. In real life, Ms. Ripa is married to Mark Consuelos, the actor who portrays Hiram in *Riverdale*.

Watch For: Multiple noir plot nods. The entire episode is an homage to the gritty crime genre. FP, finally coming around to the *Riverdale* way of thinking.

Wonder About: Is Penelope truly the multiple murderer Betty believes her to be? Angry Archie. What plot purpose does his anger serve? Hermione. What do you think she should do next?

Summary + Commentary:

Jughead's Raymond Chandler style voice-over is heard above the tapping of his manual typewriter. He summarizes the events of the season to date, and hints at the events to come. He also lets us know he's trying to get an answer to the question: Who shot Hiram?

Jughead interrogates Hermione and discovers that Hiram has been having an affair. Although that could be a motivation for her to shoot him, Hermione tells Jughead that she'd simply asked him to cease the relationship.

Betty arrives at Thistlehouse for Claudius' funeral to speak with Cheryl about how people connected with Penelope keep dying in mysterious ways, namely via poison or suicide. Toni defends her girl, telling Betty to back off. But you know she won't. While looking for Hiram's mistress at The Five Seasons, Betty and Jughead stumble into the Maple Club—Riverdale's secret sex club. Surprise! They find Penelope and call her on her exploitations. She justifies her actions by confessing her personal dark truth—the Blossoms adopted her from The Sisters of Quiet Mercy to be her brother's wife—then proclaims her innocence regarding random deaths. Over at the morgue, Dr. Curdle gives the girl sleuth some useful information— Clifford Blossom was already dead from poisoning when he hung himself.

Hiram isn't questioning anyone as he's still laid up in a hospital bed. This is causing problems for the Lodge family, because the other mobsters think the Lodges are weak now. Veronica recruits Smithers and Reggie to assist her in protecting her family's interests. Illusions are all that matters, she declares. In that spirit, she begins making the family collections herself, stepping deeper into her father's shoes.

Veronica accuses her mom of being involved in all the Fizzle Rocks stuff. The woman, as usual, defends herself, telling Veronica her plan—sell the drugs and lab. Pocket the cash.

Meanwhile, Betty tells Penelope she has proof that the woman poisoned her own husband. Penelope reminds Betty of the harm those who have died have caused—including the seizures caused by the run-off. Penelope delights in reminding Betty she isn't so innocent. Hello? Remember Chic? The kid she led to his death by delivering to the Black Hood.

Sheriff Minetta is alive and having an affair with Hermione. Jughead overhears her whispering to the not-dead man. She wants to frame FP. Jughead rushes over to tell his dad, But FP has a surprise for Jughead—he's the one who shot Hiram.

Archie doesn't care who shot Hiram. He is suffering, turning to hard physical labor and brooding. When that doesn't produce relief, he makes another scene at La Bonne Nuit. Josie gives him a cold shower and a talking to. The end result? He decides he needs to face Hiram. Ugh. What is it with these two? Archie doesn't look like such a bad-ass sneaking into Hiram's hospital room. The guy is unconscious, and so very unintimidating. Just as Archie points a gun at the unconscious man, another man enters the room with the same intent. Archie scares him off. Next, Hiram and Archie make yet another truce.

FP tells Hermione that Tall Boy is the one who shot Hiram. With Alice in the room filming the statement for her news channel, Hermione has no choice but to go along. Things get worse for Hermione when Veronica burns all the Fizzle Rocks she planned to sell, and then, to keep him from talking, she murders Sheriff Minetta.

Jughead's concluding voice-over speaks to all the deadlocked rivalries: him and Hermione; Hiram and Archie; Betty and Penelope. The secrets of Riverdale are safe and buried.

Season 3 Pop Quiz 1

1) When Hiram says the following to Veronica, what action is he referring to?

"You think I did all this to hurt Archie, Mija? Because he threatened me? No. It's because you betrayed me."

2) Who said it?

"The cyanide was mixed into a sugary drink called Fresh-Aid. Blueberry-flavored. There's something dimly familiar about this. But you asked me before if I thought this was murder, or suicide, I'm not sure what it is, but whatever it is, it's darker than what happened to Jason Blossom or what the Black Hood did. No, what we're looking at here, I believe, is the true face of evil."

3) Fill in the blanks:

Betty: "Ben's death haunts me, Jug. He didn't scream. Why not, I wonder, Because that's one of their rules of Gryphons and Gargoyles?"

Jughead: "Betty, that's what we're missing. There's no rulebook, no player's manual. What if that's the key to all this? Ethel, Ben and Dilton talked about it like a religion."

Betty: "Yeah, or a _____."

Jughead: "And every _____ has its king."

4) Who said it? And to whom?

"Someone from your club used the game to murder Featherhead. Now my classmates are dying. And the wʰ school is playing the game. I saw a creature in the woodˊ the same one you saw at the school."

171

5) Who said it?

"I don't know. I made a last-minute change to the quest. I was hoping to have the ending or answer when we got this far."

6) To whom is Hiram speaking when he says:

"I am not a 16-year-old nerd playing games to live out my overactive hormonal fantasies. I'm not the Gargoyle King. Because you know what? That's not a real thing."

6) Who said it? And to whom?

"That's weird, because real friends don't kiss each other's boyfriends."

7) Fill in the blank from Glady's line.

"All right, everyone. Go inside. Me and _____ are gonna have us a little girl talk."

8) What is Hiram referring to when he says this:

"I'll have it cleansed by a señora."

9) Which two characters exchange these lines?

"No rest for the wicked."

"Not in a wicked town."

Chapter Forty-Seven:
"Bizarrodale"

Original airdate: *February 6, 2019*
Writer: *Britta Lundin*
Director: *Harry Jierjian*

Top Quote: "Please. I have eyes. I saw you lounging together at my pool party, looking like a community theater production of *The Talented Mr. Ripley*. The Koose ship's been trouble from the gay get-go. Maybe it's time you move on."—Cheryl to Kevin when Kevin hints about with whom he's having guy trouble.

Top Trivia: The book Veronica is reading while waiting for Reggie to rob his father's car dealership, *The Girls in 3-B* by activist Valerie Taylor, published in 1959, is a lesbian pulp classic that tells the tale of three small-town girls who move to the big city. Intrigued? Get yourself a copy.

Watch For: According to *Episode Ninja*, this episode is among the top 10 worst. What do you see that could confirm this? The (other) Gargoyle King revealed! Gladys and JB return to Riverdale.

Wonder About: Did Marcus have a crush on Sierra, as she claimed? Do you care about the parents having to relive Ascension Night? Who sings better: Josie or Archie?

Summary + Commentary:

Jughead's opening voice-over: murder, mystery and candy drugs aren't the exception in Riverdale. They are the norm. Normal things, like getting married, sometimes go unnoticed.

Tom and Sierra are (finally) getting married. At least they are making plans. Toni and Cheryl are getting their SAT scores. Reggie and Veronica are getting a bill—from Hermione for the drugs they burned. Kevin and Moose are getting (secretly) hot. And it'll remain secret because Moose says so.

Josie and Sweet Pea are not getting back together. With good reason too, because she's asked him to be her date for one night, even though she knows he wants to be back together. This rejection is cause for reflection as she realizes she pushed Sweet Pea away, which is what she always does. Archie finds her alone in the music room, and soon enough, he's offering to take her to her Julliard audition. Next thing we know, he's offering to be her date to her mother's wedding.

Cheryl hunts her mother down at the Maple Club, confronting her rejection from Highsmith College. Her mother snidely informs her that a person of Cheryl's *alignment* is not suitable for Highsmith. In Cherylesque fashion, Cheryl goes forward while still going backward. At school, over the school-wide intercom, she announces her newly formed LGBTQIA Alliance, which is great, but she unintentionally outs Moose. Toni is steaming mad at her girl for crossing the privacy boundary. The scolding from Toni makes Cheryl see things differently, but doesn't stop her from blackmailing her mother—cancel the hold on Cheryl's Highsmith College application, or pictures and names of the Maple Club will be published. Later, as a result of Cheryl's misstep, Moose tells his dad about his private life.

Veronica and Reggie are feeling the pain of debt they now owe for the drugs they burned. On Reggie's suggestion, Veronica agrees to rob his dad's car dealership. The trick? A gargoyle mask to frame the Gargoyle Gang. Sadly though, Reggie gets shot, and there is a dye pack that taints the money. They take what they have to the meetup and are shocked to discover that the person picking up the money is Gladys. She accepts what they have, agrees to give them more time, and takes Reggie's car.

Meanwhile, Sierra and the rest of the parents get a threatening letter from the Gargoyle King. His demand? Reunite the Midnight Club and complete Ascension Night. They meet to deliberate. Penelope asserts her position that they must finish now, or they'll never be done. And so, the Midnight Club members arrive at school to complete Ascension Night. They drink Penelope's cyanide antidote, then begin looking for the chalices. All at once, they realize they aren't in danger. Their kids are in danger. All the parents warn their children, except Moose and Kevin who are cozy in the bunker until they are attacked by the Gargoyle King... no, wait... it's the RROTC cadets... and they have dragged the two guys out into the woods. Just as Kevin is about to drink from the chalice, Cheryl, Toni and the police arrive to save them and reveal that Moose's dad, Marcus Mason—who himself stayed at The Sisters of Quiet Mercy for conversion therapy—wanted to scare his own kid straight.

Let's tie up some loose ends. Moose is moving out of Riverdale. Sierra and Tom are finally married. Toni and Cheryl, still banished from the Serpents, are forming a new gang—the Pretty Poisons. Reggie and Veronica are giving Hermione some news. Gladys isn't leaving Riverdale any time soon. Archie and Josie are kissing.

And we're all heading into the rest of Season 3.

Chapter Forty-Eight:
"Requiem for a Welterweight"

Original airdate: *February 27, 2019*
Writer: *Michael Grassi*
Director: *Tawnia McKierman*

Top Quote: "I was reborn."—Alice, recounting her near-death baptism experience with the women from the Farm.

Top Trivia: The original Archie of the Archie Comics was also a boxer. He was not the buff, mean, fighting machine of the Riverdale ring, but he occasionally stepped into the ropes.

Watch For: Archie going back and forth with his prizefighting goals and plans. More, yes, more manipulations by Hiram. The sinister ceremony at the Farm.

Wonder About: Scale from one to five, how weird is it for Alice to wear her wedding dress for her big event at the Farm? Why has Gladys (really) returned to Riverdale? Are Josie and Archie end game?

Summary + Commentary:

Jughead's opening voice-over tells of rivalries and mythological forces—Gryphons and Gargoyles, Serpents and Ghoulies.

Gladys is up to something. She's staying at the trailer and is suddenly acting like an actual caring mom.

Who isn't acting like a caring mom though? Alice. She's making the final arrangements to be baptized into the Farm.

Hiram, who we know cares nothing about being a caring parent, wonders what happened to his drugs. Veronica plays dumb, then later, at a chit-chat at La Bonne Nuit, tips Gladys off that Hiram thinks she's the cause of her troubles. Gladys makes her an offer—if Veronica helps Gladys get the guy out of her way, she'll take over the drug trade, giving them they both want—the Lodges out of it.

Attempting to smooth the rippled baptismal waters, Betty tells her mom she thinks the atrocious white baptism dress is pretty. Then, Betty draws the line on the if-you-die-it-isn't-our-fault legal form her mother must sign. At school, Betty goes to Kevin, telling him that her mom is joining a cult, and nobody cares. Too late for sympathy from him though, as Kevin is thinking of joining the Farm too. Never one to give up, Betty starts calling Farm escapees, wanting to find out something she can use to convince her mom not to go through with the baptism.

Josie and Archie are cute, but living different lives. Josie has a meeting with her college advisor and Archie has his first fight. Sort of a fight. More like a performance, because he's agreeing in advance to take a dive. His coach, Tom, doesn't approve, and neither does Josie. Archie tries to back out of throwing the fight, but Elio laughs in his face. Archie asks Tom for help, or he'll die. Tom agrees. Archie gives Elio the money back and tells him the deal is off.

Gangs are alive and well in Riverdale. Hiram wants to regain control of the Ghoulies and Jughead wants Toni back in the Serpents. The gang numbers are so low because of the Pretty Poisons. He's even thinking about recruiting Ghoulies. Too bad there is only one left—Verne. The rest are playing G&G with some guy named Kurtz. Jughead hunts down Kurtz and the others, who are holed up in an abandoned house. He invites the Gargoyles to join the Serpents. Kurtz responds that they are living a prophecy, and the Gargoyle King will choose who is worthy to ascend.

Meanwhile, in the bunker, Betty meets with a Farm escapee, Martha. The woman tells Betty of a near-death ascension ceremony—the baptism. Across town, Alice's baptism has begun. Polly guides her mother into the water, and holds her down as she struggles for air. Betty arrives to find the ceremony in progress, her mother no longer breathing, with only just enough time for her to perform CPR, saving her life.

At the boxing gym, Archie takes a beating and loses to Randy Ronson by a split decision. Josie arrives to watch the end, inviting Archie for a milkshake at Pop's. Instead, they go to his house and have sex. The perennial question lingers, where is Fred?

The fact that Hermione pulled a fast one on Hiram is getting to be a real hassle. Veronica hides her mother's betrayal from Hiram, by agreeing to work side by side with him—if he gives up the drug trade and focuses on the prison. It holds him off for a bit, but after the Governor's call, he knows Hermione was working against him. Veronica defends her mother yet again, by coming clean about burning his drugs. Hiram, the ever-loving and kind father he is, tells Veronica she owes him $75,000.

Instead of realizing that the women from the Farm could have killed her, Alice embraces the Farmie life. She's going to sell the Cooper home to move to the Farm.

Jughead just heard from his mother that the Ghoulies are now under her command and is too distraught to offer a concluding voice-over.

Chapter Forty-Nine:
"Fire Walk with Me"

Original airdate: *March 6, 2019*
Writer: *Aaron Allen*
Director: *Marisol Adler*

Top Quote: "I sold the house [...] In true Riverdale fashion, some anonymous buyer."—Alice to Betty when she tells Betty to start packing.

Top Trivia: This episode was dedicated to Luke Perry (Fred), who passed away March 4, 2019, two days before this episode aired.

Watch For: Betty discouraging home buyers despite Alice's effort to stop her. Cheryl reading 1952 novel, *The Price of Salt* by Patricia Highsmith. The story's happy ending was among the first in lesbian literature and contrasts with Cheryl and Toni's mounting tension. More manipulations by Hiram, but that goes without saying at this point.

Wonder About: How many scars does Archie have now? Is the child services plotline realistic? Cheryl and Betty. Will Veronica be the next one to reach for the matches?

Summary + Commentary:

Jughead's opening voice-over describes the Cooper house, now up for sale.

And yet, things are not going smoothly for the Farmies. Betty supports her mom's efforts to sell her family home by telling potential buyers that it's the home of the world-famous Black Hood. At school, Evelyn and her Farmies battle with Cheryl and her Poisons.

Josie and Archie, as a couple, are limping along with their relationship. They bond over finding a starving little boy, Ricky, hiding in the closet at the gym. They take him to Pop's, but at the mention of social services, the kid bolts. He doesn't want to go back to the Santa Lucia Shelter, so Archie takes him home, letting him sleep in the garage. They bond over having the same I'm-a-sacrifice brand burned into their skin. The next day, Archie takes the kid back to Pop's.

Jughead calls a meeting of the Serpents. Unfortunately, it turns out they robbed Riverdale High's chem lab as part of a G&G game, and to make things even worse, it seems there is still bad blood between the Gargoyle Gang and the Serpents. Jughead demands that they return the stolen equipment, but Kurtz refuses. Later, Jughead complains to his dad about the sad state of affairs. His dad offers some mad knowledge—make the gang your own and give the crew something to get excited about.

The next day, Ricky bolts from Pop's, but leaves a comic-level style Gargoyle King drawing behind. Setting aside the promise not to call social services, Archie and Betty meet Ms. Weiss, from social services, and tell her about the brand they saw on Ricky.

Kevin is getting more involved in the Farm at this point. Betty follows him into the woods and tries to stop him from walking across burning coals, prompting careful bingers to wonder how many times Betty has tried to stop Kevin from doing something he wants to. As per usual, she isn't successful. Later, when Betty writes an article about the Farm, Kevin and Evelyn tell her that if she publishes it, they'll tell everyone about the Shady Man. Ouch.

Veronica makes a deal with her dad. If she entertains a VIP client on Casino Night at La Bonne Nuit, he'll shave off some of her debt. She also makes a deal with Gladys—if the woman gets to sing at La Bonne Nuit, she'll shave off some debt. Ugh. It doesn't go well. Gladys is not as impressive on stage as she believes herself to be, and one of the VIP guys starts something, causing Reggie to toss him out. Veronica is annoyed because her dad and tacky Gladys are ruining her classy joint. But she needs some protection from both her father and Gladys to return to happier, classier days. She offers full-time employment to Toni and her Poisons, to which Toni accepts. Now Gladys is not allowed in the club and Daddy isn't either. Problem solved.

Jughead and Archie find run-away Ricky in the abandoned house. Archie takes the kid to the gym to teach him to fight because, he says, running isn't going to solve anything. Remembering his dad's advice, Jughead uses the tension to motivate the Serpents. Jughead tells the Serpents they lack focus, and that he has an answer. The Serpents will be deputized and assist FP. In return, they get money and school credit. Kurtz refuses and walks out instead.

Archie, Jughead and the Serpents return to that abandoned house and begin cleaning up, preparing it to be the new HQ for a new, improved Serpents. Archie, aka the Red Paladin, reflects on how he's been marked for death. Betty and Jughead, always the good friends, assure him they'll help with… whatever.

The Cooper house is on fire. Is Betty the second Riverdale gal to set her home ablaze?

Jughead's concluding voice-over is absent. Note the memorandum for Luke Perry.

Chapter Fifty:
"American Dreams"

Original airdate: *March 13, 2019*
Writer: *Roberto Aguirre-Sacasa*
Director: *Gabriel Correa*

Top Quote: "Since when is taking care of my family a selfish act?"—Gladys, explaining to Jughead why she took over the drug trade in Riverdale.

Top Trivia: MLJ Comics, the shop where Betty, Jughead and Archie interrupt a G&G game, takes its name from M.L.J. Magazines, the company that created, and later became Archie Comics.

Watch For: Cheryl and Toni. The whole episode. Bare-chested, bloody Archie—again. Gladys. Keep an eye on her.

Wonder About: FP stuck in the middle between Gladys and Alice. Does he make the right choice? Veronica denies Reggie. Does she make the right choice? That steamy moment with Cheryl and Toni…was it simply to cater to the fans?

Summary + Commentary:

Jughead's opening voice-over asks: what is the American Dream?

Gladys Jones, the anonymous buyer, bought the Cooper's house so that Betty can just stay in her own room. Or not—she'll stay with Veronica. This is complicated.

At Pop's, Jughead, Archie and Betty look over the multiple "Kill the Red Paladin" G&G cards someone has printed out. Archie stops by Hiram's always-dark study, queries Hiram, and discovers, that yes, Hiram printed out a dozen of the cards a while back. So, since they are on truce mode at present, he gives Archie a list of possible locations where the players holding a card may be.

FP tells Alice the obvious—he and Gladys are still married. So, it's over between them. Meanwhile, Gladys tells Jughead she's looking for a chance to be a real family. It seems Jughead should be suspicious, but he's busy. The recently deputized Serpents are in training. Jughead, working with his dad, goes to Pop's where some Fizzle Rocks user nutted out. He suspects his mother is the one behind the reintroduction of the drugs.

Reggie wants to be Veronica's business partner, but she declines. She's too in debt, she says. Despite how helpful he's been. How very Lodge of her. Later, she gets even more Lodge when she gives him an envelope of cash, which he rejects and dips. Veronica is on a roll. Later, at the Pembrooke, she tells Betty that Jughead's mom is taking over the Riverdale drug trade. No surprise, Betty tells Jughead.

Jughead, Archie and Betty come up with a way to redirect the G&G players who are out to kill Archie. Archie goes to Hiram to request a location to end his Red Paladin challenge—a place to be the mountain top. Hiram gives him the keys to his boxing gym. Jughead distributes the new quest and asks the Serpents to also keep a lookout for anything about the new drug trade hot spots. Soon the boxing gym, aka The Iron Mountain, is filled with challengers. Bare-chested, bare-fisted Archie—aka the Red Paladin—beats them all one at a time. When Archie gives Hiram the keys back, the older man tells Archie to keep the keys and the gym as compensation for his wrong-doings. Hmmm… is this a trick?

Things are tense between Cheryl and Toni, as Cheryl feels left out. Things don't get better when she sees how much fun Toni is having at La Bonne Nuit. Feeling her girl slipping away, Cheryl heads back, looking hot and ready to ignore Toni. The ploy works. She gets Toni's attention and the two of them have a sexual adventure. Toni thinks Cheryl is controlling, while Cheryl thinks Toni is ignoring her. The end result is not happy—Cheryl tells Toni to move out of Thistlehouse.

Gladys brings Reggie to La Bonne Nuit and squeals on him. He tried to steal his car back. Veronica turns into her own dad, scolding the guy over a freshly poured drink. Later, Veronica and Reggie discuss their situation. He doesn't like being her errand boy, but she doesn't want to give him anything other than directions. Well, she does give him his car back, which she bought back from Gladys.

Jughead confronts his mom about her involvement in the drug trade, which she acknowledges. Then she and Jughead head to FP's 50th birthday party, where Jughead offers the official, I'm-proud-of-you-dad, Happy Birthday speech.

Instead of offering a concluding voice-over, Jughead enlists Betty's help in his plan to run his mom out of town.

Chapter Fifty-One:
"Big Fun"

Original airdate: *March 20, 2019*
Writer: *Tessa Leigh Williams*
Director: *Maggie Kiley*

Top Quote: "I invented red. I am red. Sorry, but this school's not big enough for both of us, faux-Pink Lady. And I was here first. So, go to Centerville High, or Westerberg. I don't care. But you have until first bell Monday to clear every trace of yourself out of these halls. Copy?"—Cheryl, to Toni, when she encounters her ex in the hall wearing red.

Top Trivia: Betty Finn and Veronica Sawyer of *Heathers* were named for Betty and Veronica of the original Archie Comics.

Watch For: Josie, when she claims that yes, she would fight for Archie. Remember that one a bit later. Another home goes up in flames. And Edgar Evernever finally makes his first appearance.

Wonder About: Can Archie, KJ Apa, sing? What about Jughead, Cole Sprouse? Fans did not like this episode. Many stated it was boring and hard to follow. Agree? Are Hiram and Hermione truly divorcing?

Summary + Commentary:

As promised at the end of the last episode, it's *Heathers the Musical*! Hermione, as mayor, is not happy about it. Kevin, singing, defends. The adults don't realize what the teens are dealing with. Consider, for

185

example, Jughead's goal for the week is to find his mom's drug lab and shut it down. So, yeah, they are that miserable except maybe Cheryl, HBIC.

The cast gathers, and Kevin announces that Evelyn is Kevin's co-director and surprise—Toni is the choreographer. Cheryl, angry and full of attitude, resists Toni's efforts right away, but she fights back by being amazing. Evelyn takes the rehearsals as an opportunity to do weird Farm stuff, and Betty, snide and full of sass, resists Evelyn's efforts right away. Evelyn fights back by inviting the entire cast to an in-costume get together at The Sisters of Quiet Mercy.

Hiram and Hermione are separating. Why? Hiram found out Hermione sold the drugs out from under him while he was in the hospital. Really, Lodges? *That's* the final straw? Shocked and sad, Veronica heads to the cast party at the Farm's new location—the building formerly known as The Sisters of Quiet Mercy. Later, she (finally) hooks up with Reggie.

At the cast party? Here's a tip: don't eat the brownies. Too late, Kevin did. He also hallucinates Midge, sharing the experience the next day at rehearsals, Farm style—which requires emotionally revealing self-disclosures. One of the truths to come out is that Archie and Josie are (sort of) dating. But Josie will not make it official. That's sad. Veronica, using Reggie to feel better, is also sad.

When Betty finds out that Evelyn has called a closed rehearsal in the Gargoyle Chamber, she snags Jughead's camera and snaps photos, which she delivers to Principal Weatherbee. After meeting with him, she's sure the man is connected to the Farm.

Cheryl takes it upon herself to kick Toni out of Riverdale High, so Toni sings about wanting to rebel as she dances through the hallway, ultimately running out of the school. Later, at Thistlehouse, Toni takes an olive branch to Cheryl, insisting that it's not too late for them. This is good news, because we viewers don't like the fighting Choni.

Who also isn't normal? The Lodges. Hermione tried to have Hiram killed, who declares that Veronica and her mom betrayed them, so there is no family anymore. Apparently, he doesn't remember the evil crap he did to Veronica—and to Archie. Apparently, neither does she. She asks them to come to the play's opening night for one last happy family memory. Wait, what? Were there any happy family memories?

FP arrives home scratched up from crossing paths with a guy high on Fizzle Rocks and is now determined to find who is cooking the stuff. Maybe, that night he should check his own bed.

Jughead and Betty go to the trailer and reflect. How did their lives get to this point? Drug dealing, serial killing parents? Betty, wanting to test the theory that the right song solves everything, sings about being normal. This is one time the right song doesn't solve everything. Need proof? Betty and Jughead burn down his childhood home. Archie, you're next up to light your house on fire.

It's opening night. At the close of the play, Edgar Evernever rises from his seat, clapping. He's joined by others from the Farm, who rise one at a time, wearing white and clapping in unison.

Jughead, still onstage, has no time to offer a concluding voice-over.

Chapter Fifty-Two:
"The Raid"

Original airdate: *March 27, 2019*
Writer: *Greg Murray & Ace Hasan*
Director: *Pamela Romanowsky*

Top Quote: "How many times did you try to kill Archie?"—Veronica to her dad when she is trying to convince her parents to seek marriage counseling.

Top Trivia: Jonathan Whitesell (Kurtz) is one of the many Canadian actors on *Riverdale*. *Chilling Adventures of Sabrina* fans will recognize him as the mysterious Robin Goodfellow.

Watch For: Gladys is trying to be the new worst mom in Riverdale. Yet more fantastic sweaters for Betty. Many people sneaking into many places.

Wonder About: Can you count how many people Jughead has roughed up? Cheryl Blossom and the Farm. What? Why? What will Betty uncover at the Farm?

Summary + Commentary:

No opening voice-over from Jughead, because he's busy training with FP and Tom.

Meanwhile, Veronica is struggling with the divorce and ignoring all the evil stuff her father has done to her, and to the people she cares about.

FP is surprised to find out that their burned down former home had drug cooking materials in it. Jughead and Gladys aren't surprised. The war between the two of them is out in the open now, and he is determined to continue amping up his efforts to get rid of her and the Gargoyles. He enlists the Serpents.

Hiram's new prison is opening, and all the juveniles from the detention center are being moved. Mad Dog calls Archie asking for help. Archie turns to Veronica, who taps the governor, luring him to the Pembrooke for a chat. Archie tells the governor that he'll tell the press about the underground fight club, unless the man pardons the teens, thus freeing them. It works. The guys who have no place to go, get an invitation from Archie to stay at the gym.

Elsewhere, Jughead and the Serpents are doing their best to cause Gladys problems. After Sweat Pea asks for some *game enhancement* at the MLJ Comic shop, Jughead threatens the clerk to get info on where the Gargoyles are selling. Fang and Sweet Pea start clearing the corners where they're told the sellers are located, ultimately getting into trouble by FP, who was staking out the corners himself.

Betty and Veronica take a tour of the Farm, led by Kevin. Betty runs into her mom, who has no interest in talking. Betty does a short interview with Evelyn, but it nets no new info. So, Betty talks Cheryl into going undercover to get inside the Farm. Her attempt to sneak into the Farm backfires though, when Edgar steps in to do her interview. Betty still plans to use Cheryl as her in to find out where he stores the tapes he records during the self-disclosing conversations. Cheryl's queries make Edgar suspicious, so he takes her to a closet. The next day, when Betty asks what was in the room, and suddenly Cheryl informs her she is done being a mole.

Archie tells Jughead the Gargoyles have taken over the apartments where Mad Dog's family is living. Jughead plans to talk to the Serpents to see if they want to raid the building. They do; there is a lot of fighting, but nothing really seems to happen. Later, he confronts Gladys—she doesn't care that he and his friends were shot at. He's not giving up.

After Hermione is threatened, Veronica again asks her dad not to divorce her mom. Reluctantly, he invites his wife to the ribbon cutting of the prison. How romantic. But later, Veronica finds out the marriage has been annulled. The upside to this is that according to mob custom, Hermione remains under Hiram's protection. Downside for Veronica, her parent's marriage is truly over.

Turns out, Betty doesn't need Cheryl. She sneaks into the Farm and steals the interview tapes of Polly, Alice and Cheryl herself. Turns out, the tapes aren't the only lure. The Farm can also help people see the dead, like Cheryl seeing Jason. And Alice talking to Charles. Betty finally gets to meet Edgar, telling him she wants to know everything from the beginning.

The Gargoyles are busy as ever, with Jughead and Archie finding a chalice with baby teeth inside it. FP finds Baby Teeth, aka Brandon Morris, sacrificed in the woods.

So much is going on—you know you just have to hit Next Episode, right this minute.

Chapter Fifty-Three:
"Jawbreaker"

Original airdate: *April 17, 2019*
Writer: *Brian E. Paterson & Arabella Anderson*
Director: *Gabriel Correa*

Top Quote: "I will kill you. And if you don't believe me, ask around. People will tell you what I'm capable of."—Betty, to Evelyn, after she slams her into a locker, then lets the Farmie know what will happen is she comes around Alice or Betty again.

Top Trivia: Randy Ronson is a genuine Archie Comics character. Randy *Van* Ronson is a rival of Katy Keene's boyfriend, K.O. Kelly. However, the Randy Ronson depicted in *Riverdale* is quite different from the wealthy, well-connected Randy *Van* Ronson seen in the Katy Keene comics and TV series.

Watch For: Betty casually telling Toni, 'hold on a second I think this is my dad' on the phone. Alice's deepening involvement with the Farm and Betty's deepening intent to get her out. Toni and Cheryl struggling to stay together.

Wonder About: How *does* Alice see and talk to her dead son? How *does* Cheryl see and talk to Jason? Who is behind the tainted Fizzle Rocks?

Summary + Commentary:

No opening voice-over from Jughead—he's busy with Baby Teeth, dead from Fizzle Rocks. The new twist: the guy is missing his teeth. Copycat killer or is the real Gargoyle King back and sending a message?

Betty meets with Edgar, and asks him to tell her everything. He tells her how his life used to be different. He was in shambles until he came across a farm where he worked and found purpose in his life—building a place where he can welcome lost souls are open to change. Naturally, this convo sends Betty to visit someone who'd understand a man with a twisted mind.

At the El Royale Fight Club, Archie is doing what he can to boost the fighters' spirits. Later at school, he asks Veronica for help to get his boxers into the Gilded Gloves—a tournament organized by Elio. She approaches Elio, but he shoos her away. Meanwhile, Archie prepares for his rematch with Randy Van Ronson.

Cheryl, wearing white instead of her trademark red, is touting the benefits of the Farm. At the same time, Betty is trying to find a way to expose the cult and get her mom back into reality. Toni also wants to get someone to see reality—her girl Cheryl. Neither is successful. Why not? They both think they are talking to dead people: Alice to her son Charles, Cheryl to her brother Jason. Betty won't take no for an answer. She chloroforms her mom and locks her in the bunker.

While FP and Jughead are meeting with Penelope to ask why a pack of Maple Club matches was lodged in dead Baby Teeth's throat, their meeting is disrupted by a man foaming at the mouth from Fizzle Rocks. The brothel guest fills FP and Jughead in. Kurtz is the cook making the bad Fizzle Rocks.

Toni and Evelyn have a hostile moment in the girls' bathroom, While Betty and Evelyn have a hostile moment in the hallway. Betty confronts Edgar, maintaining that Alice is on a journey, finding her truest self. When Betty's efforts to unwash her mom's mind fail, she delivers Alice back to Evelyn.

But the Farmies don't approve of indecision. Cheryl is forced to make a choice between Jason or Toni. The only way she can be with both, is for Toni to join the Farm—so Toni joins. Right after being accepted, Toni heads right to Betty to affirm they both want the same thing—a loved one back in their life.

Mad Dog gives Archie a tip—Randy Ronson is on a performance enhancer. He gives Archie a bag of a little something to even the odds, just in case. The boxers are set to enter the tournament, each fighting in Baby Teeth's honor.

At El Royale, Archie and Randy duke it out. Drug-induced Randy nearly wins, but Archie lands a knockout punch that leaves the guy flat—and not getting up. FP catches Kurtz outside the El Royale, where he and Jughead grill him. The cook hems and haws, ultimately tipping the two off that Jellybean, the little princess, is the feature of the ultimate quest. She is in danger and must be saved. Thus, no voice-over.

Chapter Fifty-Four:
"Fear the Reaper"

Original airdate: *April 24, 2019*
Writer: *Janine Salinas Schoenberg & Will Ewing*
Director: *Alexandra La Roche*

Top Quote: "I'm going to dog-walk that lying cad."—Veronica, telling Archie not to worry.

Top Trivia: This is the final episode that features, Josie McCoy, an original Archie Comics character. After saying goodbye to Archie, Josie crosses over to the spinoff series, *Katy Keene.*

Watch For: Gladys, Jughead and FP, an unlikely trio, working together. Betty forms an unlikely but reasonable alliance. This is the final episode with Luke Perry (Fred) on screen.

Wonder About: Betty and Veronica's request of Hiram about Hal? Does that make any kind of sense? How many revenge-against-Archie plans has Hiram cooked up? Gladys—is she at all sincere? Do you hope to see her again?

Summary + Commentary:

We pick up right where we left off, with Jughead busy looking for Jellybean. Kurtz insists FP, Gladys and Jughead play G&G to get her back. Right away, things get bad for the Jones family. As a result of the first challenge, Gladys is forced to admit she is the new Fizzle Rocks dealer in Riverdale.

Meanwhile, Veronica invites her dad to La Bonne Nuit for a

chat. Betty asks Hiram to move her dad into his new prison. She's heard there are lovely waterfront rooms that face Sweetwater River, and she'd like him to be transferred there. Satisfied that she's done all she can for her dad, Betty turns her attention back to her mom, who's preparing to marry Edgar. For some reason, Edgar plans to adopt Juniper and Dagwood. Doesn't that make Alice both stepmother and grandmother? That's... disturbing. Thankfully, Grandma Penelope talks Edgar out of one of the twins. Not both. Just one. So now it's only half as disturbing.

As part of the G&G game, FP, Jughead and Gladys rob Pop's. Then Kurtz sends them on another challenge—Gladys must fight... surprise... Penny, who is still alive. Jughead stops his mom from killing Penny, and out of patience, insists that Kurtz take him to Jellybean. Why didn't he just lose his patience sooner?

By the way, Randy didn't survive Archie's knockout punch, and Elio declares that it's Archie's fault the fighter is dead. Archie is tormented by guilt, so Veronica suggests they do a benefit concert to raise money for the Ronson family at La Bonne Nuit. That's good. What is not good? Archie gets caught with a bag of drugs at his gym.

At school, Betty snoops into Evelyn's file. She discovers that Evelyn has been repeating her junior year, pretending to be seventeen for over a decade. Handy Ms. Weiss confirms that Evelyn is 26, and is Edgar's wife, not daughter. Betty is more determined than ever to get back into the Farm. Once in, Betty grabs Juniper only to discover that Toni tricked her. Betty tells her mom Edgar is already married, but her mom doesn't care. Then, while the Farmies chant "join us," Edgar encourages Betty to join them. She flees instead.

Kurtz has yet another final challenge for Jughead. He must get into the ice tomb—a refrigerator. Jug does so at gunpoint, as he hears Kurtz give Ricky the order to kill the princess. Jughead fights his way out of the containment only to find Kurtz dead. However, Jellybean is safe.

Let's tie up some loose ends:

Josie breaks some news to Archie. She's going on tour with her dad. They aren't endgame; she tells him. We bingers are not surprised.

Gladys finally catches on that she isn't welcome in Riverdale. For no real reason, Jughead tries to get her to stay, but she knows she's already overstayed her welcome.

Hiram believes there are two Archies. The good and the bad. So, he can break the truce. Yes, that is real logic. At least inside Hiram's twisted mind it is.

Let's create a new loose end:

Veronica delivers some bad news to Betty. While her father was being transferred to Hiram's new prison, there was an accident that left no survivors. Is he really, truly dead? Does anyone truly die in Riverdale?

Chapter Fifty-Five:
"Prom Night"

Original airdate: *May 1, 2019*
Writer: *Britta Lundin & Devon Turner*
Director: *David Katzenberg*

Top Quote: "Prom is this weekend? We still do things like that here?"—Veronica, probably speaking to the viewers.

Top Trivia: In case you have been wondering, yes, KJ Apa is social media famous for his abs. This New Zealander eats a low-carb diet, trains continually, is 5'11", and keeps his weight around 165. And—in scenes where he's seen eating, he has a bucket stashed to spit the food out.

Watch For: The compelling power of wanting to be Prom Queen trumping everything else. The Black Hood! The Gargoyle King!

Wonder About: Will Hal ever really get what's coming to him? Will Hiram ever stop deceiving his daughter? Did the writers do a good job swapping Mary in for Fred?

Summary + Commentary:

Once again, we pick up where we left off: Betty and Veronica arriving at the crash site to ponder Hal's death. Betty heads to the Farm to tell Alice that Hal may be on the loose.

Dr. Curdle, after getting DNA from a hand, assures Betty that her father is, in fact, dead.

Jellybean, instead of seeing that her drug-dealing mom being gone is a good thing, feels abandoned. After Jughead tells her no more G & G, she discloses that the Gargoyle King personally gave her and Ricky a quest—to find the Gospel. Jughead finds the Gospel in an abandoned school bus and becomes very interested in the contents. It's full of myth.

Ready to create a story of her own, Cheryl is campaigning for her and Toni to be Junior Prom Queens. But the Farm forbids such campaigning, so she gives it up. But she's also considering giving up on the Farm.

Archie has mere days to lose five pounds, to make weight for a fight his mom told him he could not. But he forged her signature on the permission form, so technically he can. So...Archie takes on a grueling training regimen designed to help him lose the pounds.

Betty and Jughead visit a tattoo artist, getting some inside info on guys getting inked with G&G symbols. They mull over what they have learned and, in the end, decide Edgar is the Gargoyle King. But—he doesn't have the tattoos on his back, so maybe they are wrong.

Archie's mom wants him to meet with a navy recruiter. That's random, but he complies. The recruiter gives him the hard sell, and he agrees to do an exhibition match for her. So now he has two fights planned for the same night. Losing the tournament match, he arrives for the exhibition match only to get knocked out with the first punch. Instead of discouraging him, now Archie knows for certain he doesn't want to go to college or join the navy. He just wants to box.

The Serpents and the Pretty Poisons come together for the prom. Their goal is not to have fun—it's to catch the Gargoyle King. While dancing at the prom, Veronica tells Archie what she just heard from Pop. Her father owns Pop's and La Bonne Nuit, and he gave her a fake deed. In a very Lodge-like manner, her plan is now to manipulate him and win in the end. Across the dance floor, Betty receives a summons from the Gargoyle King. In the girls' bathroom, she finds two chalices. She finds the King, asks him what he wants, then slides a gun from her purse. The Black Hood attacks. While fleeing, she finds two dead bodies. Finally, Jughead finds her.

Apparently, the Black Hood's return makes Mary decide to stay in Riverdale and to support Archie's boxing. Um. Okay. What about her life in Chicago? Speaking of the Black Hood, his return sends Betty to the Farm yet again to warn her mother. Edgar invites her to stay at the Farm, to which she agrees.

Chapter Fifty-Six:
"The Dark Secret of Harvest House"

Original airdate: *May 8, 2019*
Writer: *Cristine Chambers & James DeWille*
Director: *Rob Seidenglanz*

Top Quote: "Now you just sound cuckoo-pants. Why would Edgar cause us pain, just to take it away?"—Cheryl to Betty, after Betty tells Cheryl and the others that Edgar is harming them during hypnosis.

Top Trivia: In the original Archie Comics, "Big Ethel" was a long-standing character with a huge crush on Jughead. Ethel Muggs was often shown chasing after Jughead.

Watch For: Ethel saying to Jughead, "Help me, Jughead Jones. You're my only hope." Finally, being able to piece together Edgar's entire evil plan. Archie, finally, maybe, beating Hiram—or rather helping Veronica beat him—at his own manipulation game.

Wonder About: Again, who is the Gargoyle King? Transferring emotional pain into physical pain… does that make sense? How random is that news that Betty has the serial killer gene?

Summary + Commentary:

Jughead's opening voice-over tells of the deadly prom night—The town needs answers.

The first one comes from Dr. Curdle: the Black Hood faked his own death.

Alice delivers a fun bomb to Betty—The girl has the serial killer gene. Not to worry though, Edgar will help via hypnosis, so she can confront her darker self. After her first session, she calls Jughead, tells him about it, and insists that there is a connection between the Gargoyle King and the Black Hood. Later, over a Farm healthy meal, Betty questions Kevin, Fangs, Toni and Cheryl about the treatments they've been having. He's turning their emotional pain into physical pain. How great is that?

The ultimate mobster, Hiram, wants to buy Riverdale, as in the whole town. That will put Hermione out of a job, so naturally she is against it. Veronica isn't waiting around to lose her place in the Riverdale underworld landscape either. Cooking up a plan to get her father into legal trouble, she enlists her favorite carrot-top. Archie bursts into a steam room filled with mobsters, to tell Hiram he's going to kick his ass. How? A boxing match. Of course, Hiram agrees. That's good because this match is all part of Veronica's take-down-daddy plan.

Over at the place formerly known as The Sisters of Quiet Mercy, Betty has another session with Edgar. She asks to see her other half, to find out what the darker side of her wants. What her darker side wants is not at all surprising—it mocks her and calls her a killer.

Using a map Jellybean made, Jughead heads to Fox Forest to find Ricky. A hoard of Adventures Scouts, aka the Lost Boys, chase him through the woods, sending Jughead to seek shelter in the bunker, where he finds Ethel and convinces her to get the Lost Boys to stand down.

Meanwhile, by seeing Evelyn hooked up to a medical machine, crafty Betty figures out that Edgar is butchering his own disciples. She sneaks around and finds a freezer filled with blood bags and organs.

Mary surprises Archie by gleefully telling him that she wants to watch whatever bad stuff he and Veronica have planned for Hiram. She attends the fight, watching as Archie and Hiram box. Meanwhile, over at La Bonne Nuit, Veronica performs and waits for the FBI to raid the place. She plans to tell them her father—the actual owner of La Bonne Nuit—allows illegal bets to take place there. Then, she plans to send them over to La Royale, where the same man is participating in an illegal bare-knuckle fight. One thing leads to another, and soon, FP arrests Hiram. Hiram is sincerely amazed that his own daughter betrayed him. Curious how he forgets how he's constantly betraying her.

Back at the Farm, Betty shows Cheryl a heart from the freezer. Cheryl is finally convinced that *maybe* something is wrong there, so she rushes off to put a halt to Toni's treatment, which was set to begin. Fangs and Kevin are not convinced, however, and they prevent Betty from leaving—she wakes up in the infirmary, chained to an operating table.

Archie, probably feeling connected to Veronica since they just took down her dad, arrives at the Pembrooke, ready to tell her how he feels about her, but finds Reggie already there. Veronica invites him to stay. Super awkward. He leaves.

As a thank you to Jughead for helping her, Ethel reveals the identity of the Gargoyle King—Jason Blossom. So yeah, now Jughead is on his way to dig up Jason's body. Shocker! Jason Blossom's casket is empty. Jughead has nothing to say about that.

Chapter Fifty-Seven:
"Survive the Night"

Original airdate: *May 15, 2019*
Writer: *Roberto Aguirre-Sacasa & Michael Grassi*
Director: *Rachel Talalay*

Top Quote: "Who doesn't wanna be king? Who doesn't want blood sacrifices made in their name?"—Chic to Jughead, explaining why he's taken on the role of Gargoyle King.

Top Trivia: The motto on the gate of the Blossom family estate reads, "radices currere abyssi." Translated from Latin to English, it is, "roots run deep." This episode shows that is true.

Watch For: The third, final, Gargoyle King revealed! Penelope with a gun and knowing how to use it. The cliff-hanger at the very, very end.

Wonder About: All that fighting, but no consistently visible wounds. Should Nana Rose been more consistently present throughout the season? Penelope was a mastermind behind it all... do you buy it?

Summary + Commentary:

Over tea prepared, by a known poisoner, Toni insists that Cheryl is in danger. Of course, the tea knocks Toni out. Penelope heads to the farm, interrupting Edgar right before he carves into Betty. She tells him that she wants to buy organs—in bulk. Edgar, knowing they have been outed, begins to prepare for the ascension.

In Riverdale, Hiram has been arrested and placed in custody.

Now, Veronica and her mom officially co-own Pop's and La Bonne Nuit. Now, maybe, we will all get a break from his manipulations. Then again, maybe not.

Archie, Jughead, Betty and Veronica all receive invitations to the Blossom Hunting Lodge. Betty is there, thanks to Penelope buying her from Edgar. The others arrive voluntarily. Other guests include Hal and Chic—aka the fake Jason and the Gargoyle King. Turns out, Penelope has a grudge against the entire town of Riverdale and plans to take it out on the four teens. She delivers them to the woods to play one final round of G & G. The task is to make it through the quests by the end of the night. If they try to escape, they will be killed.

First, Archie defeats the grizzled beast, completing his challenge. Veronica appears to have bested her challenge, only to be told it was a trick. As a result, both she and Betty are now poisoned. As they move on through the woods to the next challenge, we get a bit of romance when Archie professes his love for Veronica. Jughead completes his challenge and, knowing that Betty and Veronica are both poisoned, they move on to the final challenge.

On their way to save Cheryl, Toni and the Southside Serpents find Nana Rose, who tips them off that bad crap is happening in the woods. Soon, they all race to rescue the four from Penelope.

Meanwhile, Betty has the final challenge—she is faced with killing her own father. She shoots him, but not to kill, leaving Penelope to tidily finish the man off. Betty, after watching her father die, retrieves the antidote. Yay, they are all safe. Oh, wait, no, they are not. Even though they have won, Penelope orders her minions to kill them. Thankfully, Cheryl and the Pretty Poisons have arrived just in time to charge the minions and save the gang.

By the way, Alice is finally beginning to have concerns about life and goings-on at the Farm. She confronts Edgar, who begins to admit his half-truths and lies. However, Cheryl busts in and interrupts him. He has her confined and tells Evelyn and Alice that it's time to ascend. Alice grabs Juniper and helps Cheryl escape, soliciting Cheryl to look out for Betty, because she is staying back for Polly. Later, after making it through Penelope's Hell Path, Betty arrives at the Farm to find Kevin alone. Everyone else is gone.

Jughead's concluding voice-over sums up the arrests, and deaths, and the escape of Penelope Blossom. The future now belongs to the righteous. And also to Cheryl, who is welcoming dead Jason home. Next, we get a sip of what's on tap for Season 4.

Hermione is arrested for conspiracy to commit murder. In the jail-yard, Hiram gloats about the bad time his daughter is about to have. Archie is also planning the future. He will turn the El Royale Gym into a haven for at-risk kids. Alice is actually amazing. Turns out, she's been working with the FBI, and the guy she's working with is Charles, Betty's actual brother. Oh, right, he's also Jughead's actual brother.

At Pop's, Archie, Jughead, Betty and Veronica clink milkshakes as they vow to make their senior year the best time ever. Bingers know that will be true, but simply not the best time as in good time.

Viewers' first piece of evidence is the episode ending with the four of them gazing into a fire, discussing a plan to burn all their clothes—including Jughead's beanie—and to never speaking of that night again.

Season 3 Pop Quiz 2

1) What two characters exchange these lines?

"You set out to abduct and terrorize your own kid. How'd you talk your cadets into helping?"

"I made it a quest. The Gargoyle King told them their brothers needed help. 'When you are weak, I am weak.'"

2) Who said it?

"Oh well. The truth will shake out. It always does."

3) Who is Ricky speaking to when he says:

"I thought this would be the last place they'd look for me. I'll never escape them. I'm marked for death. Isn't that what this symbol means? And you have it, too?"

4) What two characters are speaking?

"Well, what do we have here?"

"Lying in wait for me? Color me shocked."

"Oh, please. Earlier tonight, you were casing the place. And you wanted me to know it.

"So, what are you going to do now?"

5) Who said it? And to who?

"Um, did you have a lobotomy for breakfast? You're wearing my signature color."

6) Who said it?

"This is between you and me, kiddo. Mano a mano."

7) Who said it?

"Brawny young men, shirtless and in shorts. Go on."

8) Fill in the blank. Hint: Jughead is speaking to Kurtz.

"If everything is parallel for Riverdale, then the Tavern is
_____."

9) Fill in the blanks:

"I am not a part of you. You are a part of me. I am the real
_____ _____. You are the illusion."

10) Which two characters exchange these lines:

"We won, didn't we? We survived the night. We proved
we're better than this town."

"That may or may not be true. Kill them. Kill them all!"

RIVERDALE

SEASON
FOUR

Chapter Fifty-Eight:
"In Memoriam"

Original airdate: *October 9, 2019*
Writer: *Roberto Aguirre-Sacasa*
Director: *Gabriel Correa*

Top Quote: "I have to go get my dad."—Archie, to Veronica, after waking from a dream.

Top Trivia: This episode is a tribute to Luke Perry, better known to Riverdale Bingers as sexy dad, Fred Andrews. It has intentionally been written as a stand-alone.

Watch For: Cheryl sharing the morning news with Jay-Jay. Bare-chested Archie. Why wear a shirt when hammering nails? Shannen Doherty, good friends with Luke Perry, appears in the episode as the woman Fred helped with car trouble.

Wonder About: Does anyone in Riverdale drive a modern era car? Where is Alice? Did Hiram do a kind thing?

Summary + Commentary:

Jughead's opening voice-over lets us know the tough times are in the past. While the terror of the Farm has not been forgotten, life is returning to normal. July 4th is approaching, and for the first time in three years, there will be a parade through town. No fireworks, but plenty of celebration.

What he could have said: Dear viewers, this is a stand-alone tribute episode and doesn't hook into the overall storyline of the show. Die-hard fans leave the remote on the table. You may be connected to the characters enough to shed a tear or two.

Jughead's concluding voice-over is replaced by his tribute to Fred, which, it seems, is also a tribute to the actor who played him. Jughead finishes by saying, "Fred left Riverdale better than when he found it. That's his legacy." Well said.

Chapter Fifty-Nine:
"Fast Times at Riverdale High"

Original airdate: *October 16, 2019*
Writer: *Michael Grassi & Will Ewing*
Director: *Pamela Romanowsky*

Top Quote: "Oh, you mean like when you dragged me by my ankles to get a lobotomy?"—Betty clarifying to Kevin what he was sorry about while under the influence of Edgar the Farmies.

Top Trivia: The previous principal of Riverdale High School was Mr. Weatherbee. In the comics, the nickname used for Weatherbee was "the Bee." Bees make Honey, ergo, the new principal's name is Mr. Honey.

Watch For: Jay-Jay. He's only dead, not gone. Many 1980s pop culture references. Reggie and Archie shifting from (sort of) enemies to (sort of) allies. More to come on this.

Wonder About: How uncomfortable do you (still) feel watching high school kids having hot, hot sex? Kevin waited *months* to reconnect with Betty? But wait, is Kevin still involved with the Farm? Scale from one to five, how understanding and patient is Toni? Or could you handle being Cheryl's girlfriend?

Summary + Commentary:

Jughead's opening voice-over tells us that by the last day of summer vacation, Archie has moved on from losing his father and is doing what he does best—encouraging others and boxing.

Many other things are the same in Riverdale: Alice is still at the Farm, Veronica is still dealing with her criminal parents, and Betty is still trying to make sure everything is exactly right.

Here's something that's new: Cheryl has brought dead Jay-Jay home and is making a habit of talking to him. No, apparently it doesn't matter that he's dead.

The four friends start off their senior year by being late for the first day of school. In the hall, they meet Mr. Honey—the new principal—who promises order, discipline and consequences. Good thing he wasn't at the Pembrooke the night before, when these same kids were drinking wine and pairing up for sex.

Later that day, things are tough on the football practice field. Reggie's dad humiliates him. Veronica is also humiliated in the locker room, when a pervert tries to snap a picture of her. The tabloids have gotten wind of the latest Lodge scandal and are hounding Veronica. Mr. Honey questions her about an article that unpacks her family's troubles and suggests she take a sabbatical from Riverdale High.

Kevin feels dumped by the farm. When Betty finds out that Kevin was under surveillance by the FBI, she pairs up with Charles and plans to use Kevin as an FBI asset. Bingers are probably not amazed to discover Kevin is in touch with Fangs, who is loyal to Edgar and the other Farmies. He relays the intel he got from Betty, that there is a witness who will testify against the Farm. Sadly, for Kevin, Fangs keeps him at an arm's length. Also sad—Betty followed Kevin into the woods. She takes him back to Charles, and the two of them question his loyalties.

Later that week, Reggie's dad humiliates him on the football field. Archie stands up for him, telling Mr. Mantle to get off the field, but Reggie acts as many abused—denies it and stands up for the abuser. Speaking of abuse, Veronica goes to prison to see her dad. He mocks her.

The week ends with Cheryl's Back to School Party. It's the perfect place for Betty to tell Kevin, that Alice is undercover at the Farm, and suggests that he tell Fangs that Penelope Blossom is the informant—even though that isn't true. Not much else gets to happen because Mr. Honey manages to ruin the party by calling in a complaint that FP acts on.

After the party, Reggie opens his heart to Archie, admitting that his dad beats him. He needs to take a stand, so he does the one thing he thinks will get his dad's attention—he smashes up his dad's car. Reggie tells Archie it worked, and the two hug and declare bros for life.

Veronica, tired of being hounded by the scandal-loving press, breaks down and invites the press to La Bonne Nuit. Later that night, after a steamy performance of "All That Jazz" she declares her love to her parents, admits to doing bad things under duress, and states that now she stands only for herself. She then completes her application to Harvard, using her mother's maiden name since the Lodge name is tainted.

Jughead may not have to worry about uptight Mr. Honey—he's been invited to transfer to Stonewall Prep. He declines, but FP insists Jughead at least visit the school. While on a school tour, an in-class conversation about *Moby Dick* causes Jughead to reconsider his attitude. The other kids have read the book! Jughead, dressed in the required school uniform, heads off to Stonewall Prep. Right after his dad wishes him well, we flash into the future to see a search party in progress, looking for... wait for it... Jughead.

Jughead is off to school, or missing, and thus has no concluding voice-over.

Chapter Sixty:
"Dog Day Afternoon"

Original airdate: *October 23, 2019*
Writer: *Ace Hasan & Greg Murray*
Director: *Greg Smith*

Top Quote: "Mija, I own that jail. I come and go as I please."—Hiram, to Veronica, when she arrives home to find him at his desk.

Top Trivia: Season 4 had the lowest viewership of all four seasons of Riverdale.

Watch For: The Car Wash Scene. All kinds of hotness. Edgar, wearing his red-white-and-blue jumpsuit, climbing onto his rocket. Alice—redeemed!

Wonder About: How exceptional is a show that references both *Dead Poets Society* and *The Full Monty* in the same episode? Should Toni have caught on sooner to the truth that to dead Jason has been residing in the basement? The circular plot with Veronica deciding whether to change her last name and ultimately deciding not to, but to go with something entirely different. What was the point?

Summary + Commentary:

Jughead is all moved into Stonewall Prep. What the hell!

Moose, now known as Marmaduke, is also at Stonewall. Remember when Moose's dad dressed up like the Gargoyle King and tried to scare Moose straight? After that happened, Moose had to reinvent himself. And he picked Stonewall. The place is okay, but things quickly get testy. During class, Jughead and Bret insult each other's work. Later, Donna advises Jughead to watch his back around Bret. You just know it—Jughead and Bret will not be buddies.

Munroe, the guy formerly known as Mad Dog, reminds Archie of his plan to turn the El Royale into a community center. Mary is a bit of a downer about the work involved, but Archie is determined. The gang cooks up ways to make money. Veronica's first idea is a car wash. The event is visually appealing but only nets a sudsy $400.

After Charles sends an undercover FBI agent to deliver pizza to the hotel where the Farmies are staying, Edgar calls Betty. He tells her that Alice admitted she is an informant, and proceeds to offer up his list of demands. Too bad the Governor won't negotiate with cults. Also too bad Edgar strapped bombs to Polly, and sent her to Charles and Betty. Why is Betty, not FBI agent Charles, the one to cut the bomb's wires? She taps Veronica for money, Toni for fake passports, steals a school bus, loads it with food and water, and heads to the motel. There, Evelyn knocks her unconscious.

In the middle of the night, Toni and Cheryl are awakened by a shrieking Nana Rose, who mistakes Cheryl for Penelope. So, it's life as usual at Thistlehouse. When Toni does a reasonable thing—hires an oversized hottie night nurse for Nana—Cheryl gets unreasonable fast and warns him not to go into the chapel in the basement.

Mary is a downer again when she asks Archie to come back to Chicago, telling him that Riverdale is a losing proposition. He tells her he's determined to make a difference in his hometown. Then, like a real man, he sneaks out his bedroom window, covers his face with a bandana, and confronts Dodger, the guy in town who is exploiting kids.

Veronica gives Mary 40K for the community center, which Mary rejects, telling her that the center weighs Archie down. Turns out, Archie stole Dodger's money. Munro suggests Veronica clean it for them, but she counters: burn the stolen money, which apparently has a voodoo curse on it, and let her pay for the renovations. Cause that all makes sense.

Here's something else that makes sense. Betty wakes up in one of Edgar's motel rooms, to hear her mother telling her that Edgar has been building a rocket. He'll take off in the rocket while Evelyn kills everyone, by driving the bus off a cliff. Betty comes up with a better, less insane plan. She'll load the Farmies on the bus and drive it off, but not off a cliff. Alice goes after Edgar, killing him when he draws on her. Sadly, we don't get to see the rocket launch. This binger, in particular, feels very cheated.

Mary has a sudden change of heart. She's staying in Riverdale and wants to help the community center, free of charge.

Veronica also had a change. She's changing her last name to Luna—Hiram's original last name.

No changes for Jughead, but he does get a gift. While home catching up with Betty, he receives a VHS tape on his doorstep. What's on that VHS? Keep watching…

Chapter Sixty-One:
"Halloween"

Original airdate: *October 30, 2019*
Writer: *Janine Salinas Schoenberg*
Director: *Erin Feeley*

Top Quote: "I told you. Its Jay-Jay. He's angry and now he's haunting us."—Cheryl to Toni when they find the doll version of Jason back in the basement chapel after Toni threw him out.

Top Trivia: *Riverdale* creator, Roberto Aguirre-Sacasa, had planned for each season's Halloween episode to have an *Afterlife* vibe, based on the *Afterlife with Archie Comics* series. However, this one from Season 4 was the first to actualize that vision.

Watch For: During the convo about needing costumes, Veronica's crossover mention and shout out to Katy Keene. Archie and his Pureheart the Powerful costume—it's the same one that he wears in the *Archie's Super Teen* Comics. Bret really starting to settle into his extra-annoying smug personality.

Wonder About: Would Toni and Cheryl really start making out after going to all that trouble to perfect those costumes? Seriously, how patient is Toni? Or: Is Toni too indulgent? That shocking ending… could it be true?

Summary + Commentary:

Jughead's opening voice-over tells of the VHS tapes showing up on doorsteps all over town. They all contain the same thing—hours and hours of front doors. Probably not what you were hoping for.

217

That morning in the Riverdale student lounge, Betty and Veronica chat about being on edge. Kevin and Reggie plan to TP Mr. Honey's office, but Archie and Munroe offer a different perspective. They want to keep kids safe on Halloween, so they plan to have a party at their community center.

Over at Stonewall Prep, Bret and Jughead bicker about horror writers, when Jughead asks Mr. Chipping about the Stonewall Four.

Earlier that morning, Toni said what we've all been thinking— it's time to say goodbye to dead Jason. Cheryl reluctantly agrees to bury him in the family plot, but when they come back inside and find a creepy Jason-like doll on the couch, Cheryl tells Toni it's a warning that Jason's ghost is now unhappy.

Halloween night, while Betty waits at her house for Jughead, Jughead—after being drugged by Donna—wakes up in a closed coffin. Betty gets a call from someone claiming to be… wait for it… the Black Hood.

After Mr. Honey catches Kevin TPing his office, they have a chat. He tells the kid that he isn't likely to get into NYU Tisch, his dream school, because of his problematic musicals, *Carrie* and *Heathers*, and now *this*. He then chats with Reggie, asking him if he takes on the clown persona to hide the pain caused by his father's cruelty.

Dodger and his crew crash Archie and Monroe's party at the community center. The guy tries to take Eddie, only to be blocked by Archie and Munroe. Archie calls FP.

Back over at Thistlehouse, Toni and Nana Rose aid Cheryl in her séance. Always one to add cheer, Nana Rose drops some old Blossom knowledge—the ghost haunting them isn't Jason, it's Julian, the third baby who Cheryl absorbed before birth.

Over at the house formerly belonging to the Coopers, the guy claiming to be the Black Hood calls back. Charles, who just happened to stop by with pizza, offers to help Betty trace the call, which they do, back to Shady Grove Treatment Center—Polly's current residence. Betty calls her sister, scolds her, then, acting like a little sister, abruptly hangs up.

Over at Pop's, Veronica realizes the man she let into the restaurant after hours is a serial killer called The Family Man. When he comes after her, she lights him on fire. Rock on! Lighting a man on fire is almost the same as lighting your house on fire. So now

Archie is the only one remaining who needs to burn something. Or someone.

The day after Halloween:

Jay-Jay is back inside Thistlehouse.

Jughead is back in the classroom. After getting out of that coffin, Mr. Chipping explains that it's just a Stonewall tradition. No harm, right? Bonus! Now he's one of them. How great is that? Sort of great—except now Moose is missing.

We end on an eerie flash forward—Jughead is in Dr. Curdle's office, and he's dead.

Chapter Sixty-Two:
"Witness for the Prosecution"

Original airdate: *November 6, 2019*
Writer: *Devon Turner*
Director: *Harry Jierjian*

Top Quote: "You're like *Beautiful Mind*, but... for serial killers."—
Kevin to Betty when she continually identifies serial killers in
FBI training photos.

Top Trivia: The Baxter Brothers and Tracy True YA mystery series
are a nod to the famous and long-loved Hardy Boys and Nancy
Drew books. Both series were written by ghostwriters and
published under a pseudonym.

Watch For: Jughead learning a secret about a family member.
Veronica learning of a secret family member. FP delivering a very
confusing pep talk to Jughead.

Wonder About: Are the Veronica vs. Hiram plotlines overdone?
What happens to the community center when Archie and Munroe
graduate? There is indeed an FBI Junior Special Agent Program.
Hmmm...

Summary + Commentary:

Jughead's voice-over describes Archie, high school kid by day, crime
fighter by night.

Over at the community center, Archie and Reggie have their
hands full trying to manage and protect the kids. Archie, who has

taken to the streets to keep them safe, tells the kids they aren't welcome at the club if they run with Dodger's Crew. Not comfortable with that boundary, Toby and another kid bail.

In the hall at school, Betty derails Kevin's plans to cruise bathrooms, by inviting him to enroll in the Junior FBI program with her. Once there, Betty soaks up the serial killer training. She finds that she has the serial killer gene, but lies about it to Kevin. Learning that serial killers torture animals as children, she recalls being told she killed the family cat, Caramel.

Jughead and Betty are going wild over Jughead's old stash of Baxter Brothers books. His interest in the books being rekindled after discovering that Mr. Chipping is the latest in a long line of Baxter Brothers ghostwriters. Bonus, Francis DuPont—the original Franklin P. Paxton—works at Stonewall, and there is a contest to select the next ghostwriter. Jughead digs into the past and discovers that Francis DuPont knew Jughead's grandfather, and that the man was a great writer. Jughead asks his dad about his grandfather, but instead of getting some feel-good info, he finds out the man was a mean drunk who skipped out on the family.

Veronica is having a busy week. Aside from running her businesses and doing her schoolwork, she has two goals: get her mom out of jail and make sure her dad stays in. Hermione's trial isn't going well. Veronica suggests her mom change her plea to guilty, while, *asking* the governor to pardon her mom. Her offer to the miserable guy? It will be the last time she blackmails him.

After a shocking memory resurfaces—and seeing some disturbing drawings in her diary—Betty confesses to Kevin that she lied to him. The FBI training triggered a memory of her dad making her kill her cat, Caramel, because the cat was dying after being hit by a car. Kevin suggests they withdraw from the program.

After Bret tells Jughead that he's only at Stonewall as a welfare case, Jughead attacks the guy, fully establishing their rivalry. Jughead takes all his stuff and goes home. FP tells him to stop being a quitter, acting like his grandfather, and to go back.

Betty also says she's quitting. When she tells Charles why, he tells her that he too has the serial killer gene, and that the program will help her keep the darkness in check. It's then that Betty wonders about Charles. He's keeping secrets.

Minutes after being told that her mother is being released from prison, Veronica discovers she has a sister—the woman seated across from her at La Bonne Nuit. The same woman who has many recordings of Veronica and her dad plotting. That same information has been used to free Hiram and allows him to run for mayor.

FP arrives at the community center to inform Archie that locals are complaining about the kids at the center, suggesting Archie reach out and invite the locals to a clambake. Instead, he has a press conference where he invites them to help or get out of his way. Turns out, the locals have been paying a protection fee to Dodger; Archie confronts Dodger and advises him to leave town.

The episode ends with a flash-forward to the arrest of Betty, Veronica and Archie for the murder of Jughead. Now that's a good twist!

Chapter Sixty-Three:
"Hereditary"

Original airdate: *November 13, 2019*
Writer: *James DeWille*
Director: *Gabriel Correa*

Top Quote: "Is that foreplay or punishment?"—Hiram to Hermione when she slaps him for threatening to have her killed.

Top Trivia: The mention of Dr. Sapirstein, the doctor who took care of Dagwood after he supposedly swallowed a ping-pong ball, is a call over to the *Chilling Adventures of Sabrina.* In both instances, the name is a nod to Ira Levin's famous horror novel, *Rosemary's Baby*, which features an evil doctor of that name.

Watch For: Cheryl's surprise visitors. The Stonewall preppies reaction to Mr. Chippings' sudden departure. Charles... and Chic! What!

Wonder About: Compare Season 1's first couple episodes to Season 4's first couple episodes. Scale from one to five: How uncomfortable and disturbing is that scene with Hiram and Hermione getting back together? Considering that Cheryl has been talking to her brother's dead body, fussing about ghosts, and trusting in circles of salt, is she incompetent as her family claims?

Summary + Commentary:

Jughead's opening voice-over tells of Dodger's system for using the young to do his dirty work. And also, Jughead's own personal dilemma—the blank page.

Speaking of dilemmas, everyone is facing one. Archie and Reggie arrive at the community center to find it ransacked, believing it to be the work of Dodger. Archie interviews Eddie and Toby, discovering arcade games are a big part of Dodger's allure.

Veronica is not keen on Hiram's latest idea. Now out of prison, he wants to bury the hatchet and have the Lodges—plus the newly arrived half-sister—work together. Jughead is discovering a riddle embedded in the Baxter Brothers mysteries. He believes his grandfather wrote the first book, and he's looking for proof. Betty is digging into Charles' life, sending her to visit Chic at the Lodge Detention Center. There, Chic tells her that Charles, under the force of Jingle Jangle, stabbed their ménage partner to death.

Cheryl continues to be haunted by Julian, the doll. She circles the thing with salt, then goes to school with worried Toni. No sooner than she arrives at school does she find out that Dagwood has swallowed a ping-pong ball. (Is that even possible?) She arrives home to scold Julian's ghost, only to discover her Aunt Cricket and Uncle Bedford have arrived. She faints.

Thinking it's a reasonable request, Betty gives Charles a poly-graph test. Charles claims it was Chic who killed the guy, and under duress, he confesses that he's a recovering addict. After she left, Chic apparently reported the murder of the Shady Man.

It turns out Cheryl's relatives want her to sell the family maple business. She blames ghost Julian for their return, so she drowns him—the doll—in a tub of water. Aunt and Uncle aren't giving up though, planning to have Cheryl declared unfit, then sell the house.

Hiram shows up at the community center to offer Archie his condolences for Fred's death and that he'd like to make a memorial donation. Next, he surprises Hermione with his bare-chested, threatening self, and tells her that he needs her and wants her by his side. We get a glimpse of how their abusive relationship got started in the first place as she concedes. Their cycle of dysfunction continues, with Hermione telling Veronica she's invited Hiram back to the Pembrooke and into their lives. Things get even cozier when half-sister Hermosa gets her claws into Riverdale. After stopping by Pop's—to invite Veronica to Hiram and Hermione's wedding vow renewal—she hangs her own portrait oil painting above Hiram's desk.

On a brighter note, Archie's lure of food and free arcade games works—the kids swarm the community center. Things don't stay bright for long, though, as Dodger shows up to reveal Archie's masked identity, retreating when Veronica calls the police.

Jughead tells DuPont he knows the man didn't write the first Baxter Brothers book—his own grandfather wrote the book. But DuPont doesn't take it well. Jughead gains a new enemy at Stonewall, a place where anything can happen. Like this: after apologizing to Jughead for not being able to help himself, Mr. Chipping throws himself out a beautiful stained-glass window. Bret, Donna, Jonathan and Joan sit quietly watching, not calling for help despite Jughead's insistence they do so. We conclude the episode with some twists.

Charles meets with Chic to let him know their plan worked out. Turns out, the two of them are still a thing. Archie and Reggie find Dodger outside the community center. This time he's not looking for a fight. He's beaten and unconscious. Over at Stonewall Prep, we find out who will replace Mr. Chipping. Its creepy Mr. DuPont. That isn't much of a stunner, but it pulls the strings of that plotline tighter.

Chapter Sixty-Four:
"The Ice Storm"

Original airdate: *November 20, 2019*
Writer: *Arabella Anderson*
Director: *Alex Pillai*

Top Quote: "You know what I think, Carrot Top? I think you've got a hero complex."—Darla, Dodger's mom, informing Archie that she believes he's the one who beat her son into a coma.

Top Trivia: This episode takes its name from Rick Moody's novel of the same name, later, the film of the same name (with Joan Allen, Kevin Kline, Sigourney Weaver, Christina Ricci, Elijah Wood, Tobey Maguire and Katie Holmes!). Fans of dark humor, retro style, and stories of awkward sexual situations should give it a read—or watch.

Watch For: Mary Andrews makes a big move! Yes! Mary! FP *finally* going after Hiram, telling him "the truth" everyone In Riverdale knows he deserves *it.* Cheryl's solution to her unwanted guests.

Wonder About: How marvelous is Nana Rose? Did Donna really have an affair with Mr. Chipping? How much therapy will those kids who came to the community center for Thanksgiving dinner need?

Summary + Commentary:

Jughead's opening voice-over reflects on Thanksgiving—Archie's first without his dad, Hiram's grab for power, and Dodger's family aching for revenge.

FP and Alice, who are having Thanksgiving dinner at the diner, invite Hiram and Hermione to join them. Why are the Lodges at Pop's instead of the Pembrooke? Because Veronica threw their meal to the floor. How charming is that? After the meal, Hiram suggests they go downstairs and toast Fred.

After Mr. DuPont blows off Jughead, he enlists Betty's help to dig into Mr. Chipping's suicide. At Stonewall, he tells her about the Quill and Skull—a secret society that appears to exist at Stonewall Prep. When Bret tries to scare Betty, he gets knocked out instead. After Betty stitches the guy's head, she suggests that they play a drinking game. The secret goal? Finding out if Bret and Donna are members of a secret society.

Munroe and Archie give the kids the news that the community center will serve Thanksgiving dinner. FP has orders from the mayor, Hiram, to shut Archie down, but Archie holds the feast anyway. Thanksgiving dinner at the community center is tense, as Dodger's family arrives to cause trouble and make threats. Darla forces Archie to his knees and demands he admit to beating Dodger. Trying to save Archie, one at a time, the boys claim they are the ones who wear the mask. All heck breaks loose when the turkey cooker explodes. If you've been waiting for a time to like Mary Andrews, you finally get it when she grabs the loose gun, aims it at Darla, and orders her out.

Meanwhile, over in the basement of Pop's, FP tells Hiram that he's not his puppet, and breaks a bottle in half to threatens the smug guy. So much for toasting Fred.

Over at Thistlehouse, after helping Cheryl dispose of Uncle Bedford's body, Toni enjoys Thanksgiving dinner Blossom style. Nana Rose tells the tale of the first Blossom Thanksgiving, when the starving Blossoms ate each other to survive. Cheryl uses the tale as a threat to Aunt Cricket. Who would buy a place where cannibals lived?

Things are also weird at Stonewall. Betty and Jughead accuse Bret and Donna of covering up Mr. Chipping's suicide. Donna explains that she and Mr. Chipping were having an affair. She broke it off, so he killed himself. Simple. But Betty isn't convinced, and neither are we. As she tells Jughead that, we the viewers, see the very obvious blinking red light of a video camera.

Now that the bad people have been chased from the community

center, everyone settles down to share company and eat. Acting like that other stuff never happened, the episode ends on a sweet note: Mary tells Archie his father would be proud. The moment gets even sweeter when Archie dedicates the community center to him, and we see the photo of Fred, aka Luke Perry, displayed on the wall.

Chapter Sixty-Five:
"In Treatment"

Original airdate: *December 4, 2019*
Writer: *Tessa Leigh Williams*
Director: *Michael Goi*

Top Quote: "I won't be psychoanalyzed by someone who doesn't know the phrase 'tilting at windmills.' It's about recognition. It's about not letting some ascot steal my family's achievements. My grandfather could have been Gatsby rich. You know what he was instead? He was a mean drunk who beat my father in a trailer."—Jughead to Mrs. Burble, when she tells him he has a persecution complex, then asks him if he's insecure as a writer.

Top Trivia: Mrs. Burble is a character from the original Archie Comics. The *Riverdale* character is similar, but the comic version is easier on the gang, less direct, and doesn't challenge their thinking.

Watch For: Alice claiming that Betty having a sex life is the reason Betty didn't get into Yale. The outcome of each session with Mrs. Burble. Hiram and Veronica trade tantrums.

Wonder About: Is Mrs. Burble getting ready to do something sinister? Alice telling Betty she loves her best. Scale from one to five, how messed up is that? Is Veronica, as Mrs. Burble declares, trying to be her father?

Summary + Commentary:

Jughead's opening voice-over lets us know that Riverdale's Watcher has left a second round of videotapes, causing anxiety and stress for Riverdale seniors.

Mr. Honey is worried about the kids, so he asks Mrs. Burble—the school's guidance counselor—to add extended office hours to assist the stressed kids. First up are Betty and Alice. Alice seems to think that the birth control pills she found in Betty's room are an indication as to why Betty didn't get into Yale. Once that's on the table, she and her mother unpack all the crazy things of the past few years. Mrs. Burble agrees that Alice's statements of "I love you" don't erase the smothering of Betty's entire childhood. Later, Betty follows up by telling her mother she loves her the most. We'll be watching to see if Alice backs off.

Archie also goes to talk with Mrs. Burble. He hasn't applied to college, because he plans to stay in Riverdale to clean up the town. When he continues to tell her everything—the mask and secret identity—she tells him his behavior sounds like an addiction and hero complex. He tells her he hurts all the time, and that he's angry. We bingers already knew this. Instead of heeding the woman's advice though, to not go out at night, he goes further into his hero world. Archie moves into the community center and sets up a hotline. When he gets his first call, it's a boy who needs help. He digs the recently discarded mask from the trash and heads out.

Cheryl is also wrestling with demons, and now Mr. Honey is threatening to take the Vixens away. So, it's off to Mrs. Burble, where Cheryl informs the counselor she's being haunted by a devil doll. The end result is that Cheryl loses the Vixens, but learns there is a test that can let her know whether she absorbed Julian in the womb. Cheryl takes the test, the results are negative. She isn't crazy or haunted by Julian, because she did not absorb him.

Next up, it's Veronica's turn in Mrs. Burble's hot seat. She unleashes her anger and frustration with her father, who continually hurts and manipulates her. Mrs. Burble claims it isn't hate—its obsession. After suggesting The Oedipus and Electra complexes, she tells Veronica that she should ghost the man. And so, even after being accepted, Veronica rejects Harvard. She won't have her life mapped out by daddy. Next, she will kill him through business. The rum business.

Lastly, Jughead finds his way to Mrs. Burble via his need for letters of recommendation for college admissions. After some ranting, he admits that he hasn't been sensitive to his father's feelings. Unlike the others, he immediately acts on his thoughts by zipping home, hugging his dad, and saying thank you. Then he digs deeper into the lives, and potential murders, of the Baxter Brother ghostwriters.

We end with a flash forward. Bret and Donna identify Archie, Betty and Veronica as the kids who killed Jughead.

Chapter Sixty-Six:
"Tangerine"

Original air: *December 11, 2019*
Writer: *Brian E. Paterson*
Director: *Gabriel Correa*

Top Quote: "You're not gonna arrest me, are you?"—Archie to FP, admitting he is the vigilante in photos.

Top Trivia: The episode title ties back to the word used by Farmie age-imposter Evelyn Evernever to activate the sleeper cells, cells in the brain that can trigger action.

Watch For: The return of Penelope and the answer to the question who has been haunting Thistlehouse. Hiram gets slapped. Yes! Jughead gets a new understanding of his grandfather.

Wonder About: Do you buy Grandpa Forsythe's reasons for being bitter and cruel to FP? Toni asking Cheryl, *are you sure*, instead of screaming, *yeah, no doubt*, when Cheryl says it might be time to bury Jason. Betty! What did she do with that rock!?

Summary + Commentary:

Jughead's opening voice-over is replaced with him reading aloud from his Baxter Brothers manuscript. He's granted the coveted ghostwriting contract, but is uncertain if he'll accept it. First, he must know the truth about his grandfather. He enlists Charles, who seems to only ever exist as a character to get information for people. As always, Charles delivers. Apparently, Jug's grandpa lives in a forest, and he finds the grisly old man living in a converted bus.

Meanwhile, it's a usual day in Riverdale. Archie confesses to FP about setting up a community hotline, Pop's liquor license is revoked, and Betty sees some security footage of Polly attacking a nurse named Betty.

Here's what happens first: Charles, again doling out the info on everything, tells Betty the call that triggered Polly and made her freak out came from Shankshaw Prison. Crafty Betty pieces things together. Evelyn, dead Edgar's wife, is held there.

Archie and FP take on (beat up) the Dickenson brothers, before getting some pie at Pop's. Cause that's a normal thing to do.

Jughead discovering that his grandfather sold his Baxter Brother manuscript for $5,000 is a nod to the ghostwritten Hard Boys and Nancy Drew Mystery Stories. Why weave that in? Maybe to get you to watch the CW's Nancy Drew TV show.

In response to La Bonne Nuit's liquor license being revoked by the mayor's office, Veronica makes plans to fight back by, you guessed it, having a blowout party at the speakeasy. Conveniently, Veronica's grandmother provides her with the secret family recipe for crafting rum. Later, at La Bonne Nuit's big party, Veronica performs as Veronica Luna at La Bonne Nuit, while a recruiter from Columbia University watches. Um. Okay.

After FP gets shot at Pop's, Archie beats the crap out of Dodger and threatens to kill both him and Darla if they don't leave town—even though they were already on their way out. Toby and some other kids from the community center witness the ass-kicking. It seems they don't think Archie's protective actions are all that heroic.

Cheryl, not willing to be shown up by the rest of the high schoolers who have exciting, wild lives, fakes her suicide. No, actually, she's trying to gas out the mystery person tormenting her. As the poison gas steams up and out—threatening to kill everyone within the walls of Thistlehouse—Penelope emerges, revealing that she is the one gaslighting Cheryl into thinking she is crazy. Cheryl locks her mom in the bunker. Then, in a riverside ceremony, burns the already dead Jason while Toni, Betty, Jughead, Veronica and Archie watch.

Betty visits Evelyn and discovers the trigger word, causing Edgar's former disciples to turn into Light Betty. When transformed into "Light Betty" they seek out "Dark Betty," who they are programmed to kill. Hoping to put a stop to this, she turns to Charles, who uses the word on her to no effect. With the aid of ever-helpful Charles, Betty goes back in time and kills her shadow self before it is born. Jughead goes back to the bus in the forest, but his grandfather has left.

Four weeks later, Archie declares Jughead dead while he stares at Betty's blood-soaked hands.

So, obviously, there is no concluding voice-over.

Chapter Sixty-Seven:
"Varsity Blues"

Original airdate: *January 22, 2020*
Writer: *Aaron Allen*
Director: *Roxanne Benjamin*

Top Quote: "It tastes like money."—Veronica, to Cheryl, on the mixture that is her rum and Cheryl's maple syrup.

Top Trivia: The Vixens perform at the start of the big game. The song *Cherry Bomb*, was originally recorded by The Runaways, an all-female teenage band, in 1976. It peaked at number six on the *Billboard* 100. You can find it on YouTube.

Watch For: Betty finds out Jughead is keeping something from him. The Vixens cheer to *Cherry Bomb*! Betty finally gets something from Mr. Honey.

Wonder About: Ick. That weird sexual tension between Mr. Honey and Miss Appleyard. Uncle Frank's fake beard. And… Uncle Frank at all, appearing from out of nowhere. Restaurant owners buying rum made by a 'kid' still in high school.

Summary + Commentary:

Jughead lets us know its spirit week at Riverdale High, and there is much to celebrate.

The episode gets off to a slow start, until Mr. Honey replaces Cheryl with a new cheer coach, Mrs. Appleyard. There is a moment of confusion for fans of USA Network's *Dare Me*, thinking some scripts got duplicated, but that's eased when the scene cuts to Betty, at *The Blue and Gold* office, interviewing the Bulldogs who inform her that the Stonewall Stallions play to hurt.

After reporter Betty digs into the Stonewall Prep players' dirty tricks to hurt guys on the opposing teams, Munroe is attacked by a squad of guys wearing bunny masks. Who did that? Here's a tip: Bret arrives late to Jughead's Quill & Skull society initiation. After the other members connect by disclosing sexual abuse experiences, Jughead admits to being homeless and watching Doc get beat up. Meanwhile, shades of USA Network's *Dare Me* continue in the tension between Cheryl and the new coach, as the two fight for squad dominance. Intrigued? Check that show out.

More tensions are building as the Riverdale vs. Stonewall game grows closer. Archie gets put in jail for standing up for his friend Munroe, and Betty thinks Bret is behind it. She taps Veronica for help, sending her to a Stonewall Prep party to use her femme fatale charms to get some dirt for her exposé article. The strategy works... until Jughead shows up at the gathering and ruins it. He also ruins his own secret about being in a secret society.

By the way, Archie's Uncle Frank showed up at the Andrews house out of nowhere, and he's been there a while. Archie, being Archie, offers him a job, but Mary is not happy. See, Uncle Frank took advantage of Fred's kindness. Archie confronts him, but Uncle Frank gets teary, so soft-hearted Archie shrugs off the transgression.

Veronica is courting buyers for her rum and moving ahead with her production plans, but receives a cease and desist order delivered directly by Hiram himself. She rejects his offer to work together, instead of against. Too much damage has been done, she declares.

Things aren't going well for Betty, either. Mr. Honey won't print her exposé.

As kickoff time looms closer, Lucky Jughead gets an invitation from DuPont to sit in the alumni section during the game. Jughead passes. How much fun would that (not) be? Uncle Frank offers the still injured Munroe some pain pills which Munroe gladly accepts. He also gets recruited by Notre Dame.

But wait—there's more. Cheryl locks Mrs. Appleyard in her office, then leads the Vixens in a cheery rendition of "Cherry Bomb." The Vixens shine—the Bulldogs get beat. We all wonder: what is the point of the Mrs. Appleyard plotline?

After the sad end to the game, Mr. Honey nearly drools with excitement when Betty lets him know she'd like to form a Riverdale High quiz team to beat Stonewall's quiz team. Jughead finds out he has been accepted to Yale. Things are looking up for Betty until we see her crying over a photo of her and Jughead. Bret witnesses her tears and tells her to stop weeping. Jug won't be going to Yale. It will just be her and him cracking the books in New Haven.

As we are led to believe something terrible has happened to young Mr. Jones, there is no concluding voice-over this time either. Sniff.

Chapter Sixty-Eight:
"Quiz Show"

Original airdate: *January 29, 2020*
Writer: *Ted Sullivan*
Director: *Chell Stephen*

Top Quote: "Why have you come for me, nightmare child?"—Penelope, to Cheryl, when Cheryl arrives in the bunker with a proposal.

Top Trivia: Maple rum is available on the market already, but you can make your own by pouring two ounces of dark rum, half an ounce of maple syrup, and top with a dash of bitters.

Watch For: Mary's prediction about Uncle Frank coming true. Charles digs up some dirt on Bret for Betty. Alice ruining Betty's life—again.

Wonder About: If the Baxter Brothers novels are like the Hardy Boys series, does a dark, serial killer storyline make sense? What is Betty's busting of Bret's chops really about? Is Penelope perfect for the role of live-in manager of the Maple Club?

Summary + Commentary:

Jughead's opening voice-over: Quiz show fever has struck Riverdale. Especially Betty, who is determined to beat Stonewall Prep.

Its Uncle Frank's first day on the job at Andrews Construction. When Archie offers his father's tool belt to Uncle Frank, the man refuses, saying he can't take another man's gear. This seems paradoxical since Frank is apparently okay with taking the man's style, facial expressions, beard, house and son. Come back to this point later in the episode when Frank has brought home the guys from work for beers and conversation, acts like they are all the best of friends, but is planning to not give the crew their annual bonuses.

Betty and Cheryl ask Riverdale's chemistry teacher, Dr. Beaker, to analyze their rum recipe to ensure it is different enough from Lodge Rum to avoid being sued. The question of why neither of these hotties have an NYU-level chemist hitting up their socials, and have to resort to this guy is quickly replaced with: how did Jughead not know his book would need a dark, edgy villain? He's already completed the first draft. Who the heck is the bad guy in there now? Doctor Spectro? We find out soon. It's the *Fishmonger*. Seriously bingers, how dull does that sound?

After a chat with the panel from the publishing company—thanks to some super quick thinking on Jug's part—he creates a new villain: The Brown Hood. How does Betty find out her own boyfriend uses her serial killer dad as fodder for his new character? Bret tells her, of course. After her fight with Jughead, Betty learns she was denied acceptance to Yale, due to her father's serial killing. While she's smashing his headstone, Alice shows up and hugs Betty. Like that will make everything okay.

Over at La Bonne Nuit, things are hopping, until Hiram, as mayor, raids the place and smashes all the bottles of rum on hand. Cheryl suggests to Veronica that the two of them relocate the business to The Maple Club—her mother's former brothel. The two of them stop by the bunker to offer Penelope a job as a live-in manager. Of course, Penelope accepts. Did you think she'd rather stay in that bunker sipping tea?

Finally, it's quiz show time. A recruiter from Yale—brought in by Jughead—shows up to watch Betty. Her mom shows up with the question's answer, and Betty, being Betty, simply tosses the answers in the green room trash basket. Where someone can easily find them. And they do. Riverdale's win is soon overturned, and Betty—even though she didn't use the answers—gets suspended.

Archie fires Frank for taking money from the business, telling his uncle: "when you took that money, it was like you were stealing from my dad." Still suffering from the boundary issues caused by his abusive relationship with his music teacher, Archie doesn't get that Frank stole the money from him, not his dad who is dead.

Maybe Betty has been right all along. Maybe one of these days, someone does need to get through to Kevin about at-risk behavior. Bad things do happen in beautiful hotels. Like when someone says 'trust me' then gets out a video camera. Later, Kevin invites Fangs to join him in a video. Cringe. This isn't going to go well.

Jughead confronts Bret about disclosing what he found in Betty's green room trashcan, then invokes the code of the society of founding fathers. That is as corny as it sounds—a duel to settle the dispute. Subsequently, Jughead disappears. At least this time, Jughead seems to be dead and Betty isn't holding a blood-soaked rock. She is declaring to Archie that she doesn't know how she's going to keep going.

Jughead's concluding voice-over is absent, as he continues to be.

Chapter Sixty-Nine:
"Men of Honor"

Original airdate: *February 5, 2020*
Writer: *Ariana Jackson*
Director: *Catriona McKenzie*

Top Quote: "This school is insane."—Kevin to Archie, after Archie is attacked in the boys' room by Ted Bishop, the crazed guy who tried to kill Uncle Frank.

Top Trivia: This episode features guest star Lucy Hale, the star of *Katy Keene,* the Riverdale spin-off based on another Archie Comics character. Unfortunately, though, the *Katy Keene* show was canceled after only one season.

Watch For: Comings and goings of Uncle Frank. The very obvious ad for *Katy Keene,* which aired for the first time the night after this episode aired. Toni being bad-ass.

Wonder About: After everything, all that he's done to ruin her, why oh why, would Veronica decide to tell Hiram about her interview with Barnard College? Jughead tells Bret that he will, somehow, lose a chess game, because Jughead is a better writer; how does that actually make any sense? Lastly, Donna's big secret finally being revealed just makes you wonder what she's actually up to.

Summary + Commentary:

Jughead's opening voice-over is replaced by a scene showing Bret and Jughead planning their duel. They will both fence and fist-fight.

Later in the episode, they are tied, so a tie-breaker chess match is added.

Meanwhile, Veronica is planning a trip to New York, where she has an interview at Barnard College. This may cause some viewers to wonder what month it is in Riverdale, because it seems a bit late in the senior school year for college application interviews. But then we remember we gave up on reality a while back, so it's all good.

When a friend of Uncle Frank's, Ted Bishop, arrives to let Frank know a fellow soldier died, Archie—not bothering to wonder why the guy didn't call instead of randomly show up—invites him to stay overnight. In the morning, instead of having coffee like a normal person, the guy tries to stab Uncle Frank. Archie returns home for his forgotten phone just in time to save his uncle. Naturally, Archie asks his uncle why one of his friends would try to kill him, to which Frank rambles on, but the bottom line is that Uncle Frank is bad news. But Archie, being Archie, continually tries to help.

Betty and her mom, who is acting much less bizarre and manipulative these days, are working together to investigate Stonewall Prep. The two of them interview Mr. Chipping's widow, who gives them a box of personal effects from his office.

After a sparkling series of scenes of Veronica shopping with her fashion-designing friend Katy Keene, we are back to the dreary mess that is Uncle Frank's life. FP and the Serpents have snagged would-be killer Ted and locked him in a cell, telling him the FBI is on the way.

At Pop's, Moose—now in the military—meets with Betty and her mom. He tells them of a videotape Bret videotaped, of Moose having sex in his dorm room and used the video to blackmail him. Naturally, Betty wants to know if there is a Betty sex tape. Naturally, Bret denies it.

Over in New York, Veronica and Katy gush and catch up. Honestly, it's kind of an ad for the new Katy Keene show. But we're okay with that.

Back in Riverdale, Uncle Frank—wearing yet another quilted flannel and henley—tells Archie he's leaving town. Coincidently, Ted is out of the cell. The guy attacks Archie in the high school bathroom. Terrible Ted is as un-killable as that hockey-masked Jason. Thankfully, Uncle Frank reappears to save Archie. Maybe that last-minute rescue explains why Archie genuinely believes Uncle Frank when the guy says he will turn himself over to the Feds.

Now back from the city, things are up and down for Veronica. First, the bad news: her dad has a degenerative disease that will break him down. Now the good news: Veronica will be going to Barnard in the fall.

When Bret tries to up the ante with Jughead, telling him he wants to give up the Baxter contract, Jug delivers the cruelest of cruel insults. He tells his nemesis, *I'm the better writer*. While Bret and Jughead battle it out on the chessboard, Betty sneaks into the basement, finding the tapes, but Bret finds her. No worries, as Jug blows the chess match and tosses aside his chance to remain a Stonewall Man of Honor. The end result—he's out of the Quill & Skull. He may be out of the secret society, but that doesn't mean the society's secrets can't still haunt and harm him and the rest of the gang.

Season 4 Pop Quiz 1

1) "Who said it?
"He died a hero."

2) Which two characters are speaking?
"What are you doing? That guy just made you look like a damn fool."
"He's fast."
"It's unacceptable. That was an embarrassing display. Go out there. Come on, man! Show me something!"

3) Who said it?
"Everyone looked down on us because of that name. So, I took a name that people would respect."

4) Who said it?
"I'm back out on the street 'cause I have to be. A lot of us are. I have two options: Either I roll with Dodger... or hide from Dodger."

5) Who said it?
"You see, our father needed help […] so I came."

6) Which two characters exchange these lines?
"Hey, how'd it all go?"
"Smooth as cream, babe. FP led me right to where he buried the body, we moved what was left, and everyone was appropriately grateful."

Melissa Ford Lucken

7) **To whom is Betty replying when she says:**
"Oh, well, I'm not as sweet as you might think."

8) **Who said it?**
"Maybe I should, uh… put down the conspiracy theories and just do my homework."

9) **Which two characters exchange these lines?**
"It's damn good."
"It's my special shimmy on Abuelita's recipe."

10) **Which two characters exchange these lines?**
"It's a welcome gift from the Quill and Skull. Speaking of which, meet us in the basement tonight, 10:00 sharp."
"Dare I ask why?"

246

Chapter Seventy:
"The Ides of March"

Original airdate: *February 12, 2020*
Writer: *Chrissy Maroon & Evan Kyle*
Director: *Claudia Yarmy*

Top Quote: "You think you're close to the truth, don't you? You and Jughead, teen detectives?"—Donna, to Betty, as Betty questions her about her involvement with DuPont.

Top Trivia: January 2020, The CW gave *Riverdale* an early renewal for a fifth season. *Riverdale* spin-offs, *The Chilling Adventures of Sabrina* and *Katy Keene,* were both canceled July 2020.

Watch For: Hermosa in a bad wig, trying to fake her way into getting some intel. Poor Jughead! Then FP's response. Then Betty having an idea. Betty calling Donna a bitch. Finally.

Wonder About: Is Mr. Honey right about not allowing non-graduating seniors to walk with their class? What's really going on with Veronica? Archie, seeking advice from Hiram, yet again. Seriously?

Summary + Commentary:

Archie is facing two harsh realities: his grades haven't been good, and he hasn't applied to any colleges.

Veronica is so disturbed by her reality—high school is ending soon, and she and Archie have not discussed their next steps—that she seeks out Archie and initiates sex right then and there, in the otherwise empty music room. Thankfully, now that these kids are seniors, viewers don't have to feel quite so skeevy about watching.

Jughead also gets some harsh news: he's been officially kicked out of the Quill and Skull, *and* his Baxter Brothers manuscript has been rejected. He gets to work on a new project, whipping up ten pages describing his experiences at Stonewall Prep, to which Mr. DuPont is neither impressed nor threatened. Jughead remains determined to write more.

Later that night, Hermosa Lodge, wearing a white bob wig and cat-eye glasses, has a meeting with Toni at La Bonne Nuit. After hearing what the frosty-haired woman has to say, Toni agrees to meet the mysterious woman to discuss the secret rum bar.

Jughead reappears in front of DuPont and a circle of the usual Stonewall students. He reads new pages, detailing more of the scandalous events that've taken place at the school. Minutes later, he's accused of plagiarizing the story that got him accepted into Yale. Now he has another, bigger, fight on his hands. As per usual, he turns to Betty and FP for advice and help.

While working out at the gym with Hiram, Archie talks about something we viewers already knew to be true—high school students can't run two businesses, manage a community organization, and complete high school coursework at the same time. Over the next few days, he waffles on the idea of unloading one of his responsibilities, but in the end, doesn't.

At school, when Mr. Honey confronts Veronica about a flask of rum he found in her locker, Archie takes the blame. After telling her that he has nothing to lose, while she has everything, he asks her what's up with her sudden aggressive sexuality. She brushes off the question and leaves.

Over at La Bonne Nuit, Cheryl and Toni provide some eye candy action when they sexy dance with Hermosa. That done, they lure her to the suite where Veronica, tipped off by Cheryl, waits. There, Hermosa drops the emotional bomb—their father told her he was ill before telling Veronica. Veronica storms out and heads home. Archie appears at the Pembrooke, asking her what's wrong, where she breaks down and tells him that her father has a debilitating disease. Forgetting how poorly Mr. Lodge has treated them both, they conclude together that Veronica is the one to get the dying man fired up enough to live.

After Jughead and Betty discover that his original Baxter Brothers manuscript has been rewritten by his classmates—thus cutting him out of the project he'd been told wasn't worthy of publication—they revisit the murder board. Was Mr. Chipping driven to suicide by Mr. DuPont? Over milkshakes at Pop's, Betty advises Donna to come clean. Meanwhile, Jughead tells Bret that he plans to let the toxic genies out of their bottles. Bret counters by telling Jughead if he does tell tales at the tribunal, he'll let loose his sex tape of Jughead and Betty. Jughead stays silent and agrees to leave Stonewall Prep.

One last hurrah is the reason why Jughead agrees to attend the Stonewall Prep party. He invites Betty, Veronica and Archie. How does Jughead get ready for the night? By grabbing a pocketknife and a rabbit mask.

Once at the party, Jughead is led into the woods by Bret. Betty follows Donna into the woods, and Veronica and Archie go into the woods together. Then, Jughead is found in the woods. Presumed dead. Again. This time Betty is to blame.

Jughead's voice-over is quick, reminding us that the week had started out like any other. What—what? We thought he was dead.

Chapter Seventy-One:
"How to Get Away with Murder"

Original airdate: *February 26, 2020*
Writer: *Arabella Anderson*
Director: *James DeWille*

Top Quote: "You're gonna regret ever meeting me."—Betty to Donna, when they meet in the woods after Jughead's body is moved to the morgue.

Top Trivia: The episode, like many others, takes its title from another production. *How to Get Away with Murder* is a television series featuring a group of law students who become embroiled in twisted murder plots.

Watch For: Alice is the only parent responding normally to a teenager arriving home in only underwear. Mary's big reveal. Various grillings and confrontations about Stonewall Prep.

Wonder About: What would happen if you arrived home in the middle of the night, wearing only underwear? Is discussing an updated will "a normal thing," and is Jughead truly dead?

Summary + Commentary:

Despite being presumed dead, we have a voice-over from Jughead. His thoughts? His three best friends should have spoken on the way home, if only to get their stories straight.

First awkward moment—Veronica arrives home in only her black panties and bra. Archie's moment, when he arrives home in his boxers, tells his mom a different explanation for not having clothes.

Betty, also wearing her bra and panties, tells her mom a mixed bag explanation. So yeah, Jughead was right. They should have planned better. Now they have a real mess on their hands. Their solution? Charles of course. He will save them. Again. Their question? Why do the Stonewall Preppies want Betty framed for the murder of Jughead?

The Naval Academy, thanks to his mom, is the new possible opportunity looming in Archie's future. The bigger surprise, Brooke Rivers—the woman offering to help Archie with his application to the Naval Academy—is Mary's new girlfriend. He's surprised his mom has a girlfriend, but is fine with it.

Hiram's will. That's what is on Veronica's breakfast plate. After Hermosa and Veronica go at it, tossing insults across the table, Hiram interrupts and proclaims discussing his will is normal. Veronica tears her copy of the document in half and storms out.

Meanwhile, while Charles listens, Betty calls Jughead's dad and lets him know she's worried because she hasn't heard from Jughead. Once that task is completed, Betty grabs a mic, seeks out Bret and Donna, and plants a bug in Bret's room, before heading to Shankshaw for a chat with Evelyn.

At Betty's request, Archie zips off to Stonewall Prep to pick a fight with Bret. Archie gets in a couple punches, before Donna breaks things up. The bug is discovered as a consequence, and destroyed. When she hears about the *incident*, Mary personalizes the whole thing and thinks Archie went after Bret because he's upset with her for dating a woman. Archie sidesteps the real issue by telling his mom about Veronica's dad being sick.

When FP finds Jughead's phone in Betty's jacket, she whips up another jumbled excuse for what happened that night, then suggests Mr. Jones officially make Jughead a missing person.

Disturbing as it is, Veronica's dad confesses to her that he didn't tell her about his illness, because he didn't want her pity. More disconcerting, she sets aside all his cruelty and declares she wants to be a source of strength for him. Additional bonus for Hiram, he's gotten Veronica to agree to get along with Hermosa. Later, the two sisters approach Daddykins with a proposal: they want to be named co-executives of his estate.

After getting a call from FP about a hiker finding a bloody rock in the woods, Betty proves again that she is terrible at hiding secrets by asking Jellybean for some fake blood, to create a new bloody rock. Charles gets the actual rock from Mr. Jones, then swaps it for the hand-crafted one Betty made. Speaking of rocks, Veronica grills Betty about the rock, and admits she may have blacked out. So, they turn to the ever-handy Charles, who hypnotizes Betty, helping her remember that Donna blew *Devil's Breath* in her face. This new awareness makes Betty decide they need to organize a search party so Sheriff Jones can find his son's body.

Later, at home, Mary tells Archie she is so sorry about what happened to Jughead. He closes his bedroom curtains, telling her he has something to confess. Betty meets with Donna in the woods, telling the evil preppy that's she's coming for her.

As Jughead is still presumed dead, he has no voice-over for us.

Chapter Seventy-Two:
"To Die For"

Original airdate: *March 4, 2020*
Writer: *Roberto Aguirre-Sacasa*
Director: *Shannon Kohli*

Top Quote: "She told me to. You heard her."—Brett, at Jughead's wake, revealing he is Donna's puppet, unable to think for himself.

Top Trivia: The Sherlock Holmes short story Betty reads from at Jughead's wake, *The Final Problem,* describes a final match between Holmes and his nemesis, Moriarty, and tells of the declared death of Sherlock Holmes despite the absence of a body.

Watch For: Cheryl placing Betty under a suicide watch, in turn making the gang's plan more difficult. Donna, who already knows the truth, looking irrational. Kevin, speaking for some viewers, when he claims there is a secret community that believes Betty should be with Archie instead of Jughead.

Wonder About: Since Betty is only getting into Yale because Jughead is dead, does that mean she won't get to go if it turns out Jughead is still alive? Do college admissions staff really have that much time on their hands? Is there plumbing in the bunker?

Summary + Commentary:

Alice is documenting FP's death via film clips and interviews. Found footage effect is used throughout the episode to reveal facts and responses.

FP, thanks to an anonymous tip, finds Jughead's tie pin in Donna's room at Stonewall. Donna, faux tears not quite streaming down her face, tells FP that she saw Betty holding a bloody rock over Jughead's body. FP then heads to Riverdale High and immediately arrests Betty, Veronica and Archie. Hand-cuffed, Betty is glad for the arrest and hopeful this will put their plan in action. She's waiting for the Stonies to trip up.

The questioning begins. The sheriff grills them, one at a time. The best moment from the interviews: Betty's mom thinks that Betty did it. There isn't much time for Betty to be insulted though, as after finding out the test results, FP reveals that the red stuff on the rock was not blood. This is shocking news to Donna and Bret, because they saw Johnathan smear Jughead's blood on the rock. So, why not call Betty and tell her she thinks Jughead is still alive, and the whole thing is a scheme to buy time, so Betty can continue to look for evidence of attempted murder?

It's a battle of retro style between Veronica and Hermosa. Veronica trying to keep her life in order; Hermosa is trying to find the other girl's weakness.

Jughead's wake is a collection of threats: Betty to Donna and Bret, and tears, everyone else, and silent toasts, the Serpents. Not one to be bothered by occasion, Hiram suggests FP take a leave of absence. FP quits.

All around Riverdale, people are saying Jughead is alive. Kevin tells Betty, who tries to stop the rumors by crying with Archie at Pop's, while Cheryl eavesdrops. Somehow it works. The next day at school, there is a shrine of flowers covering Jughead's locker. Archie, seeing Betty shaken by this, follows her into the music room. Ghosts of Ms. Grundy, anyone? Not Betty. She kisses Archie, and he kisses her back. Cheryl snaps a pick and blasts it out on text to everyone—except Veronica. She shows it to Veronica in person.

Minutes later, in the student lounge, Betty accepts the blame, telling Veronica she kissed Archie. *Betty and Veronica* comic readers may wonder about the legitimacy of this fight. In the comic world, those two pretending to fight to make something happen is a long-time plot standard. Later, in an Alice interview, Kevin affirms the kiss proves Jughead is dead.

Later that night, Donna appears at the office of the *Blue and*

*Gol*d, insisting Jughead is alive and helping build a case from behind the scenes. Her threat—you'll trip up, and I'll be there to watch you fall. This confrontation is just what Betty needs. She sneaks to the bunker, knowing Donna will follow. Donna does, but she doesn't find Betty and Jughead—she finds Betty and Archie. She flees, and so does Archie, right back into Veronica's arms. They celebrate the success of their rouse.

Next celebration—Betty and Jughead making out in the bunker. Yes, he's alive, and she's knit him a new beanie.

While preppies Donna and Bret argue, Hermosa delivers some good news to Veronica—Donna Sweet isn't who she claims to be.

Chapter Seventy-Three:
"The Locked Room"

Original airdate: *March 11, 2020*
Writer: *Aaron Allen*
Director: *Tessa Blake*

Top Quote: "No one ever really dies in Riverdale."—Cheryl to Betty on why she isn't surprised to discover Jughead is still alive.

Top Trivia: The day this episode aired, Warner Bros. Television announced it would suspend production of *Riverdale* due to a team member being in contact with a Coronavirus patient. That person ultimately tested negative. Production did not resume.

Watch For: Hermosa imagining Betty and Veronica are secret girlfriends. Editorial goof: Betty and Jughead reveal the pieces of his attempted murder. The blood Alice spotted on Betty's bra isn't there. Joan bailing on the other Stonies.

Wonder About: How glad are you that the *Is Jughead dead?* question has been finally answered, and the plot can move on? What will happen with FP and his dad? Archie's proposed vow over shakes at Pop's and the lingering question, will Jughead and Archie graduate from high school?

Summary + Commentary:

Jughead's voice-over comes from Dilton's bunker and contains his reflections on what it's like to be fake dead, and how he and Betty continue to analyze the evidence against Bret and Donna. Not who did it. But *why* did they do it?

In addition to the inner circle, Jellybean, Sheriff Keller, Mary and Hermosa know that Jughead lives. Hermosa has been the most helpful, having uncovered the truth about Donna, allowing Betty and Jughead to make their move. The two of them burst in on a cozy class at Stonewall, just as the preppies are about to discuss *Crime and Punishment*. Betty locks the door and Jughead tells them to get comfortable. Then he recounts the events, Agatha Christie-style, revealing how the sins of one generation have been delivered onto the next.

Betty and Jughead toy with their captives, questioning and revealing, taunting and teasing. The controversy centers around the ghostwriters of the Baxter Brothers books murdering students to get awarded book contracts. The question on the table is, who killed, or tried to kill, Jughead? Turns out, they were all in it together. Who failed? Jonathan. He was responsible for checking Jughead's pulse.

Archie, Betty and Veronica worked together to revive him. When Jughead refused to go to the hospital, their plan began. Ever-helpful Charles assisted and provided the next steps: burn their clothes and clean the scene.

Once Mr. DuPont finally gets to speak, Jughead cuts him off at each turn, revealing the truths to each of the old man's lies. The final nail in his coffin of secrets comes in the form of Jughead's grandfather, who has been collecting evidence of DuPont's murders for decades. FP appears too, then Charles. All the evidence has been dug up, tied together, and now DuPont is under arrest. Unwilling to submit, the old man dives through the repaired window Mr. Chipping used to commit suicide.

Charles sorts through the remaining lies via interviews. Joan and Donna don't cause much trouble, and Bret ends up getting punched in the face by Jughead. Once his face is bloody and broken, he agrees to give over the Bughead sex tape.

Betty congratulates Donna on getting away with everything, and on taking over the Baxter Brothers series. When Donna scoffs at the possibility of her masterminding the things that have happened, Betty fills Donna in on what she's learned. DuPont murdered Donna's grandmother. She acknowledges that truth, then adds one of her own— DuPont stole her grandmother's character concept, Tracy True. Betty makes the girl an offer: walk away from the Tracy True contract and Betty won't tell the world the identity of Donna's grandmother.

Jughead, Betty, Archie and Veronica meet up at Pop's. What's the good news? Jughead's grandfather is back in his life. What's the new goal? Graduating high school. They have three months. As long as no one gets murdered, they should be fine.

Chapter Seventy-Four:
"Wicked Little Town"

Original airdate: *April 15, 2020*
Writer: *Tessa Leigh Williams*
Director: *Antonio Negret*

Top Quote: "Hedwig is not a niche show. It celebrates identities, genders, expressions of all kinds. And it speaks to my entire generation. We are relentlessly slammed with crisis after crisis. And we take it, and we're numb, yes, but also screaming on the inside. Please, just... Just listen to us. We're people, not numbers. We're generation Z."—Kevin to Mr. Honey, when the principal insultingly rejects Kevin's act for the variety show.

Top Trivia: Due to the pandemic, the show was off the air for four weeks. Apparently, some viewers had too much time on their hands and used the empty hours to get really angry about Betty, a fictional character, kissing Archie, another fictional character. They also spent time speculating on the state of the real-life romance of Lili Reinhart (Betty) and Cole Sprouse (Jughead), starting a social media uproar of ugliness and privacy invasion.

Watch For: Kevin's denim jumpsuit. The band, The Archies, of cartoon and recording fame of the late 1960s finally making it to *Riverdale*. Whatever made this the lowest-rated episode of the series.

Wonder About: Who can truly sing? Which song and dance sequence is your favorite? Are these decent reasons for Betty and Veronica to get mad? Or just a ploy for the writers to get Betty and Archie to kiss?

Summary + Commentary:

Jughead's voice-over tells of the third round of sinister videotapes. All across Riverdale, a wicked little town, families watch the videotapes found on their front steps, and so begins the annual *Riverdale* musical episode.

Hiram is not singing—he's in denial, avoiding doctor's appointments and reality. At the gym, when he calls Archie for help, the man denies having "a condition."

Jughead is also in denial. Due to pretending he was dead, he is behind on assignments and thus may not graduate. Betty has prepared a color-coded graduate high school assignment book, but instead of diving in, he hooks up with Charles to watch some of the mysterious videotapes.

Over at Riverdale High, Mr. Honey rejects Kevin's variety act from *Hedwig and the Angry Inch*. Fangs encourages Kevin to go rogue, which he does, taking over the music room to sing and dance. Mr. Honey pulls the plug and kicks Kevin off the variety show. Understandably, Kevin is bummed, and Cheryl vows to convince Mr. Honey to put Kevin back into the lineup. Cheryl's attempt to change Mr. Honey's mind is not only unsuccessful, but it also deepens the already deep animosity.

When Veronica discovers that her father has been working out at the gym, and that Archie knew Hiram hadn't been going to the doctor but didn't do anything about it, she gets angry. Guess she forgot that the man framed Archie and got him sent to prison, and pretty much ruined his life.

Betty is also angry with her boyfriend. She's mad that he isn't studying as much as she thinks he should be. Guess she forgot she isn't his mother.

The kids at Riverdale High are angry too. Everyone is angry. Mr. Honey cancels the variety show.

When Betty arrives at Archie's house to practice their song, he tells her that practice has been canceled. Betty suggests they practice anyway, their singing leading to a passionate kiss.

Meanwhile, Jughead reconsiders his actions and turns to his assignments. He finishes his essay, then apologizes to Betty.

Veronica apologizes too, telling Archie she'll be hosting the variety show at La Bonne Nuit. The Archies, a band spontaneously created by the man himself, includes Archie, Jughead, Betty, Veronica and Kevin, and will still go on.

And they do. And Mr. Honey shows up.

Afterward, Jughead, having completed his past due essays, provides a voice-over during which he puzzles over the sinister, filmmaking voyeur.

Chapter Seventy-Five:
"Lynchian"

Original airdate: *April 29, 2020*
Writer: *Ariana Jackson & Brian E. Paterson*
Director: *Steve Adelson*

Top Quote: "Um, yes. In between being attacked by the Black Hood at junior prom and being hunted by the Gargoyle King before the Farm was raptured, I volunteered to be in charge of the yearbook."—Betty to Mr. Honey, upon him giving her a photo of himself, clarifying that she is editor of the yearbook.

Top Trivia: In a February 2020 video for BuzzFeed, KJ Apa, Archie, declares his belief that the idea of Archie and Betty being endgame is cool, and that fans would like it. They are iconic as a couple. He also said he likes 'Bughead' and thinks fans love 'Bughead.' He also thought Archie being single and focusing on himself would also be good.

Watch For: Alice cluelessly asking Betty what she could possibly have to cry about. References to the works of David Lynch throughout. Archie singing his song to Betty and Betty's reaction.

Wonder About: Betty and Jughead? Betty and Archie? Veronica and Archie? The cause for Archie's eyebrow scar finally revealed. Is the online tickling ring Mr. Honey's business?

Summary + Commentary:

Jughead's voice-over reflects on the macabre that is Riverdale, and the videotape showing someone wearing a mask of him being bludgeoned to death by someone wearing a mask of Betty. So, yeah, it's things as usual.

Across town, over morning coffee at the Pembrooke, Veronica and Hiram spar over business ventures. Hiram is excited by his venture with Elio's family, while Veronica is excited about her new line of affordable rum products, Maple Claw.

After Jughead and Charles watch some of the voyeur videos, Jughead questions Ethel in the chemistry lab about the tape showing Betty hitting him with a rock. She claims to know nothing. Now, he thinks the voyeur is more of a filmmaker, someone who has an artistic vision. He and Charles change tactics and soon are back to suspecting Ethel.

While Cheryl and Veronica are distributing their new products at the Maple Club, the Malloy family stops by to threaten them. Apparently, the rough-looking guys have been servicing the college crowd, and now the girls, via their new line, cutting into their profits. Soon, the club gets trashed. Cheryl, Penelope and Veronica assume Hiram is behind it, yet he says he isn't. He offers to clean up the mess with the Malloys for her. She passes, but he goes after Mr. Malloy anyway and gets a beat-down alley style.

Kevin and Fangs confess to Reggie that they make tickle videos for Terry. And Reggie wants in. After a taste of cash, he insists they break out on their own. So, Kevin tells Terry he wants out. Meanwhile, Reggie is trying to recruit other hot boys and girls. Toni proposes Vixens tickling Bulldogs with the girls in charge. Soon, names are drawn, and the first two head to the tickle suite. Hmmm. Seems no one pondered the different audience for girl-boy tickle tapes.

By the way, Archie and Betty have been stewing on their dilemma—limitations and love. Betty continues to read entries from the childhood editions of her diary, and Archie, telling her he can't stop thinking about her, doesn't help. Cheryl offers Betty some sound concrete advice—Jughead is real, a fantasy perfect romance is not. Still, Betty meets Archie at the bunker where they lie side by side, discussing their love for their partners.

After discovering that Ethel is a regular at the creepy video rental place, Charles finds a tape at Ethel's house and gives it to Jughead. Brace yourself—it's the sex tape of Betty and Jughead. Ethel tells him the tape came from the Scarlet Suite, a local place specializing in 'rare films.' Ever helpful Charles soon has an FBI warrant. He and Jughead search the store and find the video of Clifford Blossom killing Jason.

Once Terry finds out Kevin set up his own business, suddenly the previously easy-going guy is rough and demanding 40% of their profits. Reggie's counter plan is to threaten Terry at the Five Seasons. Soon, Mr. Honey is telling them to take the website down. His stance? The Vixen and Bulldog uniforms make the school look bad.

Archie invites Betty to the bunker to sing a song he wrote for her. Betty stops him from finishing it. It's over, she tells him. His response to that is to join the Naval Academy. Hers is to burn all but one of her diaries.

Cheryl wants out of the maple rum mess—the joint venture with Veronica just isn't fun anymore. Now that Cheryl is out, Veronica goes into business with Hiram, who she believes has changed to become more moral. Apparently, she doesn't know her father shot Jinx Malloy.

While Jughead delivers the disturbing news to Betty about their sex tape, Cheryl asks them over to Thistlehouse. There, she shows them yet another video, a faux, stylized snuff film of Clifford killing Jason. And on we go into the season finale.

Chapter Seventy-Six:
"Killing Mr. Honey"

Original airdate: *May 6, 2020*
Writer: *James DeWille & Ted Sullivan*
Director: *Mädchen Amick*

Top Quote: "You kids have been through a lot."—Mary to the gang, in the understatement of all times, as they toast the upcoming prom.

Top Trivia: In a 2017 interview with *Glamour*, Camila Mendes, Veronica, points out that because her character has seen a darker world, she has strength and understanding, and those qualities are ultimately good for Archie and can help him.

Watch For: Kevin giving the nod to viewers and fans by commenting on Jughead and Archie couple ship fanfiction. Miss Bell filling the gang in on another view of Mr. Honey. Mary, Alice and Hermione's pumped-up hall march.

Wonder About: On a scale from one to five: How great is it that Ms. Amick, the one and only Alice Cooper, directed this episode? Do you like seeing the gang taking their revenge on Mr. Honey? This episode was the season finale due to the COVID-19 pandemic. But does it work as a finale?

Summary + Commentary:

As he, Betty and Charles ponder who the voyeur could be, Jughead's opening voice-over reflects on the art that is imitating life. Also, what does the tape creator want?

Mr. Honey turns down Betty's yearbook. She delivered it two days late. He doesn't care about fair. His decision is final. She heads to the lounge to vent. There, they discuss the heinous villain that is Mr. Honey. Each student, except Archie and Jughead, has been banned from prom. Archie isn't allowed to walk at graduation. Betty, a la Riverdale style, suggests they scare him enough to leave town. They craft some possibilities. Reggie suggests a classic senior prank. That's how the man ends up glued to his chair with his phone glued to his hand.

All this imagining helps Jughead, who needs inspiration. He needs another writing sample for his University of Iowa application. So, he begins penning *Killing Mr. Honey,* and we viewers get to watch the story as he creates it.

Meanwhile, in the real Riverdale, Betty meets with Charles, who shows her yet another snuff film. This one presenting a depiction of Midge's on-stage death.

In a case of a few ruining something for all, Mr. Honey, fed up with the gang's antics, cancels prom. After some sleuthing, Betty discovers he's canceled prom at every school where he's worked. The gang heads home to tell their parents the bad news, quickly enlisting the adults to help fight back. The next day, Mary, Alice and Hermione arrive at school to confront Mr. Honey. Hiram, as mayor, is there to back them up. The principal doesn't back down. He stands by his decision. Next thing we know, though, at Pop's, Cheryl announces that prom is back on, and the adults are toasting the kids and declaring themselves proud.

Oh wait—now prom is off again, due to a threatening videotape Mr. Honey claims was delivered to the school.

But wait, prom is back on. Betty spotted Mr. Honey in a glass reflection in the threatening video. Now Mr. Honey is fired. As the man exits the building, a cardboard box of belongings in hand, he tells the gang he was doing everything to protect them. The danger and depravity in Riverdale is *not normal.* After he leaves, Ms. Bell comes to his defense. The cherry on top—a letter the man wrote to the University of Iowa on Jughead's behalf. After reading the letter, Jughead rushes to his keyboard to change his story in progress.

After Betty and Jughead reflect on their attitudes toward Mr. Honey, they're interrupted by Jellybean, who found a new VHS tape on their doorstep. After watching it, they head to the location depicted, the Lodge's cabin, to discover yet another video. What they find is another snuff film, this one a re-creation of the murder story Jughead himself wrote.

Season 4 Pop Quiz 2

1) Which two characters exchange these lines?

"I understand you've been asking about our other establishment."

"Why, yes. I'm Rosa Jevon. I consider myself a connoisseur of rum, and I've heard rumblings of a secret rum bar with ties to this establishment. Needless to say, I'm intrigued."

"Tell you what, since I like your vibe so much, I'll talk to my partner about it. She'll want to meet you, too. Maybe tomorrow night right here?"

"It's a date."

2) Who is Archie speaking to when he says:

"My dad was a decent, good guy. He worked hard. He loved me. He loved his life. I believe he slept peacefully, you know? Unless I was out doing some dumbass thing. Some days he won, and some days he lost. But, usually, it was a draw, and that was enough for him."

3) Which two characters exchange these lines?

"We're also terminating your Baxter Brothers contract, for failure to deliver satisfactory material by March 15th."

"This Friday? As in The Ides of March? It's only Monday, I still have time."

"Your rejected novel took you months to write. What makes you think you can write an entirely new one in five days?"

"Watch me!"

4) Who said it?

"I'm sorry, Donna... but I am the ultimate wild card. I am the daughter of The Black Hood, the nightmare from next door. I'm training with the FBI, and I'm coming for you, you psycho bitch. Not Joan, not Jonathan, not even Brett. Just you."

5) To whom is Donna speaking when she says:

"In case you've forgotten, I'm the brains of this operation. We still have a job to finish and a meddling girlfriend to pin it on."

6) Who said it?

"While you were in here playing Agatha Christie, my team was combing through DuPont's house for the last hour. Given the trophies of your victims that we found in your hollowed-out OED and your ghostwriters lawyering up... not to mention Forsythe's detective work...."

7) Which two characters exchange these lines?

"When I saw that signup sheet... I flashed back to sophomore year. I was on stage, freezing up from stage fright. Until I saw my dad. And suddenly, I could just... play. He gave me the biggest hug afterwards."

"He was so proud of you. He was always so happy whenever you played. Look, just because Veronica and Jughead aren't here doesn't mean we can't rehearse."

"All right."

8) To whom is Terry speaking when he says:

"You lied to me. You weren't getting out of the tickle business. You were setting up your own shop."

9) Who said it?

"These are your childhood memories, honey. They're precious."

10) Who are they discussing?

Archie: "Is he okay? Is he alive?"
Veronica: "No... he's not. He's dead."
Jughead: "R.I.P."

If You Only Watch One Episode

Entertainment Weekly declared Season 3's Chapter Fifty-Seven, *Survive the Night*, the best season finale to date, and with good reason. This action-packed episode delivers some serious reveals that viewers have been waiting for. But if this is your only episode, you aren't going to care about that. Here's what you will care about.

The Sisters of Quiet Mercy & The Farm

From our first introduction, when Penelope sends Cheryl there for a *cure*, we know The Sisters of Quiet Mercy is neither quiet nor merciful. Before being closed in the middle of Season 3, The Sisters of Quiet Mercy was a home claiming to be dedicated to reforming Riverdale's troubled youths. While claiming to aspire to honest and good values—such as meaningful work and spirituality—the so-called 'Sisters' ran an illegal distillery and gave the resident teens Fizzle Rocks—a drug that induces hallucinations. Truly a rockin' place.

It turns out Betty was right when she mocked her sister Polly for joining the Farm. The group was a cult, led by Edgar Evernever, who—besides messing with the followers' heads and hearts—sought to harvest their organs.

It also turns out that Betty was confined in both institutions. She first escapes The Sisters of Quiet Mercy and, once out, learns that her mother stayed there. Betty's struggle to get away from Alice's influence and control continues with her interactions with the Farm, where she is once again confined. And again, her mother is involved—this time as a current resident.

These two plotlines, The Sisters of Quiet Mercy and the Farm—resolved in *Survive the Night*—are definitive examples of how the sins and secrets of Riverdale's adults continually influence and inspire the plotlines, pulling the teens away from each other and forcing them to protect themselves.

Gryphons and Gargoyles and The Gargoyle King

The role-playing game, Gryphons and Gargoyles, is another example of how the sins and secrets of the Riverdale adults endanger and harm the teens. All throughout Season 3, viewers have been waiting to discover the G&G Game Master's identity—the one behind the resurgence of this treacherous, decades-old pastime their own parents played but swore to never discuss again after a game-related death.

That confidence is kept until Penelope Blossom coerces Betty, Veronica, Archie and Jughead to the Blossom hunting lodge. We learn that she is the Game Master, while Chic—who isn't dead after all—is the Gargoyle King. And once again they will pay the price for the misdeeds of their parents.

Over dinner, Penelope reminds the gang that they are the sons and daughters of the original Midnight Club—the Gryphons & Gargoyles game-playing group their parents formed. Her intent is to punish the teens for what the entire town of Riverdale did to her years ago. Her revenge? One last deadly round of the game. The four teens must journey through the forest surrounding Thornhill, the Blossom estate. And these woods are filled with lethal challenges—one for each of them.

Penelope Blossom's G&G revenge journey through the woods demonstrates how the teens continually fight through the conflicts caused by the actions of Riverdale's adults. As the head of the most established family in town, the vengeful Penelope represents *Riverdale's* special brand of corrupt power, the wicked need to control, and concealed violence. Archie's quest to fight the grizzled beast, and Jughead's quest to battle the Gargoyle King, are strength-proving and individual. Betty's quest to decide whether to kill her father, the Black Hood and Veronica's quest to drink from a potentially poisoned chalice to save her friends, are character-proving. All the quests are connected to conflicts created by the town of Riverdale.

Penelope's appearance at the successful conclusion of the quests is a reminder of the town's constant threat to the friends. Cheryl's rescue arrival with her bow-and-arrow armed Pretty Poisons solidifies the truth that, in Riverdale, the teens must protect each other.

The Upcoming Season

What's that? You thought you were only going to watch ONE episode? That is madness.

With the conclusion of *Survive the Night*, The Sisters of Quiet Mercy, the Farm and Gryphons and Gargoyles are behind us but it leaves us with a new mystery, a hint of the next terrible thing that is to come. We conclude this episode with a scene at Pop's where the four friends toast to a happy, normal, upcoming senior year, along with a contrasting scene in which Betty, Veronica and Archie stand around a fire, burning their clothes—and Jughead's beanie.

In his *AC Club* review Charles Bramesco states
...the heart and soul of this show live inside Archie, Jughead, Betty and Veronica. The final scene [of *Survive the Night*] leaves a sour taste, mocking the kind of high schooler melodrama that initially launched this show into hit territory. This season's high points have come when the show most closely resembles its former self; testing anxiety, school plays, prom night.

This binger's view is that this episode's conclusion accomplishes both a promise for high school antics and the bonding of the four teens. We have the promise that, since the gang has agreed to make the most of their last year together, we'll get the usual senior year events. We also have the promise of yet another mystery that will band the gang together. It seems doubtful that viewers will believe that Jughead is *indeed dead*, so we can be certain the four of them will be together.

In a show where the initial episode reveals a teacher having an abusive relationship with a student—a boy too young to even have a driver's license—we know we're not dealing with a simple high-school melodrama. "Having a good time," is not, as Bramesco states, "what Riverdale is all about." What makes *Riverdale* work, the primary action-generating conflict, is the tension between the teens and the consequences of the adults' deeds and ideas. Bramesco is correct when he declares:
Loosen up, everyone! The killers have been disposed of, it's summertime, and a new school year's coming up. [Students] starting senior year [should] savor every moment, because it'll be over before they know it. I'd give that same advice to the cast of Riverdale:

cherish every moment in which you get to be flawed, accessible, likable kids. It's only a matter of time until it's back to the blood.

This binger will add, cherish those upcoming blood moments as well. Those are where the real growth, physical, mental, and spiritual take place, and without them, *Riverdale* would be just another nice place to live. Who wants to watch a show about that?

After You've Watched

Good news, bingers, Season 5 is out. As usual, episodes air first on Wednesday nights on The CW and stream the day after on CWTV.com. Season 5 production was delayed but began in Vancouver, Canada, as soon as the cast and crew got the all-clear from the Canadian government.

Riverdale was among the first shows to suspend filming due to the COVID-19 pandemic. In March 2020, after a team member discovered they'd been in contact with someone who'd tested positive for the virus, Warner Bros. TV decided to put the safety of the cast and crew first. The team was in the midst of filming Season 4. As a result, the creation of the 4th season concluded early.

Instead of delaying the season finale, Executive Producer Roberto Aguirre-Sacasa decided to make do with what they had "in the can" and declared *Killing Mr. Honey* the finale. Dave Nemetz, a TV reporter, got the scoop from Aguirre-Sacasa for *TVLine*.
The fun thing about [episode] 19 is all of the kids are in the story together, which is very rare for us. It had a really fun conceit that made it feel special, which is the story that Jughead is writing. And it had a really shocking, gruesome cliffhanger, which really took the videotape mystery to the next level. So I thought, 'You know what? Since we are cutting the season short, maybe the best thing to do is end with [episode] 19, which is a really strong, fun episode, and then come back and have prom as our season premiere next season.'

Agreed, we bingers ended in a satisfying spot. But we were left without prom or graduation *and* with the new mystery of the videotapes still burning in our minds. Aguirre-Sacasa assured us that the show would continue where it left off. The first three episodes of Season 5, originally intended for Season 4, covered the prom and graduation.

Prior to the premiere of Season 5, Aguirre-Sacasa told *Entertainment Tonight* that the prom episode would affect Archie and

Veronica's relationship. "We haven't heard or seen the last of the song that Archie wrote for Betty, and right at this moment where they should be celebrating everything, a lot happens," he divulged, "It's pretty dramatic what happens at prom with Varchie." No spoilers here, but it was fairly dramatic. Just not as dramatic as we were expecting.

Speaking of Varchie, no doubt you are wondering what's going to happen with one of the fan-favorite couples? And—what about the other favorite couple, Bughead? And what of Barchie? In the Season 4 finale, Betty put a wall up, reminding Archie that a relationship between the two of them would hurt two other people who also happen to be their best friends. Fans, still, want to know, is that truly the end of it? Aguirre-Sacasa, when he gave Nemetz the scoop, revealed it was not.

On a basic level, Veronica and Jughead don't know anything that happened in the bunker or in Archie's garage, so there's still absolutely that to play... Betty was reinvesting in her relationship with Jughead, and Archie was sort of more lost and confused than ever. So they were basically in very different places about it, and I think we're going to play that... But definitely, there are major, major repercussions for what Betty and Archie did that go down at prom, in true teen drama fashion. So no, we haven't seen the end of that story by a long shot.

Alright then. That makes things clear on that note.

Okay, so you know that in Season 5 you will get to go to prom and graduation. It will be electrifying and passionate. Then what? What about the remainder of Season 5? First, here's some of the speculation that vibrated across the internet at the conclusion of Season 4.

There was a lot of chatter of the new Riverdale resembling the zombie apocalypse world seen in the *Afterlife with Archie* comics. It *could* happen. Ian Cardona, CBR writer, and comic industry reporter, notes that the series' first two seasons included small hints that, perhaps one day, it could adapt the comic's zombie-invasion storyline... In the *Afterlife with Archie* comics, it was Jughead's attempt to resurrect his dog that would transform the animal into a zombie. After getting bit by his dog, Jughead would then become the city's first zombie... Since the comic book's zombie invasion started with a devastating loss, it would make sense to have Cheryl attempt to bring her dead brother back to life on *Riverdale*. This could, in turn, be the start of the television series' monster apocalypse.

Some may scoff at the idea of a zombified Jason stalking the streets of Riverdale, but if there is anything we've learned these past 76 episodes, it's that anything is possible in the Archieverse.

Next, here's what we did know.

All the main cast, the Riverdale teens, would be back. Among the parents, would be Alice, Hiram and Hermione. FP would only be around for the first few episodes, then exit Riverdale and, consequently, the show. How? No spoilers here, but we will tell you he leaves Riverdale alive.

We got the news about the now famous *time jump*. Word at the time was five years. It won't ruin things for you if we let you know, it is a seven-year time jump instead.

We were promised more of fan-favorite Toni Topaz. That means more backstory and more depth of character. Aguirre-Sacasa let us know we would get introduced to Toni's family and discover what they have to say about her being in a relationship with Cheryl.

Although there was talk of a crossover with both *Chilling Adventures of Sabrina* and *Katy Keene,* that would not be happening. They canceled both shows in July 2020. However, we used some of the information we gained from the happenings on *Katy Keene* to forecast what our characters would be up to following the Season 5 time jump. Kevin Wong, in his write-up for *GameSpot,* reminds us that "*Katy Keene* Season 1 takes place [at the same time as Riverdale's] planned time jump."

Assuming Riverdale sticks to its own canon, we know that Kevin Keller will become the drama teacher at Riverdale High. We know that Archie is still in Riverdale and keeps in touch with Josie.

We know Hiram Lodge is still alive and up to no good; he appeared in Katy Keene's series finale to shake things up. If he has time to wheel and deal in real estate, he's probably not mayor of Riverdale anymore. It also means that his potentially fatal neuromuscular disorder in Season 4 was either cured in the past five years or was a bald-faced lie from the start.

Yay for Kevin. Archie staying in his hometown offers no great shock. On multiple occasions, he declared his love of Riverdale and his desire to keep it safe. Hiram? A liar? Of course he'd manipulate the truth for his own advantage. However, if his lie is in the past, what plot point would it provide? Hmmm… something to watch for.

Lastly, is what you can wonder about as you click into Season 5.

A list of possible ponderments. Add your own!

- What will pull the straying characters back to their hometown of Riverdale?
- Will Jughead be a writer? Teacher?
- Will Archie be a boxer, working at his community center? Police officer?
- Will Betty be in criminal justice? Reporter?
- Will Veronica be a business owner? Rum maven?
- Will Cheryl bring her dead brother back to life?
- Will she and Toni remain together?
- Will Josie return to Riverdale?
- What will Alice do without FP?
- What about Hiram and Hermione? Will they still be together and as shady as ever?
- Will Penelope be redeemed?
- What of Nana Rose?
- What of Jellybean? Polly? Charles?

In an interview that aired on *The Tonight Show Starring Jimmy Fallon* right before *Riverdale* production was suspended, KJ Apa promised big surprises for the start of Season 5. He offered this nugget: "what happens will be anything but ordinary bittersweet end of high school."

That's really all you need to know for now. So, keep watching bingers!

Appendices

Appendix A: Season 1 Pop Quiz Answers

1) Moose
2) Veronica
3) Veronica
4) FP and Jughead
5) The Blue and Gold office
6) Veronica
7) My name
8) Alice
9) Betty
10) Penelope

Appendix B: Season 2 Pop Quiz 1 Answers

1) Cheryl
2) Dilton
3) Jughead
4) Kevin
5) Nick St. Clair
6) Farmer McGinty
7) FP said it to Archie and Jughead
8) executed him.
9) Veronica and Betty
10) Toni's grandfather, Thomas, the oldest living Serpent

Appendix C: Season 2 Pop Quiz 2 Answers

1) Junkyard Steve
2) Cheryl Blossom
3) Midge
4) Alice
5) Running for student body president.
6) They kiss for the first time.
7) Jughead and Betty
8) Chic and the man Betty believes was her brother
9) Cheryl and Betty
10) Polly

Appendix D: Season 3 Pop Quiz 1 Answers

1) Framed Archie for murder
2) Doctor Curdle Jr.
3) Cult
4) Betty to Alice
5) Gamemaster Jughead
6) Jughead
7) Betty to Ethel
8) Penny
9) The Sisters of Quiet Mercy building and grounds
10) Jughead and Betty

Appendix E: Season 3 Pop Quiz 2 Answers

1) Marcus and FP
2) Hiram
3) Archie
4) Cheryl and Toni
5) Cheryl to Toni
6) Gladys
7) Veronica
8) Pop's
9) Elizabeth Cooper
10) Jughead and Penelope

Appendix F: Season 4 Pop Quiz 1 Answers

1) Veronica
2) Mr. Mantel and Reggie
3) Hiram
4) Eddie
5) Hermosa
6) Charles and Chic
7) Donna
8) Jughead
9) Reggie and Veronica
10) Bret and Jughead

Appendix G: Season 4 Pop Quiz 2 Answers

1) Toni and Hermosa
2) FP
3) Mr. Dupont and Jughead
4) Betty
5) Bret
6) Charles
7) Betty and Archie
8) Kevin
9) Alice
10) Mr. Honey

Appendix H: Stay a Fan

Fandoms: Who's Saying What Online
Riverdale Fans Online
https://riverdalefansonline.com/

FANDOM's Archieverse Wiki
https://riverdale.fandom.com/wiki/Riverdale

TV Fanatic
https://www.tvfanatic.com/shows/riverdale/

Podcasts: Listen in on the After Glow
Riverdale After Dark
https://comicbookclublive.com/

Riverdale After Show
https://www.afterbuzztv.com/riverdale-after-show/

Betty2: A Riverdale Podcast
https://anchor.fm/betty2-a-riverdale-podcast

A River Runs Through It
https://ariverdalerunsthroughit.podbean.com/

XOXO Riverdale
https://anchor.fm/xoxoriverdale

Appendix I: What to Watch Next

Sabrina the Teenage Witch
Twin Peaks
Veronica Mars
Buffy the Vampire Slayer
Katy Keene
Stranger Things
DC Titans
13 Reasons Why
Jessica Jones
The Vampire Diaries
Pretty Little Liars
Little Big Lies
Dollface
The Society
Teem Wolf
Looking for Alaska
The Order

Acknowledgements

Professor of Communications and Literature Carey Millsap Spears of Moraine Valley Community College. who, over whisky and hot wings, shared Gothic wisdom and friendship.

Timothy E. Kelley, Director of Integrated English, Lansing Community College. It's good to have a good boss.

Lansing Community College's Arts and Science Leadership Team, whose collective enthusiasm and encouragement—and sense of humor—is a welcome part of my professional life.

The Popular Culture Association's Popular Culture Summer Research Institute at Bowling Green State University and the staff of the Ray & Pat Browne Library for Popular Culture Studies. Summer 2019 made all the difference, thank you.

Sources

"Riverdale" Scripts • Transcripts Series Portfolio. 8FLiX, 8FLix. https://8flix.com/riverdale/scripts/.

Archieverse Wiki. Fandom, Fandom, https://riverdale.fandom.com/wiki/Archieverse_Wiki. Accessed Mar-Aug 2020.

AguirreSacasa, Roberto. "Escape from Riverdale." *Afterlife with Archie,* No. 1, Archie Comics, 2014.

AguirreSacasa, Roberto (@WriterRAS). "And we're back. Second day of shooting #Riverdale Season 4." 9 Jul 2019, 2:36 PM. Tweet.

Amick, Mädchen (@madchenamick). "What a kind gentle soul he was. Missing you friend. Especially today." 4 Mar 2020, 11:22 PM. Tweet.

Amick, Mädchen (@madchenamick). "What an honor it was to direct these incredible actors & wonderful humans. I'm so proud to be able to call them my dear friends. Their love & support meant the world to me as I took my first step into the directing world." 7 May 2020, 2:13 AM. Tweet.

Andreeva, Nellie. "'Riverdale' Archie Comics CW Pilot Casts Its Betty Cooper & Jughead Jones." *Deadline,* Deadline, 9 Feb. 2016. https://deadline.com/2016/02/riverdale-betty-cooper-lili-reinhart-jughead-jones-cole-sprouse-archie-comics-the-cw-pilot-1201699204/.

Botting, Fred. *Gothic.* 2nd ed., Routledge, Taylor and Francis Group, 2014.

Bramesco, Charles. "Riverdale Readies for One Grim Senior Year in Its 3rd Season Finale." TV Club, 16 May 2019, tv.avclub.com/riverdale-readies-for-one-grim-senior-year-in-its-3rd-s-1834739361.

BuzzFeed Celeb. "KJ Apa Plays with Puppies While Answering Fan Questions." YouTube, 27 Feb. 2020, https://youtu.be/647AHRtlkPs.

Cardona, Ian. "Riverdale Could Still Adapt Afterlife with Archie - Here's How." *CBR*, CBR, 25 Apr. 2020, www.cbr.com/riverdale-adapt-afterlife-with-archie-comic-zombies/.

Dibdin, Emma. "'Riverdale' Creator on That Bloody Finale Cliffhanger and Honoring Luke Perry." *The Hollywood Reporter*, 15 May 2019. https://www.hollywoodreporter.com/live-feed/riverdale-season-3-finale-explained-roberto-aguirre-sacasa-interview-1210265.

Digman, Catherine. "Themes and Tropes in Gothic Literature." Culture Notebook, 4 Feb. 2012, culturenotebook.wordpress.com/2012/02/04/themes-and-tropes-in-gothic-literature/.

Drum, Nicole. "Exclusive First Look at 'Betty & Veronica' #2 From Archie Comics." *Comics*, ComicBook.com, 7 Jan. 2019. https://comicbook.com/comics/2019/01/07/betty-and-veronica-2-exclusive-artwork-archie-comics-jamie-rotan/.

Goree, Eli (@TheRealEliGoree). "The final round begins tonight!! @CW_Riverdale season finale!" 15 May 2019, 4:29 PM. Tweet.

Highfill, Samantha. "'Riverdale' Recap: The True Gargoyle King Is Revealed." EW.com, 15 May 2019, ew.com/recap/riverdale-season-3-finale/.

Lauren, Baltimore. "First Appearance of Archie In Pep Comics #22 Hits $252,100 At ComicConnect Auction." *Bleeding Cool News And Rumors*, Bleeding Cool News And Rumors, 16 Sept. 2017, bleedingcool.com/comics/recent-updates/mlj-comics-comicconnect-auction-results/.

Lucken, Melissa. "Gothic Girls Gone Wild: *Riverdale's* Recrafting of Betty Cooper and Veronica Lodge." January 14 2020.

Murray, Ashleigh (@iamamurray). "Face throwing a kiss." 7 May 2020, 9:00 PM. Tweet.

Nagy, Evie. "How Archie Comics' New Chief Creative Officer Is Reimagining Riverdale." *Fast Company*, Fast Company, 18 Apr. 2017. https://www.fastcompany.com/3028694/how-archie-comics-new-chief-creative-officer-is-reimagining-riverdale.

Nemetz, Dave. "Riverdale EP Breaks Down Season 4's 'Gruesome' Early Finale - Plus, Will We See Prom and Graduation in Season 5?" *TVLine*, TVLine, 7 May 2020, tvline.com/2020/05/06/riverdale-recap-season-4-finale-prom-graduation/.

Public Domain Super Heroes Archie Comics. Fandom, Fandom Comics Community, https://pdsh.fandom.com/wiki/Category:Archie_ Characters.

Punter, David, and Glennis Byron. *The Gothic.* Blackwell Publishing, 2013.

Radloff, Jessica. "'Riverdale' Star Camila Mendes: 'I Don't Want to Fake Who I Am to Fit a Stereotype.'" *Glamour*, Glamour, 24 Feb. 2017, www.glamour.com/story/riverdale-camila-mendes-i-dont-want-to-fake-who-i-am-to-fit-a-stereotype.

Rao, Sonia. "What Happened to 'Riverdale'?" *Daily Herald*, Daily Herald, 16 May 2019. (Heiland)

Reinhart, Lili (@lilireinhart). "#Riverdale iconic." 15 Apr 2020, 11:24 PM. Tweet.

Ringwald, Molly (@MollyRingwald). "Joining #Riverdale tonight playing #ArchiesMom." 13 Apr 2017, 9:43 AM. Tweet.

Risesman, Abraham. "Archie and Betty and Veronica and Zombies." *Vulture*, 23 Jan. 2017, www.vulture.com/2017/01/archie-riverdale-cw-c-v-r.html.

Roberts, Amy. "Why 'Riverdale' Remains TV's Most Wicked Misfit." *Film Daily*, 14 Jan. 2020, filmdaily.co/obsessions/riverdale-tvs-most-wicked-misfit/.

Series/Riverdale. TVTropes, TVTropes, https://tvtropes.org/pmwiki/pmwiki.php/Series/Riverdale. Accessed 10 July 2020.

Riverdale. IMDb, Amazon, https://www.imdb.com/title/tt5420376/. Accessed June 2020.

Tonight Show Fallon Starring Jimmy Fallon. "KJ Apa Teases Wicked Surprises After Riverdale Graduation." YouTube, 10 Mar. 2020, https://www.youtube.com/watch?v=Flu1x7neI-Q.

"Voluntary Code to Self-Regulate the Content of Comic Books in the United States." *Wikisource, the Free Online Library*, Wikimedia Foundation, Inc., 19 Oct. 2017, en.wikisource.org/wiki/Comic_book_code_of_1954.

Waid, Mark. "Archie #2." Archie. Vol 2, 2. Archie Publications. Pelham, New York. 2015.

Whitesell, Jonathan (@JonWhitesell). "Kurtz and the Jones family really don't get along." 25 Apr 2019, 12:19 PM. Tweet.

Wong, Kevin. "Riverdale Season 5: What We Know, Including Plot Details And Returning Cast Members." *Gamespot*, Gamespot, 14 Aug. 2020, https://www.gamespot.com/gallery/riverdale-season-5-what-we-know-including-plot-det/2900-3539/#1.

About the Author

Professor Melissa Ford Lucken holds an MA in Special Education from Eastern Michigan University and an MFA in Creative Writing from Boston College's program at Pine Manor College. She teaches creative writing and composition at Lansing Community College. As Isabelle Drake, she has published more than 65 novels, novellas and short stories. Her current pop culture scholarship focuses on transmediation and horror. Her academic areas of interest include creative writing, composition and program and curriculum development. Stay up to date on her work and events by visiting her site, Adventures in MFALand @ http://mfaland.blogspot.com. Find and follow Isabelle Drake on all the socials and @ isabelledrake.com.

Ready to read some Isabelle Drake?
Like Gothic horror?
- *Servant of the Undead* & *Mistress of the Undead* from Riverdale Ave. Books

Like romance on the sweeter side?
- *Cowboy for Hire* or *Not Home for the Holidays* from Riverdale Ave. Books
- *Unfinished Business* from Totally Bound Publishing

Like romance on the steamier side?
- *Everglades Wildfire* or *Satisfaction Guaranteed* from Riverdale Ave Books
- The *Invitations* series from Totally Bound Publishing
- *Make Me Blush* from Pin-Up Girl Press

Other Riverdale Avenue Books You Might Like

The Binge Watcher's Guide to Doctor Who:
A History of the Doctor Who and the First Female Doctor
By Mackenzie Flohr

The Binge Watcher's Guide to the Films of Harry Potter
An Unauthorized Guide
By Cecilia Tan

The Binge Watcher's Guide to The Handmaid's Tale
An Unofficial Companion
By Jamie K. Schmidt

The Binge Watcher's Guide to Black Mirror: An Unofficial
Companion
By Marc W. Polite

Made in the USA
Columbia, SC
03 June 2021